BECOMING INTERDISCIPLINARY

An

INTRODUCTION

to

INTERDISCIPLINARY

STUDIES

Second Edition

Tanya Augsburg
Arizona State University

KENDALL/HUNT PUBLISHING COMPANY
4050 Westmark Drive   Dubuque, Iowa 52002

Cover photos provided by Patty Barnes.

The selected painting for the cover, *South Window 8.204* (2004), explores the startling new possibilities that develop when something ordinary, a view from a window, is seen from multiple perspectives. At first glance what we see is an unattractive view of a block wall and electric wires with a small slice of sky and treetops. This wall is symbolic of the many walls or obstacles we all face in our lives. The artist Patty Barnes captured the view first with a camera and then later with paint on canvas. Looking through thick glass, Barnes was able to obtain multiple new perspectives and make the ordinary come alive. By turning the activity of looking through glass into a highly conceptual and creative act, Barnes creates with her art a visual metaphor for becoming interdisciplinary. She imaginatively captures the many ways we can see obstacles or problems in our world and transform them by means of the integrative process into the extraordinary.

To the Two Men Who Encouraged Me to Write This Textbook:

My Husband,

Robert M. Schmitz,

and My Editor,

Jay Hays

Contents

Preface

This textbook introduces students to interdisciplinary studies and is useful for students seeking a better understanding both of interdisciplinary studies and of themselves. It is written for undergraduates in an extremely readable style. It includes readings of seminal texts in interdisciplinary studies and incorporates examples from current events.

I have taken a constructive-developmental approach to introducing interdisciplinary studies, following leading education scholar Marcia B. Baxter Magolda (1999; 2001), who calls for reforming college education by fostering self-authorship in students. Borrowing from psychologist Robert Kegan (1994), who coined the term *self-authorship* in his important study, *In Over Their Heads: The Mental Demands of Modern Life*, Baxter Magolda modifies the term somewhat. Baxter Magolda (1999) asserts that undergraduates can learn "to generate their own ideas effectively, in essence to develop their mind, their voices, and themselves" (pp. 7–8). Taking Baxter Magolda's call for educational reform seriously, I make the case that interdisciplinary studies allow students to integrate the personal, the educational and the professional. *Becoming Interdisciplinary* provides a scholarly overview of interdisciplinary studies and helps students to recognize themselves as interdisciplinarians. Students are asked to reflect on their lives, their reasons for majoring in interdisciplinary studies, and their intellectual interests so that they can make better decisions regarding themselves, their education, and ultimate career goals.

Organization

Part One of this book focuses on understanding interdisciplinary studies. In Chapter One the question, "What are interdisciplinary studies?" is answered by providing Julie Thompson Klein and William H. Newell's authoritative 1996 definition as well as some historical contexts regarding the emergence of interdisciplinary studies programs. Chapter Two considers essential terms for interdisciplinary studies and explains the difference between *interdisciplinary* and *multidisciplinary*. In Chapter Three metaphor is presented both as a means for describing interdisciplinary studies and as a means to foster interdisciplinary thinking. Chapter Four lists and discusses leading characteristics of interdisciplinarians. Chapter Five addresses the challenge of telling one's story as an interdisciplinarian. Guidelines for how to write a personal narrative are provided, as are numerous readings selected to help students craft their intellectual autobiographies and create visual autobiographical maps. In Chapter Six, Thomas C. Benson's (1982) seminal "Five Arguments Against Interdisciplinary Studies" and William H. Newell's (1983) "The Case for Interdisciplinary Studies: Response to Professor Benson's Five Arguments," are included as readings and discussed in depth. Guidelines for a mock class trial on "the case of interdisciplinary studies" are delineated as an experiential learning activity designed to help students better understand the leading criticisms lodged against interdisciplinary studies and to help students articulate the advantages of their degree in an informed manner. Additionally, the integrative process discussed in the Newell reading is presented. An integrative process worksheet is provided at the end of the chapter to help students understand the process of doing interdisciplinary work.

Part Two focuses on "Doing Interdisciplinary Studies." In Chapter Seven the epistemology of disciplines is explained so that students can understand the nature of disciplines and the importance of doing disciplinary research. Readings include Hugh G. Petrie's (1976) "Do You See What I See? The Epistemology of Interdisciplinary Inquiry." A class activity based on a recent *New York Times* article about the emergence of behavioral economics allows students to practice identifying seminal theories, concepts, and research methods within disciplines. At the end of the chapter a disciplinary research worksheet is included with detailed guidelines so that students will be able to conduct disciplinary research on their own. Chapter Eight provides an overview of portfolios useful to all college students in general and interdisciplinary studies students in particular. It offers some detailed information about assembling program, electronic, and showcase portfolios. It also illustrates how student portfolios can help students track their progress as interdisciplinarians.

Part Three offers supplementary readings for introductory interdisciplinary courses. The first cluster includes a reading on transfer as a method of integration. Cluster Two offers selections pertaining to trends in the 21st century interdisciplinary workplace. Both readings are from Richard Florida's (2002) influential book, *The Rise of the Creative Class*. Finally, Cluster Three provides readings on types of intelligences (emotional intelligence and multiple intelligence) for the interdisciplinary workplace.

Special Features

Special features of this book include all of the following:

- Definitions of major terms by leading scholars of interdisciplinary studies
- A background history of how interdisciplinary studies programs emerged
- A listing of popular metaphors for interdisciplinary studies
- A detailed discussion of leading characteristics of interdisciplinarians
- A helpful self-checklist of interdisciplinary characteristics
- A discussion of the leading advantages and disadvantages of interdisciplinary studies
- An explanation of William H. Newell's 1983 conception of the integrative process
- A discussion on the nature of disciplines
- Detailed guidelines for the following major assignments: personal narrative (intellectual autobiography), autobiographical maps, disciplinary research (mapping), and student portfolios

- Numerous experiential learning class activities, such as a metaphor top-ten list and a class "trial" on interdisciplinary studies
- Readings of seminal texts in interdisciplinary studies and readings selected to increase understanding
- Discussion questions for most readings designed to help students pick out the main points of the readings
- Inclusion of actual student work as examples for class activities and assignments
- Numerous real-life examples taken from current events to increase student knowledge and interest
- Bibliographies at the end of each chapter
- A complete reference list of all works cited at the end of the book

Suggested Readings

Baxter Magolda, M. B. (1999). *Creating contexts for learning and self-authorship: Constructive-developmental pedagogy*. Nashville, TN: Vanderbilt University Press.

Baxter Magolda, M. B. (2001). Making their own way: *Narratives for transforming higher education to promote self-development*. Sterling, VA: Stylus.

Benson, T. C. (1982). Five arguments against interdisciplinary studies. *Issues in Integrative Studies*, 1, 38–48. [See Reading 7 in this volume.]

Florida, R. (2002). *The rise of the creative class*. New York: Basic Books.

Kegan, R. (1994). *In over our heads: The mental demands of modern life*. Cambridge, MA, and London: Harvard University Press.

Newell, W. H. (1983). The case for interdisciplinary studies: Response to professor Benson's five arguments. *Issues in Integrative Studies*, 2, 1–19. [See Reading 8 in this volume.]

Acknowledgments

There are a few things to say about risk-taking, which is a cherished activity among interdisciplinarians. In a sense this book is the result of risk-taking. Yet it is also the product of serendipity, of the incredibly good fortune of my being at the right place at the right time. In February 2000 I attended an academic conference in Sacramento and happened to walk by the Kendall/Hunt display. Seeing the publisher's name struck a particular chord with me as I had used one of their textbooks previously. I greeted the gentleman warmly at the display and then abruptly asked him, "What about an introductory textbook in interdisciplinary studies?" He listened carefully as I explained how I was teaching in a growing interdisciplinary studies program and that there were no introductory textbooks available. He took notes, and asked me for my card. I had no idea that I had been speaking to one of the most senior editors at Kendall/Hunt.

A year later, a young, ambitious Kendall/Hunt editor, Jay Hays, contacted me about my idea regarding an introductory interdisciplinary studies textbook. It took a year for me to commit to the project (I had to overcome, evidently, my aversion to what I perceived at the time as a risk), and another two to deliver a manuscript. Jay never wavered in his faith both in the success of this project and in my ability to pull it off. In essence, Jay is the epitome of risk-taking. I have sorely tested his patience as well as the patience of my other editor at Kendall/Hunt, Billee Jo Hefel. To both I owe much thanks.

I must also thank my colleagues at Arizona State University (ASU) for their support and suggestions over the years. I would like to especially thank Mirna Lattouf, who offered to help me complete the project at a time when it looked very unlikely that I could meet any deadline. Kevin Ellsworth needs to be thanked for allowing me to do what I do best. Monica Tucci, the interdisciplinary studies program manager, and Brian Eggen, the interdisciplinary studies program office manager, deserve much thanks as they helped me with some of the more practical matters and menial tasks that went into the making of this textbook. Frederick Corey's support over the years has been an ongoing miracle. Chris Helms of ASU Career Services has taught and helped me a great deal over the years. I owe much of my thinking on student portfolios to Chris, and her very important work has all too often been inadequately acknowledged. I am very grateful for her support, expertise, and friendship.

This project would not have been possible, let alone completed, without William H. Newell. Bill Newell's tireless efforts made the Association of Integrative Studies what it is today. It is no exaggeration to say that most undergraduate interdisciplinary studies programs, their faculty, and students owe Bill Newell a great deal. In my particular case Bill offered to read and give feedback on every draft of every chapter. His comments have been extremely helpful, and this textbook would no doubt be a much better one had I been able to take all of his suggestions in time for both the first and second editions. I will certainly endeavor to do so for the next edition! Bill was additionally kind enough to point out and correct all too many egregious errors in syntax and spelling. I personally owe him more than words can possibly say.

Many others have helped me either directly or indirectly with writing this textbook. Another giant of interdisciplinary studies, Julie Thompson Klein, has been both generous with sharing her important ideas and supportive of this project. Julie was kind enough to give me some extremely helpful feedback. Stuart Henry needs to be thanked for being my cheerleader, always offering encouragement, suggesting interesting ideas, and gently correcting my numerous oversights.

I must thank additionally Joanna Frueh for all her infinite patience and support. Joanna's example as an interdisciplinarian has been a source of great inspiration and a wonderful opportunity for learning. I am in eternal gratitude for her vision and loving generosity. Tamarra Kaida's example, support, patience, and encouragement have been undeserved and greatly appreciated blessings. Orlan's vision, insights, generosity, and many homework assignments have helped me navigate across uncharted territories in interdisciplinarity, for which I am eternally grateful.

Arthur Sabatini's sage advice over the years has been a tremendous help, as was Robert Taylor's. Rob's contribution was invaluable to me, as he shared his textbook writing experiences with me. Both Arthur and Rob brought to my attention the need to expand the first edition's scope to include the interdisciplinary arts. I should point out here that Anton Lawson's counsel on textbook writing has been extremely helpful also. Linda Weintraub, who is an exemplary textbook author, has been a source of great inspiration and encouragement. Allen Repko needs to be thanked for sharing drafts of his textbook with me. I am grateful to Patty Barnes and Bill Tonnesen for granting me permission to use numerous images of their respective artwork.

I am very thankful for my family and friends, who put up with me while I was working on this project and neglecting them. I am particularly indebted to my husband's family, who were very understanding and supportive of my obsession to finish the first edition of this book during a very tragic and unforeseen circumstance, the passing of my father-in-law, Bob Schmitz, in June 2004. My heart especially goes out to my husband, Robert M. Schmitz, who provided the support, the stability, and most wonderfully, the love that enabled this project to blossom.

Finally, I would like to thank my students, too many to name individually, who over the years offered many helpful suggestions that shaped my developmental approach to this textbook. Some of you were generous enough to be willing to share your writing with the readers of this textbook. This textbook is for all of you.

Introduction

"What are interdisciplinary studies?" Have you ever been asked that question about your choice of study? How did it feel when someone asked you that question? How did you answer that question? Chances are that the question could have made you feel a bit on edge or defensive if you were uncertain how to answer. Perhaps you felt a bit nervous answering the question, as if you were uncertain that your answer was convincing enough. Hopefully, you did not allow the person(s) who asked the question to make you second guess yourself, your decision, or your major. Nevertheless, if you do not know much about interdisciplinary studies, you are probably hoping to learn more about it so you can better explain your degree to others—whether you need to explain your degree to a friend, a parent, a relative, or a prospective employer.

The Importance of Self-Understanding for Learning

Before you can begin to understand what interdisciplinary studies are about, you need to try to get a better understanding of yourself. What led you to choose interdisciplinary studies as a major? Did you begin your college education knowing you would major in interdisciplinary studies? If you did, you are currently in the minority, although that is beginning to change as interdisciplinary degree programs are becoming increasingly popular in the United States, Canada, and Europe. The following, which are listed in no particular order, are some of the more common reasons why students major in interdisciplinary studies at Arizona State University:

- I felt limited studying just one thing.
- I was really interested in studying two or more things, and I could not limit myself to one major.
- I'm a transfer student.
- I'm an older, returning student.
- I would like the intellectual challenge of creating my own individualized plan of study.

- I changed majors numerous times, and now after many years of college, I want to graduate and move on with my life.
- I need a degree to advance in my job.
- I am interested in doing something very specific and innovative for my career and a degree in just one discipline will not be adequate for my professional goals.
- I don't know what I want to do yet, and I need more focus.
- I was unable to complete my previous degree program.
- My friends graduated with a degree in interdisciplinary studies, and they are doing extremely well in their careers.
- I want to learn how to create and use a portfolio to help me get a job.
- I like the fact that I am required to do an internship, which will give me valuable professional experience before I graduate.

Do any of these reasons apply to you? As you get to know your classmates, you may find out that your reasons are similar or very different than theirs. Students at other colleges and universities may have reasons that are specific to their interdisciplinary programs' requirements. Regardless of the individual paths that led all of you to the crossroads of interdisciplinarity, together you and your classmates are about to embark in the following pages in a journey to become interdisciplinary.

The Purpose of This Textbook

The purpose of this textbook is to introduce students to the foundations of interdisciplinary studies, so that they can better understand what interdisciplinarity is all about. Students will begin to learn how to answer the following questions:

✓ What are interdisciplinary studies?
✓ Why are interdisciplinary studies degree programs becoming so popular among college and university students?

✓ What are some characteristics of interdisciplinarians?
✓ What are the advantages and disadvantages of having a degree in interdisciplinary studies?
✓ How does one *do* interdisciplinary studies?
✓ What can one do with a degree in interdisciplinary studies?
✓ How can interdisciplinary studies help me find a job?

Learning about interdisciplinary studies is a developmental, multi-step process that involves self-reflection, self-assessment, goal setting, research, articulation of knowledge, and arguably, even a bit of personal marketing as you learn how to articulate how your interdisciplinary studies degree will be meaningful to you. Your introductory interdisciplinary studies class may be very different from other classes you have had in the past. Not only is it very likely to be writing- and work-intensive, but it may challenge you in other ways. You may have to reflect on your life and goals, identify your skills, assess your strengths and weaknesses, understand the nature of disciplinary knowledge, fully understand the disciplines you wish to integrate, identify complex problems that are interdisciplinary, and do research on interdisciplinary topics of potential interest.

By reading this textbook, students will learn the following:

■ The historical background of interdisciplinary studies
■ The nature of the relationship between traditional disciplines and interdisciplinary studies
■ Some essential terms for interdisciplinary studies
■ Some metaphors of interdisciplinarity
■ The numerous characteristics of interdisciplinarians
■ The pros and cons of majoring in interdisciplinary studies
■ Some ways of explaining and articulating the degree to others
■ How to tell your story as an interdisciplinarian
■ How to understand more comprehensively different disciplines
■ Various interdisciplinary studies methods
■ The fundamentals of interdisciplinary research
■ The strategies for identifying interdisciplinary research topics

■ Some trends in the twenty-first century interdisciplinary workplace

Students will learn some useful applications:

■ Personal assessment
■ Academic research
■ Career development

Accordingly, this textbook will elaborate on the following assignments for learning how to do interdisciplinary studies:

■ Internet Research on Interdisciplinary Studies Programs
■ The Intellectual Autobiography
■ Autobiographical Map
■ Integrative Process Worksheet
■ Disciplinary Research (Mapping)
■ Program Portfolio
■ Showcase Portfolio

While the intellectual and career interests of students will differ greatly, most if not all students are interested in their futures. This textbook will help students learn how to integrate the personal, the educational, and the professional. As Figure 1.1 indicates, all three realms are interrelated—in order to be an interdisciplinarian, you must always simultaneously consider how your choices in one area may affect the other two. In other words, interdisciplinary studies teach students how to take a holistic approach to their education.

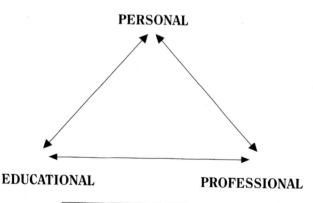

PERSONAL

EDUCATIONAL   **PROFESSIONAL**

FIGURE 1.1 Becoming Interdisciplinary Model: Students Learn How to Integrate Their Personal, Educational, and Professional Goals Doing Interdisciplinary Studies

PART ONE

Understanding Interdisciplinary Studies

WHAT ARE INTERDISCIPLINARY STUDIES?

SOME INITIAL DEFINITIONS AND HISTORICAL CONTEXTS

What a splendid book one could put together by narrating the life and adventures of a word. The events for which a word was used have undoubtedly left various imprints on it; depending on place it has awakened different notions; but does it not become grander still when considered in its trinity of soul, body and movement?

Honoré de Balzac (qtd. in Frank 1988, p. 139)

Learning Objectives

After reading Chapter One of *Becoming Interdisciplinary*, you should be able to:

1. Know that dictionary definitions for the word *interdisciplinary* are not adequate for understanding what is interdisciplinary study.

2. Understand that while the term *interdisciplinary* is a relatively recent one, the concept of *interdisciplinarity* is much older.

3. Realize that the concept of interdisciplinarity depends on the concept of disciplinarity.

4. Obtain at least an initial understanding of what is a discipline.

5. Understand why it is important for interdisciplinary studies majors to know about the history of the university, the emergence of disciplines, and the emergence of interdisciplinary study in the university.

6. Obtain a historical overview of the history of the university.

7. Understand how interdisciplinary studies degree programs emerged in the United States.

8. Recall the most authoritative definition of interdisciplinary studies, which is the one which this textbook uses.

9. Understand the difference between "full" and "partial" interdisciplinarity.

Consulting the Dictionary

According to the unabridged second edition of the *Random House Dictionary of the English Language*, the adjective *interdisciplinary* is defined as the following:

in ter dis ci pli nar y (in't r dis' pl ner'e), adj. **1.** combining or involving two or more academic disciplines or fields of study: *The economics and history departments are offering an interdisciplinary seminar on Asia.* **2.** combining or involving two or more professions, technologies, departments, or the like, as in business or industry. [1935–40; INTER- + DISCIPLINARY]

The Random House Dictionary includes an etymology of the word *interdisciplinary*, which indicates that the word is a rather recent one. The authoritative dictionary for the English language, *The Oxford English Dictionary*, defines *interdisciplinary* similarly: "Of or pertaining to two or more disciplines or branches of learning; contributing to or benefiting from two or more disciplines." *The Oxford English Dictionary* is more precise than *The Random House Dictionary* by pinpointing the exact year of the earliest example of the written use of the word *interdisciplinary* as 1937. Scholar Roberta Frank (1988) has uncovered even earlier usages of the word, dating as far back to 1926 (p. 140).

While the exact moment when *interdisciplinary* was first used may be regarded as uncertain, it is certain that the word *interdisciplinary* is a product of the twentieth century. Evidently, historical conditions in the twentieth century created a need for the adjective *interdisciplinary* and related words such as the noun *interdisciplinarity* to exist. What were those conditions? That question will be addressed later in this chapter.

The Necessity of Further Research

Dictionaries are often useful starting points, although they can be simplistic, incomplete, or otherwise inadequate in their explanations. For example, both *The Random House Dictionary* and *The Oxford English Dictionary* definitions provide students with a very rudimentary, imprecise idea of what interdisciplinary study is and does: such definitions give the misleading and inaccurate impression that when one studies interdisciplinary studies, one usually combines two or more academic disciplines in some way. Moreover, these two dictionary definitions remain rather vague regarding *what exactly* is being combined within the involved disciplines or how that combination is actually accomplished. As we will see later in this chapter, what gets combined or integrated are *disciplinary insights*, not disciplines themselves. In other words, dictionary definitions do not always provide students with comprehensive explanations. Because dictionaries are unable for spatial reasons to go in much depth, it is always a good idea to follow up consulting the dictionary with more research, such as finding out what the leading scholars on any topic say about the subject of their expertise. For example, we have to read Frank (1988) to learn about the earlier usages of the word *interdisciplinary* prior to 1937. We can also learn a great deal more from her scholarly research: Frank has been able to determine not only who were the first people to use the term but exactly where the term was first used and for what purposes. More specifically, Frank has determined that the term *interdisciplinary* was first used by members of the Social Science Research Council (SSRC) at its headquarters in midtown Manhattan on the corner of 42nd Street and Madison Avenue during the 1920s. The Social Science Research Council was created in 1923 by "visionaries . . . who thought not only that disciplinary boundaries could be transcended but that the resulting research could speak to contemporary social problems and public policy" (Calhoun 2001, p. 7). According to Frank (1988), the first recorded public use of the word occurred on August 30, 1926 in Hanover, New Hampshire by SSRC member, psychologist Robert Sessions Woodworth while he was discussing "the range of research appropriate for the Council" (p. 140). In other words, Professor Frank's research provides us with a more complete historical background and context for the word *interdisciplinary* that we would not have had had we limited ourselves solely to looking it up in the dictionary.

Did You Know? "The Social Research Council (SSRC) was the world's first national organization of all the social sciences, and from the onset its goal has been to improve the quality of, and the infrastructure for, research in the social sciences" (Worchester 2001, p. 15).

You can read more about the SSRC at its official website: http://www.ssrc.org.

The Idea of Interdisciplinarity: Some Historical Contexts

Most scholars make the distinction between definitions or meanings of the word, *interdisciplinarity*, and the concept or idea of interdisciplinarity. While there is consensus among scholars that *interdisciplinary* and *interdisciplinarity* are twentieth-century terms, there is less agreement about the history of the idea of inter-disciplinarity. Both **Julie Thompson Klein** (1990) and Gunn (1992) have independently asserted that the roots of the concept of interdisciplinarity are quite old and can be traced back as far as Greek antiquity. They disagree, however, on the reasons why. According to Klein (1990), "the roots of the concept lie in a number of ideas that resonate throughout the modern discourse—the ideas of a unified science, general knowledge, synthesis and the integration of knowledge" (p. 19). Klein believes that the twentieth-century concept of interdisciplinarity was partially already contained in some major ideas of ancient Greek philosophy. Gunn (1992) sees the roots of interdisciplinary studies more in terms of boundary crossing and borrowing, particularly from the humanities where "Greek historians and dramatists drew on medical and philosophical knowledge, respectively, for clues to the reconception of their own material" (pp. 239–240).

Interdisciplinary Studies: A Response to the Development of Academic Disciplines

Views such as Klein's and Gunn's, although compelling, are problematic to other scholars because they are anachronistic. To be anachronistic is to be misplaced in time. It is anachronistic to say that interdisciplinary studies can be traced as far as Ancient Greece when the disciplines did not yet exist! One of the leading scholars of interdisciplinary studies, **William H. Newell** (1998), addresses Gunn directly when he writes the following:

> *His claim raises the question of whether we need to make an additional distinction between interdisciplinarity and pre-disciplinarity. In what sense is it meaningful to talk about inter-disciplinarity prior to the advent of disciplines? Clearly, scholars have long borrowed ideas and in-formation from other fields, but the interdisciplinary practice of adopting the perspective of another field is less common and much more recent. Indeed, the interdisciplinary motivation to seek a more comprehensive perspective would have had little urgency prior to the development of the distinc-tive worldviews of reductionist disciplines. Thus interdisciplinarity is appropriately seen as a re-sponse to the development of academic disciplines and the intensification of specialization that dates back to the late nineteenth century. (p. 533)*

The Term *Interdisciplinarity* and Its Relation to *Disciplinarity*

For Newell and other scholars the term, *interdisciplinarity*, is historically linked to the term, *disciplinarity*. As Menand (2001) has written, "*interdisciplinarity* is not only completely consistent with disciplinarity—the con-cept that each academic field has its own distinctive program of inquiry—it actually depends on the concept" (p. 52). Newell (1998) is in accordance when he writes, "understanding the role of disciplines in interdiscipli-nary studies should be central to a full understanding of interdisciplinarity" (p. 541). Once students discover that the concept of interdisciplinarity is inextricably linked to the concept of disciplinarity then they can learn to appreciate how important it is to learn more about how those links developed historically, i.e., how disciplines and interdisciplinary studies emerged in the university. To put it differently, once students understand that in-terdisciplinary studies programs would not have been possible without the rise of disciplines, students begin to realize that learning about interdisciplinary studies involves learning about how knowledge has been organized and transmitted historically.

What Is a Discipline?

A more comprehensive discussion about disciplines will be offered in Part Two. Only a preliminary understand-ing of disciplines can be given in this chapter, enough for students to have some conceptual grasp of the term.

As we experienced at the beginning of this chapter, consulting dictionaries can lead to confusion. The first six definitions listed for *discipline* in *The Random House Dictionary* pertain more to the military than to education or learning:

1. training to act in accordance with rules; drill: *military discipline.*
2. activity, exercise, or a regimen that develops or improves a skill; training: *A daily stint at the typewriter is excellent discipline for a writer.*
3. punishment inflicted by way of correction and training.
4. rigor training effect of experience, adversity, etc: *the harsh discipline of poverty.*
5. behavior in accord with rules of conduct; behavior and order maintained by training and control: *good discipline in an army.*
6. a set or system of rules or regulations. (Flexner 1987, p. 562)

The Oxford English Dictionary is more helpful, although the first definition it lists is noted as obsolete: "Instruction imparted to disciples or scholars; teaching; learning; education, schooling." The second definition is one with which students are more familiar: "A branch of instruction or education; a department of learning or knowledge; a science or art in its educational aspect."

Such dictionary definitions really don't say much. Students want to know how disciplines impact or affect them. Moran (2002) has defined the term *discipline* rather concisely: "it refers to a particular branch of learning or body of knowledge" (p. 2). The renowned education scholar **Howard Gardner** (2000) in his aptly titled book, *The Disciplined Mind*, provides some illustrative examples in his description of disciplines:

> *It is easy for students (and teachers and parents) to be confused about the disciplines. They are often seen simply as "subjects": courses to take with discrete texts and teachers, in order to pass certain requirements. To the extent that disciplines are simply presented as sets of facts, concepts, or even theories to be committed to memory, students may remain innocent of their powers. After all, facts themselves are discipline-neutral: they acquire their disciplinary colors only when they have been pieced together in a certain way and placed in the service of a particular theory, framework, or sequence.*
>
> *For the disciplines inhere not primarily in the specific facts and concepts that make up textbook glossaries and indexes, compendia of national standards, and all too often, weekly tests. Rather, the disciplines inhere in the ways of thinking, developed by their practitioners, that allow those practitioners to make sense of the world in quite specific and largely nonintuitive ways. Indeed, once mastered and internalized, the disciplines* **become** *the ways . . . in which experts construe the phenomena of their world. (p. 155)*

Gardner (2000) makes some important points. When we pursue studying a discipline—for example, economics—we begin to see the world through the eyes or perspectives of its practitioners, e.g., economists. In other words, if we study economics, sooner or later we begin to view the world and its phenomena from the economic perspective. Viewing phenomena from the economic perspective means more that just seeing things in terms of supply and demand, two central concepts in economics. We will consider more comprehensively what it means to view phenomena, problems, or issues from a disciplinary perspective in Chapter Seven. For now it is helpful to remember the following three points about disciplines:

Table 1-1 Three Important Initial Points about Disciplines

1. A discipline is a branch of knowledge or study.
2. Disciplines are often seen as subjects or majors.
3. Disciplines help shape the way their practitioners see the world.

Other scholars have been able to make connections between the vastly divergent meanings of the word *discipline* that dictionaries do not provide. The late philosopher **Michel Foucault** (1979) saw connections between the more military meanings of the word *discipline* with the educational meaning. As Moran (2002) summarizes Foucault argument succinctly: "Foucault points out that schools and universities, where the academic disciplines are taught, are also disciplinary environments" (p. 134). Salter and Hearn (1996) suggest that "these two seemingly distinct definitions of discipline—as a branch of knowledge and as a means of social control—should always be understood together. Disciplines defined as branches of knowledge always already connote the regulation of knowledge in the service of power relations" (p. 18). In other words, studying a particular discipline involves rigorous, regimented, methodological training.

As a word *discipline* is much older than *interdisciplinary*, first appearing in English in the twelfth century. Like the concept of interdisciplinarity, the concept of discipline can be traced back to the ancient Greeks, but a bit later to **Aristotle**, who, as Klein (1990) points out, divided knowledge into areas such as politics, poetics, and metaphysics (p. 19). To understand how disciplines further developed, one has to know how universities emerged and evolved.

THE MEDIEVAL ORIGINS OF THE MODERN UNIVERSITY

To paraphrase art historian **James Elkins** (2001) in his history of art schools, it is worth knowing that universities did not always exist, and that the earliest universities were completely different from what we call universities today (p. 5). According to Briggs and Micard (1972), the earliest universities were informed by the Christian concept of the unity of knowledge (p. 186). Klein (1990) points out that "as the modern university evolved from the medieval cathedral schools, a unified whole had come to include both letters and the sciences in the customary divisions

> The university is a product of the Middle Ages.
> Swoboda 1979, p. 54.

of the *trivium* (grammar, logic, and rhetoric) and the *quadrivium* (music, geometry, arithmetic, and astronomy)" (p. 20). The earliest universities began informally during the twelfth and thirteenth centuries in various cities in Europe such as Salerno and Bologna in Italy and Paris in France where groups of students and teachers (or masters) would meet, often in rented halls or rooms. The original meaning of the word *university* does not refer to either "universe" or "universal" but rather, to the totality or unity of a group, as in a group of students (Randall 1936, pp. 4–5; Haskins 1940, p. 14; Moran 2002, p. 5). The concept of unity with regard to knowledge was crucial for the earliest universities. Briggs and Michard (1972) emphasize this last point by claiming the following: "The university rested on a conviction that there was an essential and universal unity of knowledge and through Christianity, that faith was the highest order of knowledge. The conception of the unity of knowledge influenced the pattern both of organization and teaching" (p. 186).

As Salter and Hearn (1996) point out, "the origins of the disciplines can be found in the medieval university, where the study of theology and the arts became distinct from law and medicine" (p. 18). The earliest disciplines of medical and legal studies were the result of societal or external (as in external to the university) demands rather than from purely academic or internal pursuits or research agendas (Swoboda 1979, p. 54). The learning process was rather *disciplinary* in the more military sense of the word as it was both hierarchical and dogmatic. Students were considered disciples of their teachers. According to Swoboda (1979),

> disciplina *originally referred to the instruction of disciples and was contrasted to* doctrina, *pertaining to the doctor or teacher. The disciples necessarily subordinated themselves to the teacher in a strongly hierarchical setting. Doctrines were considered final and given; this system as a whole (even granting important exceptions) was not conducive to the qualitative growth of learning.* (p. 57)

Students were all male, and sometimes were only allowed to speak Latin. Since the printing press had not yet been invented, books had to be copied by hand. Not surprisingly one book would typically be used for a year-long course (Elkins 2002, p. 6). Students were expected to memorize sections of the book and the professors' lectures on it for class, where they would be drilled by the teachers on the material. Elkins (2002) points out that "today the medieval kind of rote learning occurs in Orthodox Jewish classes on the Talmud, in Muslim schools that memorize the Koran, and to some degree in law and medical schools—but not in colleges" (p. 6).

Discussion Questions

Compare the contemporary college experience with the earliest universities. How were they different? How were they the same?

THE RENAISSANCE ACADEMY AND THE CHALLENGE TO TRADITIONAL KNOWLEDGE

The hierarchical process of learning changed little during the Renaissance and Reformation. What discussion and exchange of ideas that did occur usually took place outside the university at the academy. The word *academy*, according to Elkins, "comes from the district of Athens where **Plato** taught. The Renaissance academies were modeled on Plato's academy, both because they were informal (like Plato's lectures in the park outside Athens) and because they revived Platonic philosophy" (p. 8). Most were concerned with language, and "a few were secret societies" (Elkins 2000, p. 8). The modern art school grew out of the Renaissance academy, as did the modern scientific research institute.

The rise of modern science and rival institutions in the eighteenth century during the European intellectual movement known as the Enlightenment began to challenge the idea of a unity of knowledge. During the eighteenth century knowledge became ordered and categorized; it was during this period that the first encyclopedias appeared. By the end of the nineteenth century the idea become systematically dismantled with the rise of academic disciplines and increased secularization. As universities became less tied to religious institutions, the concept of the unity of knowledge began to be replaced by the concept of the advancement of knowledge. Briggs and Michard (1972) provide the following example: "The hero of the medical faculty, was not the 'good physician' but the innovator in the medical sciences. This bias was obviously true in the case of all the natural sciences and applied in the arts and the social sciences also" (p. 186).

THE EMERGENCE OF DISCIPLINES DURING THE NINETEENTH CENTURY

The early nineteenth century saw the rise of the modern research university as well as the emergence of many sciences and disciplines. Between the years 1807 and 1810 the University of Berlin was founded by the Prussian education reformer and linguist, **Wilhelm von Humboldt** (1767–1835). According to Humboldt, the purpose of the university was to be a site for the production of (scientific) knowledge, but it was to orient its primary focus, science, to "the spiritual and moral training of the nation" (Humboldt 1810 qtd. in Lyotard 1984, p. 32). In other words, the university's dual function was to produce knowledge and to educate young citizens to enter civilized society. By the nineteenth century science, particularly the life sciences, such as biology, and the physical sciences, such as chemistry, required laboratories, technology, and man power. The days of the gentleman scholar/scientist tinkering away at home were no longer possible.

With the rise of different sciences came competition for university resources, and universities began to organize themselves around the disciplines. Klein (1990) provides the following explanation regarding the rise of disciplines:

> *The modern connotation of **disciplinarity** is a product of the nineteenth century and is linked with several forces: the evolution of the modern natural sciences, the general scientification of knowledge, the industrial revolution, technological advancements, and agrarian agitation. As the modern university took shape, disciplinarity was reinforced in two major ways: industries demanded and received specialists, and disciplines recruited students to their ranks. The trend toward specialization was further propelled by increasingly more expensive instrumentation within individual fields. . . . Although the "Renaissance Man" may have remained an ideal for the well-educated baccalaureate, it was not the model for the new professional, specialized research scholar. (pp. 21–22)*

According to Salter and Hearn (1996), "American universities were 'reformed' in the mid-nineteenth century and were modeled after the German prototype. The integration of research facilities into the American college led to the establishment of the American university" (p. 19). These American reforms "carried the extension and intensification of specialized knowledge far beyond their German model" (Swoboda 1979, p. 73). Many American professional disciplinary academic associations were formed by the late nineteenth century: history in 1884, economics in 1885, political science in 1903 and sociology in 1905 (Hershberg 1981, p. 23; Swoboda 1979, p. 72). It might be surprising to learn that physics was scarcely recognized as a discipline until the twentieth century. Klein points out that "even holders of degrees in physics were not even officially registered as physicists until 1917" (Klein 1998, p. 286). What needs to be emphasized here is that many so called "traditional" academic disciplines are not much older than some interdisciplinary programs—in effect, the founding of modern disciplines preceded the emergence of interdisciplinary programs by roughly seventy years. Nonetheless, students are often given the impression that the "traditional disciplines" have been around since time immemorial.

THE TWENTIETH CENTURY AND THE CRISIS OF KNOWLEDGE

During the first half of the twentieth century the American university faced at least three major challenges: (1) fragmentation of knowledge, (2) change in student demographics, and (3) complex world and technological developments. First of all, as Orrill (1998) points out, by 1900 the American university found itself pressured by a reform movement, the result of the rapid growth of new knowledge. "By 1900," Orrill (1998) writes, "the new knowledge had swept forcefully into the college curriculum before anyone was sure about how the dramatically increased number of 'studies' could be organized into a coherent curriculum" (p. *xi*). Many new disciplines appeared on the horizon without regard to their possible interconnections to each other. Orrill (1998) notes, "By 1910, the typical college curriculum contained 20 or more new disciplines that had not existed in the 1880s" (p. *xi*). *This rapid proliferation of disciplines led to a fragmentation of knowledge.* While such fragmentation was often helpful to producing new knowledge for research, it was problematic for educating undergraduates seeking some coherence to their education, especially since by the turn of the century primacy was given to disciplinary research over undergraduate teaching (Swoboda 1979, pp. 76–78; Salter and Hearn 1996, p. 20). Universities and colleges responded by developing general education courses. Some universities created required "Great Books" seminars, while others developed courses that reflected some of the central civic concerns and needs of the time. For example, some "Great Books" seminars were created in response to the questions raised by the First World War.

The frenetic growth of new disciplines was only part of the story. By the 1960s there were other pressures on the university stemming from liberation movements, the end of colonialization, and women's rights movements. In other words, new populations of students were demanding to enter the university in numbers previously unseen. *The overall university student population was not only increasing by large numbers, but its demographics were beginning to change.*

Finally, complex world developments, particularly those technological in nature, made interdisciplinary inquiry a necessity. World War I and its huge number of fatalities were made possible with advances of sciences and technology. Nevertheless, it was World War II that produced a significant crisis in knowledge. Germany in the early twentieth century was considered the most civilized nation in Europe. Yet it was Germany that engineered the Holocaust—the systematic slaughter of millions of Jews and others, such as Gypsies and homosexuals. The Holocaust defied and continues to defy understanding—especially understanding from any single discipline. Think about it: what discipline would you study to try to understand the problems of why and how the Holocaust happened? Would history be enough? Hardly. One would have to understand something about German culture, with its long tradition of anti-Semitism. One would also have to understand something about Judaism. Studying politics and mass media would be helpful in understanding Nazi propaganda. Studying psychology would be helpful to understanding the crowd mentality. Reading personal narratives and Holocaust literature gives insight to the experience of being in the camps. Viewing and studying art produced by inmates of Nazi concentration camps is helpful to understand not only their experiences, but also their hopes for freedom and survival. For example, "The Last Expression: Art and Auschwitz" is an art exhibition that presents art produced at Auschwitz. The curator of the exhibition, David Mickenberg, also curated the following website related to the exhibition: <http://lastexpression.northwestern.edu>. According to Mickenberg (2003), "The exhibition posits broad questions of how art served as a document of camp atrocities and a testimony to the existence of an individual; how art served as a means of subjugation by the perpetrators or as a means of survival—physical, psychological, or emotional—for the victims; and how art reflects the multifaceted role of creativity in the lives of human beings and in the making and interpretation of history" (p. B15). Can you think of other disciplines to be consulted in trying to learn more about the Holocaust? Write them down here:

While the problem of the Holocaust is so complex that it has yet to be "solved," i.e., more racially and ethnic genocides have occurred since the Holocaust, our understanding of why the Holocaust occurred is deepened by viewing the problem more comprehensively—in other words, by considering it from multiple disciplinary perspectives and then trying to integrate them all.

Think of other complex problems such as AIDS, terrorism, or capital punishment. How can one approach such problems? What disciplines does one need? Make a list of disciplines useful to understanding each complex problem.

AIDS   **Terrorism**   **Capital Punishment**

Emergence of Interdisciplinary Programs in American Universities and Colleges

Students are often surprised to learn that interdisciplinary studies programs have existed for decades. Their formations were facilitated in part by the efforts in the 1920s and 1930s of the creation of grant award agencies "with the expressed aim of encouraging collaboration among the social sciences" (Sherif and Sherif, 1969, p. 3). During the 1930s the first American Studies programs appeared. Initially intended to combine the study of American literature and American history, American Studies quickly expanded to incorporate the study of other aspects of American culture and society. Also during the late 1930s new programs known as "area" studies sprung up at universities. Area studies began as "efforts to provide comprehensive, integrated knowledge about other geographical areas" (Klein 1990, p. 25). Depending on the program, an area studies faculty could include scholars from many different disciplines, including political science, religion, language(s), literature, history, and anthropology. Students majoring in a particular area studies program would expect to take many different courses in different disciplines in order to obtain comprehensive understanding about a particular geographical area.

Did You Know? Area studies continue to be popular types of interdisciplinary study. Current area studies commonly found at colleges and universities include programs in African Studies, Latin American Studies, Caribbean Studies, South Asian Studies, East Asian Studies, Russian Studies, Eastern European Studies, Scandinavian Studies, Basque Studies, Middle Eastern Studies, and Israel Studies.

After WWII all kinds of interdisciplinary activity flourished. According to Sherif and Sherif (1969) interdisciplinary conferences, large-scale research projects (otherwise known as mission projects) and interdisciplinary education programs became "commonplace" (p. 3). Additional types of graduate interdisciplinary programs began to appear midcentury. The Graduate Institute of Liberal Arts at Emory University, one of the oldest interdisciplinary humanities and comparative studies programs in the United States, first opened its doors in the 1950s. While there was some experimentation with interdisciplinary art education already in the 1920s and 1930s, the first interdisciplinary arts programs such as the Inter-Arts program at San Francisco State University also were created during this period. New hybrid sciences such as biophysics, biochemistry, biomedical engineering, and radioastronomy began to make their presences felt on university campuses as well (Klein 1990, pp. 32–33).

The 1960s were a time of experimentation and revolt on college campuses worldwide. A number of interdisciplinary universities were created. In Britain, the University of Sussex opened in 1961 and was "one of the first comprehensive attempts to redefine relations between academic areas" (Klein 1990, p. 157). In the United States, the University of Wisconsin, Green Bay was chartered in 1965. Green Bay was innovative for its emphasis on themes and field study rather than traditional disciplines and professional study. Its curriculum was centered on nine problem-centered concentrations within four environmental theme-based colleges (Klein 1990, pp. 157–158).

During the late 1960s and early 1970s numerous interdisciplinary undergraduate degree studies programs were founded that still exist today. For example, in 1967 Fairhaven College of Western Washington University "was created as an innovative, interdisciplinary, liberal arts laboratory for student-centered, collaborative teaching and learning" (Newell et al. 2003, p. 13). In 1971 two programs known for their emphasis on interdisciplinary individualized study, The Gallatin School of Individualized Studies at New York University and the New College at the University of Alabama, opened their doors. In 1974 the School of Interdisciplinary Studies (Western College Program) at Miami University in Ohio was created with several different tracks in the humanities, the social sciences, and the natural sciences.

Many other interdisciplinary programs started during the late 1960s and early 1970s were more focused on particular themes or problems. Only a few can be mentioned on these pages. For example, the first African American Studies programs emerged during this period. While the first women studies course was "reportedly" taught as early as 1965 at the Free University of Seattle, the first women studies program was created in 1970 at San Diego State University (Klein 1996, p. 115). Klein (1990) notes that "the Program in Social Ecology at the University of California, Irvine, started in 1970, offers integrative study of a wide range of recurring social and environmental problems" (p. 174). The Honors Mathematical Models in the Social Sciences Program at Northwestern University developed during the 1970s and "is limited to a small number of students who have high mathematical aptitude and a strong interest in social problems and issues" (Klein 1990, p. 174).

> **Sherif and Sherif (1969) had the following to say already in 1969 regarding the growth of interdisciplinary trends in higher education:**
>
> The most striking evidence of the interdisciplinary trend is its manifestation in professional and technical schools. Forty years ago—even twenty years ago—who could have imagined that some of the white-coated figures in the antiseptic corridors and wards of medical schools would be, not medics, but sociologists, anthropologists, or even philosophers? Who could have thought that social psychologists and sociologists would be in business schools along with the professors of bookkeeping, business-letter writing, and marketing? How many engineers could have dreamed in their wildest fancy that their own professional organizations would put pressure on them to give greater exposure to the social sciences than what came through the traditional university-wide lecture series supported from student-activity fees? Who could have imagined then that engineering schools would have departments of management and courses on human relations?
>
> These things have happened and they are happening. They reflect a trend in education and in research that is irreversible to the point of no return. We are living in a time of increasing interdisciplinary contact and concern, whether we like it or not. (pp. 3–4)

By now it should be evident to the reader that there are many types of interdisciplinary studies degree programs as well as various types of interdisciplinary activity occurring within universities. As Klein and Newell (1998) point out, interdisciplinary studies "can no longer be defined by pointing to a few exemplary practices and program types" (p. 3). They point out that there are numerous types of interdisciplinary study in higher education. The more traditional or visible forms and locations include the following:

- Free-standing institutions
- Autonomous and cluster colleges
- Centers and institutes
- Interdisciplinary departments
- Interdisciplinary majors, minors, and concentrations
- Mainstream and alternative general education programs
- Individual courses within disciplinary departments
- Tutorials
- Independent Study and self-designed majors
- Travel-study, internships, and practicums (pp. 6–7)

Less visible or not officially recognized interdisciplinary studies activities that occur at universities include study groups, interest groups, networks, community-based projects, problem-focused research projects, and teamwork (Klein and Newell 1998, pp. 7–8).

What types of interdisciplinary studies programs exist at your college and university? It is in your interest to research what kind of interdisciplinary studies programs exist at your college or university. It would also increase your understanding of interdisciplinary studies to compare the nature of your interdisciplinary studies program with at least one other at another college or university.

 **EXERCISE 1-2** Go on the Internet and do research on an interdisciplinary studies degree program at another college or university. If you do not know any, try Googling "interdisciplinary studies degree program" and the name of your favorite state on the same search line.

Your search line would look something like the following:

```
"interdisciplinary studies degree program" "Arizona"
```

Carefully review the search results. Click on the link to the home page of an interdisciplinary studies degree program at a school of which you are unfamiliar. Examine the website carefully. Fill out the following worksheet.

INTERDISCIPLINARY STUDIES DEGREE PROGRAM INTERNET RESEARCH WORKSHEET

Url: http://www. _____

Name of College or University:

Name of Interdisciplinary Studies Degree Program:

Graduate Program or Undergraduate Program?

Year Created:

Degree(s) offered:

Number of Students:

Number of Faculty Members:

Program Requirements:

Special Features of Program:

☐ Individualized Program of Study?

☐ Core Curriculum?

☐ Senior Project?

☐ Capstone Seminar?

☐ Program Portfolio?

☐ Applied learning opportunities (internship, cooperative learning)?

☐ Independent Studies offered?

☐ Other:

Table ⎡1-2⎤ Three Stages of the Interdisciplinary Studies Movement

(Klein 1990; Salter and Hearn, 1996, pp. 26–28)

Stage One (World War I to World War II)
Discussions of interdisciplinarity were part of educational reform. General education programs were created as "an antidote" to the increasing number of disciplines and the fragmentation of knowledge that resulted. Promotion of cooperative efforts across disciplines was discussed among scholars at universities such as the University of Chicago and organizations such as the Social Sciences Research Council (SSRC).

Stage Two (World War II to the late 1960s)
Strong debates about interdisciplinarity in the social sciences along with increased discussion about interdisciplinarity among scholars. Government and industry-funded research sponsor large mission oriented interdisciplinary projects such as the Manhattan Project. New interdisciplinary studies programs begin to appear in colleges and universities.

Stage Three (Late 1960s to the Present)
Interdisciplinary studies programs become increasingly popular in colleges and universities. Increased awareness about interdisciplinarity and professionalization of interdisciplinary studies are facilitated with the creation of the Association of Integrative Studies (1979) and INTERSTUDY (1980).

Towards a Textbook Definition of Interdisciplinary Studies

Many scholars have attempted to define and explain *interdisciplinary studies* since the 1970s, which has resulted in even more confusion. The first attempt was in 1970 with the first international seminar on interdisciplinarity organized by the international Organization for Economic Co-operation and Development (OECD). In 1972 the results of this seminar were published in book form as *Interdisciplinarity: Problems of Teaching and Research in Universities*. The book, according to Klein (1990) "remains the most widely cited reference on the subject of interdisciplinarity" even though some of the ideas and definitions provided became quickly disputed by other scholars and/or outdated (p. 36). For example, the OECD revised its earlier definition after conducting a survey of the relationships between the university and the community in its member countries as well as hosting a 1980 international conference on the topic (Klein 1990, p. 37).

The years 1979–80 were important for other reasons as well. In 1979 two professional organizations for the study of interdisciplinary studies were founded. William H. Newell started the Association for Integrative Studies (AIS) and remains today its Executive Director. As Klein describes it, "the AIS is a U.S.-based organization that promotes the study of interdisciplinary study, methodology, curricula and administration. Most of its members are teachers and scholars engaged in interdisciplinary education" (p. 37). The international organization INTERSTUDY was "formed after the first NSF-sponsored international conference on interdisciplinary problem-focused research. It has . . . focused primarily on the management of research. Most of its members come from government, industry, and primarily business and social science departments in universities" (Klein 1990, p. 37).

𝔇id 𝒴ou 𝒦now? According to the OECD (2005) website,

"The OECD grew out of the Organization for European Economic Co-operation (OEEC), which was set up in 1947 with support from the United States and Canada to co-ordinate the Marshall Plan for the reconstruction of Europe after World War II.

Created as an economic counterpart to NATO, the OECD took over from the OEEC in 1961 and since then its mission has been to help governments achieve sustainable economic growth and employment and rising standards of living in member countries while maintaining financial stability, so contributing to the development of the world economy. . . . In recent years the OECD has moved beyond a focus on its 30 member countries to offer its analytical expertise and accumulated experience to some 100 developing and emerging market economies" ("How Has It Developed?").

For more information about the OECD, see http://www.oecd.org.

Over the past few years, AIS members and leading interdisciplinary studies scholars such as Klein and Newell have dedicated themselves to producing a working definition of interdisciplinary studies from the academic perspective, thus elaborating and improving upon dictionary definitions such as the two quoted in the beginning of this chapter. Klein and Newell's (1998) scholarly definition of interdisciplinary studies is as follows:

> *Interdisciplinary studies may be defined as a process of answering a question, solving a problem, or addressing a topic too broad or complex to be dealt with adequately by a single discipline or profession . . . IDS draws on disciplinary perspectives and integrates their insights through construction of a more comprehensive perspective. In this matter, interdisciplinary study is not a simple supplement but is complementary to and corrective of the disciplines (p. 3).*

Klein and Newell's 1998 definition will serve as this textbook's definition of interdisciplinary studies. Note that their definition of interdisciplinary studies is process oriented and emphasizes problem solving. Note too that interdisciplinary studies draw on disciplinary perspectives. The aim of interdisciplinary studies is to construct (and therefore obtain) a more comprehensive perspective or understanding. These important distinctions will be further discussed in Part Two in this book. But for now, you should keep in mind that when you study a discipline, you are learning how specialists working in that particular discipline view the world, i.e., their disciplinary perspective.

ESSENTIAL FEATURES OF INTERDISCIPLINARY STUDIES

Once Klein and Newell's 1996 definition is broken down to distinct elements, five characteristics of interdisciplinary studies become apparent. These five characteristics are noted in Table 1-3.

Table 1-3 Five Characteristics of Interdisciplinary Studies

1. Means for addressing questions or solving complex problems.
2. Draws on multiple disciplinary perspectives.
3. Works toward the integration of multiple disciplinary insights through the construction of a more comprehensive perspective.
4. Goal is to construct a more comprehensive perspective in answering questions, solving complex problems, or obtaining a greater understanding.
5. Results in correcting, complementing, and supplementing the limits of disciplinary approaches.

NEWELL'S CONCEPTS OF PARTIAL AND FULL INTERDISCIPLINARITY

In his essay "Professionalizing Interdisciplinarity," Newell (1998) suggests using the terms "full" interdisciplinarity and "partial" interdisciplinarity (p. 533). **Full interdisciplinarity** would involve all five characteristics of interdisciplinarity included in Klein and Newell's definition: more than one perspective used from more than one discipline to create a more comprehensive perspective in solving or addressing a complex problem that cannot be satisfactorily addressed using one of the traditional disciplines. **Partial interdisciplinarity** occurs when at least one element of full interdisciplinarity is included, such as the utilization of multiple perspectives. Partial interdisciplinarity occurs, for example, when one signs up for an "interdisciplinary" class on a topic, say French Women in the Twentieth Century, and each week different professors lecture on their topic of specialty. One week a French literature professor may lecture on French women writers. The next week a political science professor will talk about the women's right moments in France. The week after that, an art history professor lectures on French women artists. Such a class could only be considered as interdisciplinary in a partial sense, since no integration occurs in the course (except perhaps in the minds of the students at the end of the course). To be more precise, such a course would be considered multidisciplinary rather than interdisciplinary. Further discussion on the various levels of integration, including multidisciplinary versus interdisciplinary approaches, will be discussed in the next chapter.

 **EXERCISE 1-3** Practice answering the question, "What are interdisciplinary studies?" deploying what you already have learned in this chapter. Memorize the five essential characteristics of interdisciplinary studies. Work on personalizing your definition of interdisciplinary studies by incorporating the following in your definition:

✓ Your disciplines/areas of study

✓ The multiple perspectives you are using

✓ The complex problems you are studying or wish to study

Words to the Wise

The more specific and detailed your answer to the question "What are interdisciplinary studies?" the more knowledgeable and persuasive you will appear to others. Don't worry if you cannot be specific in your answer yet. The following chapters will help you to work on defining interdisciplinary studies in a more personal and comprehensive manner.

Eminent Thinkers and Scholars Mentioned in Chapter One

In Chapter One the names of numerous thinkers and scholars were boldfaced. Table 1-4 lists all these names of eminent scholars and thinkers. These are all individuals whom you may want to learn more about by reading their work or doing research.

Table 1-4 **Eminent Thinkers and Scholars Mentioned in Chapter One**

Plato

Aristotle

Wilhelm von Humboldt

Honoré de Balzac

Michel Foucault

Howard Gardner

Julie Thompson Klein

William H. Newell

James Elkins

Suggested Readings

Briggs, A., & Micard, G. (1972). Problems and solutions. In *Interdisciplinarity: problems of teaching and research in universities* (pp. 185–299). Paris: Center for Educational Research and Innovation.

Calhoun, C. (2001). Foreword. In K. W. Worcester, Social Science Research Council, 1923–1998 (pp. 4–10) [Electronic Version]. New York: Social Science Research Council. Retrieved on July 7, 2005 at <http://www.ssrc.org/inside/about>

Elkins, J. (2001). *Why art cannot be taught.* Urbana and Chicago: University of Illinois Press.

Flexner, S. B. (Ed.). (1987). *The Random House dictionary of the English language* (2nd ed.). Unabridged. New York: Random House.

Foucault, M. (1979). *Discipline and punish: The birth of a prison.* Trans. Alan Sheridan. New York: Vintage.

Gunn, G. (1992). Interdisciplinary studies. In J. Gibaldi (Ed.), *Introduction to scholarship in modern languages and literatures* (pp. 239–261). New York: Modern Language Association.

Haskins, C. H. (1940). *The rise of universities.* New York: Peter Smith.

Hastings, R. (1936). *The universities of Europe in the middle ages.* Vol. 1. London: Oxford University Press.

Hershberg, T. (1981). The new urban history: Toward an interdisciplinary history of the city. In T. Hershberg (Ed.), *Philadelphia: Work, Space, Family, and Group Experience in the Nineteenth Century* (pp. 3–42). New York and Oxford: Oxford University Press.

Klein, J. T. (1990). *Interdisciplinarity: History, theory and practice.* Detroit: Wayne State University Press.

Klein, J. T., & Newell, W. T. (1998). Advancing interdisciplinary studies. In W. T. Newell (Ed.), Interdisciplinarity: Essays from the literature (pp. 3–22). New York: College Entrance Examination Board. Originally published in J. G. Gaff, J. L. Ratcliff, & Associates (Eds.), *Handbook of the undergraduate curriculum* (pp. 393–415). San Francisco: Jossey-Bass.

Lyotard, J.-F. (1984). *The postmodern condition: A report on knowledge.* Trans. Bennington, G. and Massumi, B. Foreword by Jameson, F. Minneapolis: University of Minnesota Press.

Menard, L. (2001). Undisciplined. *The Wilson Quarterly, 25* (4), 51–60.

Mickenberg, D. (2003, Jan. 17). Creating art in the microcosm of Auschwitz. *The Chronicle of Higher Education,* p. B 15.

Moran, J. (2002). *Interdisciplinarity.* New York: Routledge.

Newell, W. H. (1998). Professionalizing interdisciplinarity: Literature review and research agenda. In. W. H. Newell (Ed.), *Interdisciplinarity: Essays From the Literature* (pp. 529–563). New York: College Entrance Examination Board.

Newell, W. H., Hall, J., Hutkins, S., Larner, D., McGuckin, E., & Oates, K. (2003). Apollo meets Dionysius: Interdisciplinarity in long-standing interdisciplinary programs." *Issues in Integrative Studies,* 21, 9–41.

Orrill, R. "Foreword." In W. H. Newell (Ed.), *Interdisciplinarity: Essays from the literature* (pp. *xi–xii*). New York: College Entrance Examination Board.

Sherif, M., and Sherif, C. W. (1969). Interdisciplinary coordination as a validity check: Retrospect and prospects. In M. Sherif and C. W. Sherif (Eds.), *Interdisciplinary relationships in the social sciences* (pp. 3–20). Chicago: Aldine Publishing.

Simpson, J. A. and Weiner, E. S. C. (Eds.). (1989). *Oxford English dictionary* (2nd ed.). Oxford: Clarendon Press; New York: Oxford University Press.

Swoboda, W. W. (1979). Disciplines and interdisciplinarity: A historical perspective. In J. J. Kockelmans (Ed.), *Interdisciplinarity and higher education* (pp. 49–92). University Park: The Pennsylvania State University Press.

Worcester, K. W. (2001). Social Science Research Council, 1923–1998. [Electronic version]. New York: Social Science Research Council. Retrieved July 7, 2005 at <http://www.ssrc.org/inside/about>

ESSENTIAL TERMS FOR INTERDISCIPLINARY STUDIES

Learning Objectives

After reading Chapter Two of *Becoming Interdisciplinary*, you should be able to:

1. Know that there are a number of related terms associated with interdisciplinarity, and that some are more used than others.

2. Know that for some terms such as *crossdisciplinary* there are so many numerous definitions that some conflict in meaning.

3. Learn the most authoritative meanings for *multidisciplinary*, *transdisciplinary*, and *crossdisciplinary*.

4. Keep in mind that while learning the most widely accepted definitions for interdisciplinary terms are extremely important for your knowledge, those terms are "essentially contested."

5. Understand what is meant by an *essentially contested concept*.

6. Understand the distinctions between multidisciplinary and interdisciplinary.

7. Understand the distinctions between transdisciplinary and interdisciplinary.

8. Understand the differences between the following approaches to interdisciplinarity: instrumental interdisciplinary studies, conceptual interdisciplinary studies, and critical interdisciplinary studies.

Multiple Terms and Their Conflicting, Often Confusing Definitions

If trying to understand what the term *interdisciplinarity* means is not confusing enough, there are many related terms that are even more perplexing. *Multidisciplinarity* is often used interchangeably with interdisciplinarity. *Pre-disciplinary* and *transdisciplinarity* are increasingly being used among scholars, while *pluridisciplinary* less so. There are so many contradictory usages of the word *crossdisciplinary* that the word has become extremely problematic to use (Klein 1990, p. 55). Then there are numerous trendy words such as *antidisciplinarity*, *postdisciplinarity* and even *de-disciplinary* used by a number of scholars in order to reflect suspicion and even antagonism toward the continuing utility of the concept of disciplinarity.

Despite any confusion or tension, scholars continue to reach some working consensus about the meaning of words such as *discipline, disciplinarity, multidisciplinarity, interdisciplinarity,* and *transdisciplinarity* because the terms distinguish the different levels of integration, i.e, the different ways and processes of how interdisciplinary work is done. While *discipline* and *interdisciplinary* have been discussed and provisionally defined in the previous chapter, they are included again in this chapter but with additional definitions by leading interdisciplinary studies scholar Julie Thompson Klein. Klein's definitions of *multidisciplinary, transdisciplinary,* and *crossdisciplinary* are also listed in this chapter; they should be considered as the most authoritative current definitions available.

Interdisciplinary Terms as Essentially Contested Concepts

While it is good to know that Klein's definitions are currently among the most widely accepted definitions among scholars, it is important for you to keep in mind at all times that the definitions of interdisciplinary studies terms are continually being contested, vetted, and revised as the growing academic literature on interdisciplinarity develops and advances (which is a major reason why there is so much confusion). All the various meanings of *interdisciplinarity* are akin to all the different meanings of *democracy* insofar as both interdisciplinarity and democracy are regarded as achievements valued by many, yet their practices are complex enough that there is much disagreement and contestation over how they are to be achieved and/or practiced. Gallie (1962) called terms such as *democracy* **essentially contested concepts**, which "essentially involve endless disputes about their proper uses on the part of their users" (qtd. in Connolly 1993, p. 10).

You may be asking yourself why do you need to know that interdisciplinarity and its related terms are essentially contested concepts? How does such knowledge ultimately affect me? Isn't it enough to know what the most renowned scholars say? After all, isn't trying to learn and understand the definitions for interdisciplinary studies terminology challenging enough? Such relevant questions deserve some answers. While it is very important for students to know how the most highly qualified scholars define essentially contested terms such as *interdisciplinarity* and *democracy* it is also good to know that these definitions are not set in stone. Think about it: what kind of democracy would we have if there were only one definition and/or concept of democracy? As long as there is general agreement about the most important aspects, some disagreement allows for individual interpretation and collective debate that ultimately furthers understanding of what a democracy is and/or should be.

Similar things can be said about interdisciplinarity and its related terms. Since the 1970s critical debates over terminology have overall improved our understanding of interdisciplinary studies. Thus, in order for the definitions offered in this chapter to become meaningful for you, you should try to come up with your own composite "working definition" of each term based on what you have read so far. To put it differently, try to write a definition of each term using your own words. You may first want to compare and contrast Klein's definitions of interdisciplinarity and discipline with the definitions and discussions presented in the previous chapter. Following Klein's definition of interdisciplinarity in this chapter is a discussion of the salient differences between multidisciplinarity and interdisciplinarity. A discussion of the differences between interdisciplinarity and transdisciplinarity follows Klein's definition of transdisciplinarity. Chapter Two concludes with introducing and explaining the three major kinds of interdisciplinary activity.

Five Definitions of Essential Terms for Interdisciplinary Studies

by

Julie Thompson Klein

1. Discipline

The term *discipline* signifies the tools, methods, procedures, exempla, concepts, and theories that account coherently for a set of objects or subjects. Over time they are shaped and reshaped by external contingencies and internal intellectual demands. In this manner a discipline comes to organize and concentrate experience into a particular "world view." Taken together, related claims within a specific material field put limits on the kinds of questions practitioners ask about their material, the methods, and concepts they use, the answers they believe, and their criteria for truth and validity. There is, in short, a certain particularity about the images of reality in a given discipline. (Klein 1990, p. 104)

What strikes you about Klein's (1990) definition of "discipline"? Disciplines, according to Klein's definition, are particular—they have a "particular 'world view'" as well as "a certain particularity about the images of reality." Klein's definition is similar to Gardner's (2000) provided in Chapter One as both stress the idea that disciplines shape the way we see the world. Now compare Klein's definition of discipline with the following definitions of other terms.

2. *Multidisciplinarity*

"Multidisciplinarity" signifies the juxtaposition of disciplines. It is essentially *additive*, not *integrative*. Even in a common environment, educators, researchers, and practitioners still behave as disciplinarians with different perspectives. The relationship may be mutual and cumulative but not interactive, for there is "no apparent connection," no real cooperation or "explicit" relationships, and even, perhaps a "questionable eclecticism." The participating disciplines are neither changed nor enriched, and the lack of "a well-defined matrix" of interactions means disciplinary relationships are likely to be limited and transitory. (Klein 1990, p. 56)

3. Interdisciplinarity

Interdisciplinarity has been variously defined in this century: as a methodology, a concept, a process, a way of thinking, a philosophy, and a reflexive ideology. It has been linked with attempts to expose the dangers of fragmentation, to re-establish old connections, to explore emerging relations, and to create new subjects adequate to handle our practical and conceptual needs. Cutting across all these theories is one recurring idea. Interdisciplinarity is a means of solving problems and answering questions that cannot be satisfactorily addressed using single methods or approaches. (Klein 1990, p. 196)

What Are the Distinctions between Multidisciplinarity and Interdisciplinarity?

Understanding the differences between multidisciplinarity and interdisciplinarity is crucial for students in learning how to do interdisciplinary studies. All too often a project or event will be advertised as "interdisciplinary" when in actuality it is really multidisciplinary. For example, imagine a special event at your school: a panel on the future of AIDS. You enter the auditorium, and on the stage is a long table. Seated behind the table are a number of panelists, who include the following: a virologist, a public health worker, a doctor who treats AIDS patients, an epidemiologist, a pharmacologist who conducts research on drugs for a leading drug company, and a human rights activist. Each panelist gives a presentation on the future of AIDS from his or her own perspective. The virologist discusses new advances in understanding the virus. The public health worker discusses public health initiatives in South Africa and compares them with those in the United States. The doctor reports on the encouraging results of new drug therapies on his patients. The pharmacologist promises better drugs in the future with fewer side effects. The epidemiologist forecasts which countries will be affected by AIDs the most. Finally, the human rights worker discusses how making drugs available to all those infected with HIV at low cost will be increasingly a human rights issue.

When and where does the integration occur if it occurs at all? While the audience hears multiple perspectives and insights on the future of AIDS from many disciplines, the presented multiple perspectives and insights are never integrated. Consequently it is up to the audience members to think through how the perspectives of drug companies will integrate with those of human rights activists, if they ever will at all. While the panel might have been advertised as "interdisciplinary," it was actually multidisciplinary because no integration occurred during the process of the event, except perhaps at the end in the minds of the audience members.

All too often students working on interdisciplinary research projects will work in a multidisciplinary rather than an interdisciplinary manner. Students who have busy schedules will sometimes work independently on a group project, and will only meet shortly before the presentation is due to put together a joint introduction and conclusion. *To work on a class project in a truly interdisciplinary manner students would have to work together and would have to integrate their research and the insights it uncovers throughout the duration of the project.* Interdisciplinary group work can happen when students opt for a skit as a student presentation. By creating a script or dialogue, each student is contributing not only their insights from their research to the project but also ideas for how to integrate those insights coherently.

In terms of doing individual academic interdisciplinary research, you can turn to Reading 4, "Confessions of an Unconscious Interdisciplinarian," which is Thomas H. Murray's (1986) account of how he became an interdisciplinarian. Murray's personal narrative is an excellent example of learning how to do interdisciplinary research. As a psychology graduate student, Murray (1986) became interested in the ethical questions raised by his experience of witnessing social psychological experiments on human subjects. In his case the human subjects were undergraduate college students who were "tricked" as they were led to believe that "they were witnesses to someone accidentally receiving a severe electric shock" (p. 58). He began to identify a complex problem within his discipline of psychology that was being overlooked: ethical responsibility. He learned how to address the ethical responsibilities of researchers by studying other disciplinary perspectives such as philosophy, religion, and law. Murray (1986) writes of the interdisciplinarity of his graduate studies research as follows:

> *In what sense is this argument "interdisciplinary?" It is not merely an argument in moral philosophy that deceptive research is wrong per se; nor is it merely an empirical observation or theory. It requires as necessary components both moral arguments and insights from psychological theories (dealing with discrepancies between verbal and non-verbal behavior, factors affecting interpersonal interactions, the need for and methods by which self-esteem may be sustained, and the potential for self-deception in the service of avoiding internal conflict) as well as the privileged empirical observations I was able to make in my role as experimenter. (p. 64)*

You will read more about Murray's intellectual development as an interdisciplinarian in Reading 4, which can be found in Chapter Five. What should be pointed out is that Murray has continued to raise ethical questions in not only psychological research, but in other related fields such as medicine, genetics research, and even Olympic athletic training as he has served on the U.S. Olympic Anti-Doping Committee. More recently he has served as the President of the leading think tank on bioethics, The Hastings Center. You can read more about what Murray has done since writing "Confessions of an Unconscious Interdisciplinarian" by going to the Hastings Center Website and clicking on "People" and then "Staff." Murray's biography posted on the Hastings Center Website can be accessed at the following URL: <http://www.thehastingscenter.org/people/staff>.

Interdisciplinary work is also common in the workplace where people work in teams. For example, the development of new drugs in drug companies is done typically in an interdisciplinary manner. For any given health problem, such as high blood pressure, there will be an interdisciplinary team working together to put out a new drug to treat high blood pressure. Those on the project team may include chemists, doctors, pharmacologists, marketing specialists, patent lawyers, sales representatives, and project managers. All of their inputs and insights from their areas of disciplinary expertise are needed throughout the development process to put the new drug out on the market.

4. Transdisciplinarity

"Transdisciplinary" approaches are far more comprehensive in scope and vision. . . . "Transdisciplinary" approaches . . . are conceptual frameworks that transcend the narrow scope of disciplinary world views, metaphorically encompassing the several parts of material handled separately by specialized disciplines. A "transdisciplinary" approach literally transcends a particular range, breaking through disciplinary barriers, and disobeying the rules of disciplinary etiquette. Disciplines become "irrelevant," subordinate," or "instrumental" to the larger framework. (Klein 1990, pp. 65–66)

What Are the Distinctions between Interdisciplinarity and Transdisciplinarity?

Understanding the differences between interdisciplinarity and transdisciplinarity can be confusing. The crucial difference lies in their differing approaches to disciplines. Interdisciplinarity relies on disciplinary knowledge insofar as it draws from multiple disciplinary insights in the process of identifying, evaluating and solving problems. In contrast, transdisciplinary approaches to problem solving, as Klein (1990) notes, are "far more comprehensive in scope and vision" (p. 65). Transdisciplinarity relies more on theories, concepts, and approaches that literally go beyond or transcend disciplines. Klein (1996) subsequently points out that "the term 'transdisciplinary' usually labels a paradigm or vision that transcends narrow disciplinary worldviews through overarching synthesis" (p. 11). In other words, knowledge that cannot be singularly claimed as belonging to or originating in any one discipline can be considered as transdisciplinary. A good example of a transdisciplinary framework is Marxism. Karl Marx has been claimed as a major thinker in sociology, economics, political science, and philosophy. In actuality his thought has been influential not only in those disciplines but many others such as art history and literature. Other examples of transdisciplinary thinking include general systems theory, structuralism, and phenomenology (Klein 1990, p. 65; 1996, p. 11). Within the sciences an example of transdisciplinary research would be sociobiology, which according to Klein's (2004) entry on transdisciplinary in the *Encyclopedia of Life Support Systems*,

applies principles of natural selection and evolutionist biology to the study of animal social behavior. Promoted as a "new synthesis" sociobiology is rooted in the theory of genetic inheritance, which holds that genes are selected from available pool interaction with the environment over time, providing maximum fitness for individual and kin survival and reproduction. This is not the first time . . . the evolutionary model has been imported into social sciences. E.O. Wilson (1998), a proponent of sociobiology, extended the campaign to integrate natural sciences with social sciences and humanities in his theory of "consilience." The term was first proposed by nineteenth century philosopher of science William Whewell to connote the "jumping together" of knowledge by linking facts and fact-based theory across disciplines, in order to create a common groundwork of explanation. Harkening back to the ancient "Ionian Enchantment of belief in the primacy of a few natural laws, Wilson crafted an encyclopedic vision of Western knowledge that privileges biochemical explanation. (n.p.)

5. Cross-disciplinarity

It has been used for several different purposes: to view one discipline from the perspective of another, rigid axiomatic control by one discipline, the solution of a problem with no intention of generating a new science or paradigm, new fields that develop between two or more disciplines, a generic adjective for six different categories of discipline-crossing activities, and a generic adjective for all activities involving interaction across disciplines. (Klein 1990, p. 55)

Klein's definition offers a clear image of the variability that distinguishes cross-disciplinary interaction. Some examples of cross-disciplinary work, according to Meeth (1978) include "describing the physics of music or the politics of literature"(p. 10). Doing cross-disciplinary work can be difficult. According to Newell and Green (1982/1998),

cross-disciplinary inquiries, such as the physics of music, might well be conducted in an interdisciplinary way, but in practice they seldom are. The problem here is that one of the disciplines involved usually exercises complete hegemony (a kind of disciplinary imperialism) over the other in such fashion that the second discipline (or, more properly, its subject matter) becomes a passive object of study rather than an active system of thought, so that the analysis draws critically on only one discipline. Courses on the physics of music apply the principles of physics to (the subject matter of) music, but the discipline of music—its aesthetic standards and so on—is rarely considered. (p. 24)

 **REVIEWING AND DEFINING FOR YOURSELF ESSENTIAL INTERDISCIPLINARY TERMS**

Review the definitions regarding levels of integration provided so far in this chapter. Come up with your own working definition for each of the following terms. Be sure to check that your working definition is in agreement with Klein's definitions.

Disciplinarity

Interdisciplinarity

Multidisciplinarity

Transdisciplinarity

Cross-disciplinarity

More Essential Terms for Interdisciplinary Activity

While some scholars such as Newell (2001) dispute that there are different kinds of interdisciplinary activity, recent literature on the subject suggests otherwise. The following three distinct types of interdisciplinary work can be identified in recent academic literature on interdisciplinarity: (1) instrumental interdisciplinarity, (2) conceptual interdisciplinarity, and (3) critical interdisciplinarity. What is instrumental interdisciplinarity? ***Instrumental interdisciplinarity*** occurs whenever the primary focus of interdisciplinary study or work is on solving complex problems. According to Salter and Hearn (1996), "instrumental interdisciplinarity consists, for the most part, of borrowing methods and tools from across the disciplines in an effort to address needs dictated by the specific problem in hand" (p. 30). The advantage of an instrumental interdisciplinary approach is that one avoids becoming bogged down or sidetracked by purely academic or intellectual debates about how interdisciplinary work is accomplished, i.e., discussions of epistemological issues or the search for the unity of knowledge. The bottom line or aim of instrumental interdisciplinarity is getting the job done, i.e, solving an unsolved problem or achieving greater understanding, which is why instrumental interdisciplinarity is often associated with interdisciplinary work done outside of universities, such as in business, government, or government-sponsored research or mission projects. It is precisely this "hands-on" approach that initially attracts some interdisciplinary studies majors.

The second type of interdisciplinary activity is known as ***conceptual interdisciplinarity***. Conceptual interdisciplinary activity not only endeavors to understand and/or solve complex problems, but it also is concerned with how interdisciplinary work occurs, i.e, understanding the process or integration as well as the relation(s) between interdisciplinary studies and the disciplines. For example, Newell (1983, 2001, 2005; Newell & Green 1982) has made great advances in understanding the integrative process while Klein (1990) has persuasively argued that the pervasive opposition between disciplinarity and interdisciplinarity is "an oversimplified dichotomy that obscures the more subtle interactions that do take place" (p. 105). Conceptual interdisciplinarians tend to stress the importance of a strong foundation in disciplinary knowledge for interdisciplinary studies. In other words, conceptual interdisciplinarians believe that before interdisciplinarians can do acceptable interdisciplinary work, they have to have a sufficient understanding of the disciplines they are interested in integrating. While conceptual interdisciplinarians can be critical of the way disciplines are currently structured, organized and administered, they do not endeavor to do away with them or with the notion of specialization (Salter and Hearn 1996, p. 32).

In contrast, the primary characteristic of the third type of interdisciplinary work, ***critical interdisciplinarity***, is its focus: the profound critique of, or opposition to, disciplines. According to Klein (2005), critical interdisciplinarity "aims to transform existing structures of knowledge and education" (p. 56). While both conceptual and critical interdisciplinarities share the same criticisms of disciplinarity (see textbox), critical interdisciplinarians would like to see much more radical changes made in the ways research and education are conducted.

According to Salter and Hearn (1996) conceptual and critical interdisciplinarians share the following similar criticisms of disciplines:

- Disciplines fragment and dislocate knowledge
- Disciplines with their emphasis on specialization create useless units of knowledge that have no application to real life social concerns
- Disciplines encourage exclusivity
- Disciplines promote rigidity in the pursuit of knowledge
- Disciplines create cultures where specialists in a given discipline can only communicate with other specialists in the discipline
- Disciplines create disciplinary isolation (p. 34)

Discussion Questions

1. Would you agree that interdisciplinary work or study should be broken down to instrumental interdisciplinarity, conceptual interdisciplinarity, and critical interdisciplinarity? Why or why not?

2. If you do agree that it is a good idea to break down interdisciplinarity into instrumental, conceptual, and critical interdisciplinarities, which ones are you most interested in learning more about and why?

Suggested Readings

Centre for Educational Research and Innovation. (1972). *Interdisciplinarity: problems of teaching and research in universities.* Paris: OECD Publications.

Connolly, W. E. (1993). *The terms of political discourse* (3rd ed.). Oxford, UK and Cambridge, M.A.: Blackwell.

Gaff, J. G., J. L. Ratcliff and Associates. (1997). *Handbook of the undergraduate curriculum: A comprehensive guide to purposes, structures, practices, and change.* San Francisco: Jossey Bass.

Gallie, W. B. (1962). Essentially contested concepts. In M. Black (Ed.), *The importance of language* (pp. 121–146). Englewood, N.J.: Prentice-Hall.

Klein, J. T. (1990). *Interdisciplinarity: History, theory and practice.* Detroit: Wayne State University Press.

Klein, J. T. (1996). *Crossing boundaries: Knowledge, disciplinarities, and interdisciplinarities.* Charlottesville and London: University of Virginia Press.

Klein, J. T. (2004). Unity of knowledge and transdisciplinarity: Contexts of definition, theory, and the new discourse of problem solving" [Electronic version]. In G. H. Hadorn (Ed.), *Unity of knowledge* (in *Transdisciplinary research for sustainability*). In *Encyclopedia of life support systems* (EOLSS). Developed under the Auspices of the UNESCO, EOLSS Publishers, Oxford, UK. Retrieved June 2004 from <http://www.eolss.net>

Klein, J. T. (2005). *Humanities, culture, and interdisciplinarity.* Albany, NY: State University Press of New York.

Meeth, L. R. (1978). Interdisciplinary studies: A matter of definition. *Change: The Magazine of Higher Learning*, 10 (6), 10.

Murray, T. H. (1986). Confessions of an unconscious interdisciplinarian. *Issues in Integrative Studies*, 4, 57–69. [See Reading 4 in this volume.]

Newell, W. H. (1983). The case for interdisciplinary studies: Response to professor Benson's five arguments. *Issues in Integrative Studies*, 2, 1–19. [See Reading 8 in this volume.]

Newell, W. H. (2001). A theory of interdisciplinary studies. *Issues In Integrative Studies*, 19, 1–25.

Newell, W. H. (in press). Decision-making in interdisciplinary studies. In G. Morçöl (Ed.), *Handbook of decision making*. New York: Marcel Dekker.

Newell, W. H., & Green, W. J. (1982). Defining and teaching interdisciplinary studies. *Improving College and University Teaching*, 30 (1), 23–30.

DESCRIBING INTERDISCIPLINARY STUDIES

THE POWER OF METAPHORS

Whether implicit or explicit, arguments about knowledge are often guided by metaphors.

Julie Thompson Klein (1996, p. 5)

Learning Objectives

After reading Chapter Three of *Becoming Interdisciplinary*, you should be able to:

1. Understand what is a metaphor.
2. Understand what is a simile.
3. Know that there are various kinds of metaphors.
4. Become familiar with some of the more common metaphors for describing interdisciplinarity and interdisciplinary studies.
5. Learn how to utilize metaphors to conceptualize and articulate your degree.
6. Learn how metaphors encourage interdisciplinary thinking.

Understanding Metaphor

In this chapter you will learn how to utilize metaphors to conceptualize and articulate interdisciplinary studies. You will also learn how metaphors encourage interdisciplinary thinking. But before you can engage in such activities, you need to understand fully what is a metaphor and what are its numerous features. Metaphors are central to human thought and understanding. Much of language is metaphoric; indeed, language is largely impossible without metaphor. Metaphor is the most basic of all tropes or figures of speech.

What is a metaphor? According to Baldick (1990), a metaphor is one word or expression used in comparison of another thing, idea or action to suggest some similarity or "common quality shared by the two." Baldick (1990) continues as follows:

> *In metaphor, this resemblance is assumed as an imaginary identity rather than directly dated as a comparison: referring to a man as that pig, or saying he is a pig is metaphorical, whereas he is like a pig is a simile. Metaphors may also appear as verb (a talent may blossom) or as adjectives (a notice may be green). (p. 134)*

Similes are similar to metaphors but use "like" or "as." When Madonna sang, "Like a Virgin," she was using a simile.

Metaphors compare two unlike things—usually something abstract (or unknown) with something more concrete (or known). Take for example the following metaphor: my love is a rose. Love is what is being compared; it is considered the subject of the metaphor and is called the tenor. Rose is the object of the metaphor and is called the vehicle as it transports or carries away the meaning of the tenor. Metaphors thus can increase our understanding of concepts or ideas that are abstract, nebulous, complex, new, unfamiliar, or otherwise inexplicable. For example, love is certainly an abstraction; it is difficult to understand, let alone describe. There is no one definition of love—each person will describe love differently, in his or her own unique way.

For some love is understanding. For others, it is unconditional. For some, love is what you feel for a romantic partner. For others, it is the bond a parent has for a child. Some think love is passion. One can have love for their romantic partner. One can also love chocolate.

When the Scottish poet Robert Burns described love as a red, red rose in a simile, he was comparing something abstract (love) to something concrete and vivid—a rose. While love is something very difficult to picture in one's mind, a rose is very easy to envision. The connection between love, an abstraction, and a rose, a flower, may be different for each person. For instance, one person may think that love smells good. Someone else may think that love is beautiful. Another may think love is eternal, while still another may think love is so delicate that it does not last very long!

METAPHOR	LOVE	IS A	ROSE
Type of Noun	Abstract		Concrete
Observed Qualities	Unknown, Vague, Multiple or Unfamiliar		Known: Red Beautiful Delicate
Rhetorical Term	Tenor		Vehicle

FIGURE 3-1 | Diagram of the Metaphor, *Love Is a Rose*

Danish physicist Niels Bohr relied on metaphor to explain something abstract, complex, and unfamiliar: atomic structure. Bohr described something that was abstract and at the time unfamiliar, the structure of the atom, by comparing it to something that was familiar and widely understood: the solar system. As von Oech (1990) points out, "Within this framework, he [Bohr] figured that the sun represented the nucleus and the planets represented the electrons (pp. 44–45). For von Oech (1990), "metaphors are also effective in making complex ideas easier to understand. Indeed, they can be good tools to explain ideas to people outside your specialty" (p. 45).

Effective and Non-Effective Metaphors

Metaphors can be effective or non-effective. Metaphors are like jokes insofar as there can be numerous reasons why a punch line is funny for a good joke. The important thing is that the audience laughs. Metaphors need to be effective.

For example, typically students do not think of college as a "home away from home" or "heaven on earth." Similarly, if one says college is like Las Vegas, students may disagree or become confused. Depending on one's school and program, if someone said college is like a boot camp, some students would shake their head in agreement. Since large public universities such as Arizona State University are such diverse places, it is difficult to come up with a metaphor that all students at such universities can agree with. If someone says, ASU is a big parking lot—there is a well-known parking shortage at ASU—ASU students will laugh or shake their head in agreement. Nevertheless, while it may be an effective metaphor for students, it may not be an effective metaphor for faculty, administrators and/or Parking Services. The challenge with coming up with an effective metaphor is creating one that your audience will immediately understand and agree with.

Effective Metaphors Are Like Good Jokes

Philosopher Donald Davidson thinks that there are only effective metaphors and good jokes. According to Davidson (1979), "A metaphor implies a kind and degree of artistic success; there are no unsuccessful metaphors, just as there are no unfunny jokes. There are tasteless metaphors, but these are turns that nevertheless have brought something off, even if it were not worth bringing off or could have been brought off better" (p. 29).

Metaphors: True or False?

Another important observation that Davidson (1979) makes regarding metaphors is that metaphors, unlike similes, tend to be false:

> *If a sentence used metaphorically is true or false in the ordinary sense, then it is clear that it is usually false. The most obvious semantic difference between simile and metaphor is that all similes are true and most metaphors are false. The earth is like a floor, the Assyrian did come down like a wolf on the fold, because everything is like everything. But turn these sentences into metaphors, and you turn them false; the earth is like a floor, but it is not a floor; Tolstoy, grown up, was like an infant, but he wasn't one. We use a simile ordinarily only when we know the corresponding metaphor to be false. We say Mr. S. is like a pig because we know he isn't one. If we had used a metaphor and said he was a pig, this would not be because we changed our mind about the facts but because we chose to get the idea across a different way. (p. 39)*

Dead Metaphors

Metaphors that have become commonplace, or even clichés are called *dead metaphors*. For example, "the legs" of a chair is a dead metaphor. Baldick (1990) cites *"branch of an organization"* as his example of a dead metaphor (p. 134). Can you think of others?

Mixed Metaphors

Mixed metaphors are usually the result of trying to apply two metaphors to any one thing, resulting in an illogical, confusing, or just plain ridiculous comparison. Baldick's (1990) example of a mixed metaphor is apt: "those vipers stabbed us in the back." (p. 134). Vipers cannot stab anyone—they are snakes.

Interdisciplinary Metaphors

For many people interdisciplinary studies are unfamiliar and abstract. You yourself may have been unfamiliar with interdisciplinary studies before taking your first interdisciplinary studies course. Your challenge from now on as an interdisciplinary studies major is to describe your degree concisely and effectively. Possibly the best way to describe your degree is to employ effective metaphors and similes. You will have to come up with metaphors that produce vivid, clear images in the minds of others. Interdisciplinary studies can be compared to . . . what? Take a look around you. Look at your desk. What do you see? Chances are you will see some if not all of the following: a stapler, a paper clip, a day organizer, a computer, a computer diskette. What do you carry with you? Nowadays most students carry at least a wallet and a cell phone. Everyday objects such as these make some excellent effective metaphors for interdisciplinary studies. Paper clips and staplers attach two more pieces (of paper). Cell phones and computers allow for multitasking and organizing. Wallets multitask, organize, and contain financial tools. Do you wear glasses? Glasses contain two lenses—often grounded to different prescriptions—that allow you to see better and more clearly.

Are you hungry? Food metaphors can serve as effective metaphors for interdisciplinary studies. Interdisciplinary study is like a smoothie when fully integrated, or it can be like trail mix with all the elements still discrete and identifiable. Yet when all the different parts are mixed together, they create something new (and, students have pointed out, delicious). Trail mix happens to be an excellent metaphor for multidisciplinarity. Other popular metaphors for interdisciplinarity involve fruit. Fruit, fruit salad, and smoothies make extremely illustrative metaphors for understanding the differences between disciplinarity, multidisciplinarity, and interdisciplinarity. Nissani (1995) points out that fruit can be served whole side by side (disciplinary metaphor), or chopped up as in a fruit salad (multidisciplinary metaphor), or finely blended as in a fruit smoothie (inter-disciplinary metaphor). The combinations can be quite exotic and unusual, or more familiar such as mixing apples and oranges. To use another food metaphor, interdisciplinary studies can be described as a peanut and jelly sandwich, combining two elements that complement each other quite well.

While it is important to come up with an effective metaphor for interdisciplinary studies that is meaningful to you, it is helpful to know that scholars have already come up with many effective metaphors for interdisciplinarity. Many of these metaphors can be used in contrast to metaphors for disciplinarity.

For example, Klein (1990) notes the following metaphors for disciplinarity:

- Private property
- Patrolled boundaries
- Island fortress
- "No trespassing"
- Mother lode
- Territory
- Empire
- Oligarchy
- Domain (p. 77)

What kind of images pop in your head when you read these words? It is difficult not to receive images of exclusion, isolation, enforcement, or perhaps even elitism. According to Klein (1990), geopolitical metaphors constitute the dominant imagery for discipline (p. 77). In other words, disciplines are often described in terms of territory and power control. Such metaphors are not surprising, Klein (1990) points out borrowing from Lakoff and Johnson (1980), because

> The concept, the activity—indeed the very language of argument—are partially structured by the metaphor of war: claims are "indefensible, criticisms land "right on target," positions are wiped out by "strategy," arguments are "attacked," "demolished," "won," or "shot down." This tendency is only heightened in the case of interdisciplinarity. (Klein 1990, p. 78)

Indeed, contrast the disciplinary metaphors with the following geopolitical ones Klein (1990) lists for interdisciplinarity:

- Breaching of boundaries
- Cross-cultural exploration
- Excursions to the frontiers
- Border traffic
- Poorly charted waters
- Demilitarized zone
- Switzerland of academia
- Mining other fields
- Alliances
- Bridging
- Overlapping neighborhoods (pp. 77–78)

Note that these metaphors for interdisciplinarity imply challenges to both power and borders. They can imply a pioneering spirit (excursion to the frontier) but also chaos and confusion (poorly charted waters, demilitarized zone).

The Increasing Importance of Boundary Metaphors

Klein (1996) has brought to our attention the emerging importance of boundary metaphors for thinking about and talking about interdisciplinarity. She asserts in her important 1996 book, *Crossing Boundaries: Knowledge, Disciplinarities, and Interdisciplinarities*, that "*boundary* has become a new keyword in discussions of knowledge" (p. 1).

While the metaphor of boundary is geopolitically based, it is also a spatial metaphor denoting place as well as "turf, territory, and domain" (Klein 1996, p. 1). Boundaries can give individuals a sense of belonging when they are kept, and a sense of transgression when they are not. Boundaries are not necessarily fixed or permanent. Tremendous efforts must be made at times to keep boundaries firmly in place, i.e., boundary work. According to Klein (1996), when we apply the term *boundary work* metaphorically to knowledge, we are referring to "the composite set of claims, activities, and institutional structures that define and protect knowledge practices. People work directly and through institutions to create, maintain, break down, and reformulate boundaries between knowledge units" i.e, disciplines (p. 1).

Some disciplinary boundaries appear impenetrable, closed, or restricted—think of the physical sciences such as physics or some business disciplines such as accounting. They also appear to have clearly set, inflexible boundaries, although Klein (1993) has demonstrated that even the boundaries of physics have since the mid twentieth century been altered considerably. Overall, however, there is an increasing awareness that disciplinary boundaries have increasingly blurred. Many disciplines welcome interaction with other disciplines and thus are considered open or unrestricted. Other disciplines, particularly in the humanities, are said to have fuzzy boundaries as they are either considered more interdisciplinary or lend themselves to interdisciplinary work (think of art history or literature).

To do interdisciplinary work, boundaries have to be crossed. Crossing boundaries is thus a crucial metaphor for doing interdisciplinary work.

Other Metaphors for Interdisciplinarity

There is no shortage of metaphors for doing interdisciplinary work. Other theoretical realms can serve as good sources for interdisciplinary metaphors as well. Klein (1990) provides the following from mathematics and physics:

- Fission
- Clusters
- Nexus
- Fusion
- Concentric circles (p. 80)

Yet other metaphors for interdisciplinarity are organic in nature:

- Hybrid vigor
- Symbiosis
- Spill-over
- Network
- Chain links
- Overlapping fish scales (Klein 1990, p. 80; 82)

Metaphors and Interdisciplinary Thinking

When you make comparisons between two unlike things using metaphor, you encourage interdisciplinary thinking as you are presenting one thing in terms of another perspective. For example, geopolitical metaphors used when discussing interdisciplinarity compare an abstract educational concept, "discipline," from geopolitical viewpoints—in terms of territory and power. In so doing the meanings of both territory and power are expanded.

When we typically think of territory in geopolitical terms, we think of it in terms of physical space and geography. We also can think of land disputes and the political conflicts that result from land disputes, i.e., political struggle. While disciplinary "territories" may be conceptual rather than physical, their effects and consequences are just as real as those from physical territories, i.e, disputes and power conflicts. Education as a service profession is concerned with how to educate individuals, not necessarily how to understand conflict. Nevertheless, whether or not educators care to admit it or not, conflicts exist in education, especially about disciplinary boundaries. By taking into consideration how political scientists view conflicts stemming from territorial claims, educators can better deal with their own "territory disputes."

Important Metaphors for Interdisciplinarity

During the 1970s bridge building and restructuring were very popular metaphors for intererdisciplinary work. Klein (1990) describes the difference between the two as follows:

> The first, "bridge building," takes place between complete and firm disciplines. The second, "restructuring," involves changing parts of several disciplines. Bridge-building seems more common and is less difficult, since it preserves disciplinary identities. Restructuring is more radical and often embodies a criticism of not only the state of the disciplines being restructured but, either implicitly or explicitly, the prevailing structure of knowledge. Bridge-building usually assumes a grounding in the constituent disciplines and often has an applied orientation. Restructuring usually assumes the need for new organizing concepts and the methodologies or skills common to more than one discipline. (pp. 27–28)

For students studying interdisciplinary studies, bridge-building is an important metaphor, as students will try to make connections between their two disciplines. Restructuring is, as Klein (1990) states, rare, and usually requires the efforts of more than one person.

Two other important metaphors for doing interdisciplinary work are the following:

- Borrowing
- Translation

Since each is essential to understanding how to do interdisciplinary studies, each needs to be discussed in depth separately. A brief discussion of borrowing and translation can be found in the introduction to Reading 12, "Teaching for Transfer," by D. N. Perkins and Gavriel Salomon (1988).

A Note of Caution: Inappropriate Metaphors for Interdisciplinarity

Just because there are many definitions of interdisciplinarity (see Chapter Two) does not give you free license when trying to create a meaningful metaphor either to describe interdisciplinary studies or to prompt interdisciplinary thinking. Metaphors not only have to be effective—they have to be *appropriate*. For example, Klein (1996) singles out the popular metaphor of *bilingualism* as an especially inappropriate metaphor. Klein objects to bilingualism because "it implies a mastery of two complete languages that rarely if ever occurs." (p. 220). Instead of bilingualism, Klein recommends *pidgin* or *creole* as they "are the typifying forms of interdisciplinary communication." Pidgin or creole usually are hybrid languages, combining two languages by simplifying one or both of them. Klein (1996) insists that "communication competence is a condition for the possibility of interdisciplinary work," and that "studies of interdisciplinary communication reveal that most activities involve combing everyday language with specialist terms from pertinent domains" (p. 220). In other words, when doing interdisciplinary work you are very likely going to mix everyday language with particular words from what you have learned in your coursework. As we will discuss further in Chapter Seven, different disciplines may use the same word differently, so it will be essential for you to understand how each discipline uses a particular word, term, or concept.

Chapter Three □ 33

Create an original metaphor for interdisciplinary studies following the diagram provided below. Fill out the blanks. In so doing you should be able to not only create your metaphor but to be able to justify or explain it. Make sure that you are comparing interdisciplinary studies, which is an abstraction or something unfamiliar to some people, to something concrete or vivid. Avoid comparing interdisciplinary studies to a person or an animal—it is generally not appropriate to compare living things, particularly people, to either abstractions or things. In other words, it is inappropriate to say interdisciplinary studies is like an octopus or to say that interdisciplinary studies is like Bill Gates—even if you think you can make some insightful and original points of comparison (you can always say that Bill Gates–or someone else—is an interdisciplinarian). It is very important that you make sure that your metaphor is both effective and appropriate. Once you finish diagramming your metaphor, answer the following questions:

□ How does your metaphor increase your understanding of interdisciplinary studies?

□ How can it be helpful to others?

METAPHOR	INTERDISCIPLINARY STUDY	IS	_____
Type of noun	abstract		concrete
Observed Qualities	Unknown, vague, multiple or unfamiliar		_____
Rhetorical Term	Tenor		Vehicle

Come up with a "Top Ten List" of the top ten metaphors for interdisciplinary studies. Compare your list with those of your classmates. Identify the additional insight into interdisciplinary studies that each contributes. Note that some metaphors extend the meaning in the same direction, while others extend it in new directions.

Actual Student Metaphors for Interdisciplinary Studies from Spring 2003

Students in the author's spring 2003 introductory interdisciplinary studies course did Exercise 3-2 as a class activity. The class came up with the following "Top Ten List:"

10. Educational bi-polarism

9. Engine

8. Bridge

7. Relationship

6. Bifocals

5. Road map

4. Legos®

3. Zipper

2. Salt and pepper

1. Liberty and Government

Actual Student Metaphors for Interdisciplinary Studies from Spring 2004

A year later students in one of the author's Spring 2004 introductory interdisciplinary studies courses also did Exercise 3-2 as a class activity. The class came up with the following "Top Ten List:"

10. Long Island Ice Tea

9. Quilt

8. Magnet

7. Jukebox

6. Supreme pizza

5. Buffet

4. Legos®

3. Butterfly [no two degrees are alike]

2. Jigsaw puzzle

1. Orchestra

It is an interesting coincidence that both classes chose Legos® as their fourth choice!

 **METAPHORS FOR INTERDISCIPLINARY THINKING**

Exercise developed by David Thomas

Dream up some comparisons between two unlike things with metaphor in order to encourage interdisciplinary thinking. Be sure to compare one thing in terms of another. Try then to utilize your metaphor as a vehicle to ask unusual questions and/or formulate interesting hypotheses/theories. How has the metaphor increased your thinking about the connections between two disciplinary perspectives?

Suggested Readings

Baldick, C. (1990). *The concise Oxford dictionary of literary terms*. Oxford and N.Y.: Oxford University Press.

Davidson, D. (1979). What metaphors mean. In S. Sacks (Ed.), *On metaphor*. Chicago and London: University of Chicago Press.

Klein, J. T. (1990). *Interdisciplinarity: History, theory and practice*. Detroit: Wayne State University Press.

Klein, J. T. (1993). Blurring, cracking, and crossing: Permeation and the fracturing of discipline. In E. Messer-Davidow, D. R. Shumway, & D. J. Sylvan (Eds.), *Knowledges: Historical and critical studies in disciplinarity* (pp. 185–211). Charlottesville: University of Virginia Press.

Klein, J. T. (1996). *Crossing boundaries: Knowledge, disciplinarities, and interdisciplinarities*. Charlottesville and London: University of Virginia Press.

Lakoff, G. & Johnson, M. (1980). *Metaphors we live by*. Chicago: University of Chicago Press.

Nissani, M. (1995). Fruits, salads, and smoothies: A working definition of interdisciplinarity. [Electronic version] *Journal of Educational Thought* 29: 119–125. Retrieved August 1, 2005 from <http://www.is.wayne.edu/mnissani/PAGEPUB/SMOOTHIE.htm>

Perkins, D. N. & Salomon, G. (1988). Teaching for transfer. *Educational Leadership,* 40 (8), 22–32. [See Reading 12 in this volume.]

Sacks, S. (Ed.). (1979). *On metaphor*. Chicago and London: University of Chicago Press.

Von Oech, R. (1990). *A whack on the side of the head: How you can be more creative*. Revised ed. N.Y.: Warner Books.

CHARACTERISTICS OF INTERDISCIPLINARIANS

Students of interdisciplinary studies are marked by their willingness not simply to challenge, but also to cross, traditional disciplinary boundaries.

Giles Gunn (1992, p. 239)

Learning Objectives

After reading Chapter Four of *Becoming Interdisciplinary*, you should be able to:

1. Understand some of the reasons why students choose to become interdisciplinary studies majors.
2. Become familiar with some common personality traits shared among interdisciplinarians.
3. Become familiar with some psychological traits of interdisciplinarians.
4. Recognize which interdisciplinary characteristics you may have.

Introduction

This chapter will help explain to you some of the reasons behind the reasons why students choose to become interdisciplinary studies majors. While circumstances and personal situations may have played a role in your decision, probably so too could have psychological characteristics and personality traits. In the pages that follow, you may learn a lot about yourself that you did not previously, namely the characteristics that interdisciplinarians tend to share.

Characteristics of Interdisciplinarians

According to Klein (1990), the following character traits have been associated with interdisciplinary individuals:

- Reliability
- Flexibility
- Patience
- Resilience
- Sensitivity to others
- Risk-Taking
- Having a thick skin
- Preference for diversity
- Preference for new social roles (pp. 181–182)

Klein (1990) quotes Armstrong (1980), who includes the following characteristics:

- High degree of ego strength
- Tolerance for ambiguity
- Considerable initiative and assertiveness
- A broad education
- A sense of dissatisfaction with monodisciplinary constraints (Klein 1990, p. 182)

Petrie (1976) (see Reading 10 in Chapter Seven) makes some similar claims. According to Petrie, interdisciplinary individuals share the following psychological traits:

- Self-secure
- Competence in one's field
- Adventurous
- Broad interests
- Need for achievement
- Ability to work in groups
- Sense of adventure of the unknown (pp. 32–33)

When we compare Klein's discussion with Petrie's, we cannot help but notice some overlap. Nonetheless, it is helpful to discuss each characteristic more in depth.

RELIABILITY

It makes sense that interdisciplinary individuals are reliable. After all, interdisciplinarians tend to be self-motivated (the by-product of the sum of their characteristics) and therefore attend class regularly. While you may take regular attendance for granted, many employers do not as employee absenteeism can be a big problem. Many college students today work either part-time or full-time. Many also juggle family commitments. Reliability is thus more important than one would initially think. If one is not reliable one cannot be trusted or considered dependable. Who wants to work with someone who is not reliable, especially when teamwork is part of the job?

FLEXIBILITY

Many students are attracted to interdisciplinary studies degree programs for the flexibility they allow in designing one's program of study. In most interdisciplinary studies programs students can choose the areas/disciplines they wish to study and the courses they can take. In so doing, they enjoy a greater level of flexibility than other degree programs may allow.

CONSIDERABLE INITIATIVE AND ASSERTIVENESS

With flexibility comes responsibility. Students must choose their areas of study and what courses they will take. They will have to explore unfamiliar territory with their studies, reading, studying, and researching new material. In interdisciplinary studies degree programs that require internships, students are responsible for finding their own internship. They will have to overcome fear in order to ask someone for an informational interview in order to do career research. All these requirements and assignments help students to improve initiative and assertiveness.

PATIENCE

Rome was not built in a day. You will not become an expert interdisciplinarian overnight. It takes time to become a competent interdisciplinarian, let alone an expert one. Lattuca (2001) reports that interdisciplinary teaching and research projects among university and college faculty members generally begin with the faculty members reading in more than one discipline. After reading widely they then tend to seek opportunities in which to engage others in interdisciplinary conversation and collaboration. A number of those interviewed by Lattuca described the process as quite lengthy. Because of the length of time involved, both aspiring and accomplished interdisciplinarians have to be patient when pursuing interdisciplinary activity, whether that activity is in education, research, or the workplace.

TOLERANCE FOR AMBIGUITY

Complex problems are complex, often utilizing multiple approaches and terminology that cannot be singularly defined. Many people see the world in black or white, in terms of dualities such as either/or. Interdisciplinarians can see that sometimes solutions to problems are best phrased as both/and, which produces ambiguity.

RESILIENCE

How do you react when your plans are thwarted? Do you fall into a deep depression because your original plans did not originally work out? Did you become resentful? What good did such attitudes do? A much better approach to handling life's disappointments is picking yourself up and finding alternative paths to reaching your goals. As a student of interdisciplinary studies, you have more control of your choice of study. In so doing, you can feel confident taking alternative paths that others would be either afraid or hesitant to take. Because studying interdisciplinary problems at times involves trial and error, interdisciplinary studies majors learn not to become discouraged by temporary setbacks. In order to bounce back from setbacks, let alone failures, one has to be resilient.

RISK-TAKING

Without a doubt, interdisciplinary studies majors are risk-takers—especially those students who had no idea what interdisciplinary studies are before declaring it as their major. Only risk-takers could major in something that they did not quite know what it is or involves! Nevertheless, risk-taking is not the same as gambling. You probably took a calculated risk: you had heard good things about interdisciplinary studies from other students or alumni.

SENSE OF ADVENTURE FOR THE UNKNOWN

Interdisciplinary studies majors do not have to follow well-trodden paths. Many prefer to be trailblazers, forging their own path in their educations, their careers, and their lives. A sense of adventure goes along with taking risks—but even when charting new ground, adventurers and explorers need their research tools and knowledge for navigation. So too do interdisciplinary studies majors.

HAVING A THICK SKIN

Interdisciplinary studies majors have thick skin—how else could they put up with the comments and criticisms of others who lack knowledge and understanding regarding the newest trends in education and the workplace? Many people cannot take criticism well—those individuals would have a very difficult time being interdisciplinary studies majors so they would end up changing majors very quickly.

High Ego Strength

SELF-SECURE

Having high ego strength goes hand in hand with having thick skin. One has to have a strong, stable ego—a sense of self—to be able to withstand criticism and perhaps even disapproval. Interdisciplinarians have confidence in their ability to make choices for themselves—they do not need others to make decisions for them. Nor do they necessarily need approval from others to feel good about themselves—although, of course, such approval is always appreciated!

SENSITIVITY TO OTHERS

Your interdisciplinary studies classes embrace diversity. Often times challenging topics are discussed, and students learn how to discuss intelligently challenging and controversial issues with respect for the opinions of others. Furthermore, the teamwork you do in your coursework trains you to work and respect others.

PREFERENCE FOR DIVERSITY

By studying more than one discipline, one becomes attracted to variety or diversity, whether that diversity is manifested in one's education or in dealing with different types of people.

PREFERENCE FOR NEW SOCIAL ROLES

Interdisciplinary studies degrees are relatively new and untested. Students must decide how their education is going to work for them. Along the same lines, many jobs or careers are new or just emerging. Interdisciplinary studies majors tend to be attracted to the new and emergent, whether in education or career choices. Obviously, students will have preference for those new social roles that provide flexibility, risk, and diversity.

A Broad Education

A SENSE OF DISSATISFACTION WITH MONODISCIPLINARY CONSTRAINTS: BROAD INTERESTS

Many students chose interdisciplinary studies because they could not decide on just one major—they enjoyed learning about two or more areas. Often times, two areas complement each other such as African American studies and history. By studying African American studies, students can learn what is left out in regular history classes. Moreover, students then get the benefit of learning more about African American culture, psychology, literature, music, religion, etc. Students can then better situate African American culture and history in relation to other histories and cultures.

COMPETENCE IN ONE'S FIELD

Interdisciplinary studies majors need to do their homework. Success absolutely depends on how well they can articulate the knowledge and skills learned in their program of study. Students will not sound very convincing if they can only articulate their degrees on a superficial level. For example, it is extremely superficial to say that one studies business and communication because in order to do business one has to communicate effectively! One has to be able to explain what effective communication means under which context. One has to know how to solve specific communication problems within numerous business contexts (i.e., viewing sexual harassment as a communication problem as well as a legal, business, managerial, and human resources problem).

Occasionally students sign up to take the introductory course in interdisciplinary studies with only taking the minimum number of courses in each of their declared study areas or disciplines. When that is the case, students do not always know much about the disciplines they wish to integrate. In the introductory course students are expected to do research on their chosen disciplines so that they know the important terms, concepts, methods, thinkers, and texts. The more knowledge you have, the better you can identify an interdisciplinary research topic and problems and work towards possible solutions.

ABILITY TO WORK IN GROUPS

Much interdisciplinary work both inside and especially outside academia is done in groups. Pursuing interdisciplinary studies gives students excellent preparation for working in groups and experience in teamwork.

CHECKLIST FOR INTERDISCIPLINARIANS

Check all the traits and characteristics you share with interdisciplinarians. Provide examples that illustrate you having that characteristic.

Once you are comfortable with the traits you have, review the traits you do not have at the moment. Ask yourself why you are lacking in this trait. Ask yourself also if you would like to have this trait. What can you do to obtain it?

- ☐ Reliability
- ☐ Flexibility
- ☐ Patience
- ☐ Resilience
- ☐ Sensitivity to others
- ☐ Risk-taking
- ☐ Having a thick skin
- ☐ Preference for diversity
- ☐ Preference for new social roles
- ☐ High degree of ego strength
- ☐ Tolerance for ambiguity
- ☐ Considerable initiative and assertiveness
- ☐ A broad education
- ☐ A sense of dissatisfaction with monodisciplinary constraints
- ☐ Self-secure
- ☐ Competence in one's field
- ☐ Adventurous
- ☐ Broad interests
- ☐ Need for achievement
- ☐ Ability to work in groups
- ☐ Sense of adventure of the unknown

Suggested Readings

Armstrong F. (1980). Faculty development through interdisciplinarity. *JGE, The Journal of General Education*, 32 (1), 52–63.

Gunn, G. (1992). Interdisciplinary Studies. In J. Gibaldi (Ed.), *Introduction to scholarship in modern languages and literatures* (2nd ed.), (pp. 139–261). New York: The Modern Language Association of America.

Klein, J. T. (1990). *Interdisciplinarity: History, theory and practice.* Detroit: Wayne State University Press.

Lattuca, L. R. (2001). *Creating interdisciplinarity: Interdisciplinary research and teaching among college and university faculty.* Nashville: Vanderbilt University Press.

Petrie, H. G. (1976). Do you see what I see? The epistemology of interdisciplinary inquiry. *Journal of Aesthetic Education*, 10, 29–43. [See Reading 10 in this volume.]

TELLING YOUR STORY AS AN INTERDISCIPLINARIAN

WRITING AN INTELLECTUAL AUTOBIOGRAPHY/ PERSONAL NARRATIVE

Life is interdisciplinary; students of life must be interdisciplinarians.

Jerry L. Petr (1986, p. 21)

Life, however, is not naturally interdisciplinary. It is a neutral assortment of phenomena that are ordered through human thought and action.

Julie Thompson Klein (1996, p. 12)

If you want to know me, then you must know my story, for my story defines who I am. And if I want to know myself, to gain insight into the meaning of my own life, then I, too, must come to know my own story.

Dan P. McAdams (1993, p. 11)

Learning Objectives

After reading Chapter Five of *Becoming Interdisciplinary* you should be able to:

1. Understand better why you chose interdisciplinary studies as your major.
2. Explain to others why you are an interdisciplinarian.
3. Tell your life story as an interdisciplinarian.

Telling Your Story as an Interdisciplinarian

You have learned all of the following:

1. definition(s) of interdisciplinarity;
2. how to answer the question, "What are interdisciplinary studies?";
3. how interdisciplinary studies programs emerged;
4. various levels of integration;
5. how to use metaphor to explain interdisciplinary studies; and
6. characteristics of interdisciplinarians.

re you going to tell your story as an interdisciplinarian? By now you should start to think of your story of an interdisciplinarian. It is important for you to be able to reflect the events and circumstances that brought you to this point in life, so that you can better plan where you want to go from here. Being able to see a clear path is critical for your academic success as an interdisciplinary studies major, as you will need both to reflect on your college career thus far and to plan the rest of your college career, i.e, your path to graduation. You should be able to understand why you chose your particular areas of study—in other words, you should understand your academic interests and how they tie in to your personal interests and professional goals.

Different instructors will ask students to tell their story as an interdisciplinarian in different ways. Some instructors will ask you to write a personal narrative. Some will ask you to reflect on your identity as a researcher. Some will ask you to consider your identity in terms of your goals and mission statement. Others will ask you to write your "intellectual autobiography"—sort of an odyssey of the mind. Layne Gneiting asks his students to create visual autobiographical maps in addition to writing their intellectual autobiographies, and his assignment is included at the end of this chapter.

The word *autobiography* has three parts to it etymologically:

Auto > Greek prefix meaning "self"
Bio > Greek root meaning "life"
Graph > Greek root meaning "write"

The word *autobiography* thus means to write the life of one's self. What is surprising to most students is that autobiographies are not necessarily considered true. In fact, according to Lejeune (1975)—autobiographies are to be considered fictions because they involve selection. Nevertheless, as Ibarra and Linebeck (2005) point out, autobiographies are not intended to be "tall tales." An autobiography is a story, but "by 'story' we don't mean 'something made up to make a bad situation look good.' Rather, we're talking about accounts that are deeply true and so engaging that listeners feel that they have a stake in our success" (Ibarra and Linebeck 2005, p. 66).

What should you select to write about your life? One cannot possibly write everything about one's life—life is too short for such an endeavor. Students certainly cannot write their life stories down in four, five, or even six pages. They have to select what is most important for their ultimate aim—to tell a story with a particular message.

The message you want to tell is that you have had a life that lends itself to being interdisciplinary. Accordingly, you would want to stress the following:

✓ Your interdisciplinarian characteristics
✓ Your understanding of your self-identity
✓ Why you wanted to study more than one discipline
✓ Why you chose your areas of study
✓ The key events, situations, influences that led to your academic interests
✓ What is it exactly that interests you about your academic interests (be sure to be as specific as possible and include specific concepts, topics, methods, or perspectives of interest)
✓ Your values, skills, strengths (and if relevant, weaknesses)
✓ What interdisciplinary problems you are interested in
✓ How you plan to use your interdisciplinary knowledge and skills in your future, especially in your future career plans or goals

You should review the discussion of interdisciplinarian characteristics in Chapter Four. Be sure to do the checklist at the end of the chapter. This way you will familiarize yourself not only with characteristics of interdisciplinarians, but those characteristics that you may have. Try to mention which characteristics you have in your narrative if possible. For example, the reason why you were attracted to interdisciplinary studies was because you were dissatisfied with monodisciplinary constraints. Why? It is not enough to state the characteristic—you need to analyze how it developed. What experience(s) did you have that led to such dissatisfaction? Are they relevant? If so, be sure to explain the reasons why you have a particular characteristic of interdiscipinarians.

Also, you may want to read Reading 17 as well as Reading 18 in Part Three of this textbook. Reading 17, "Success Secret: A High Emotional IQ," by Anne Fisher introduces the concept of emotional intelligence. Jennifer James in Reading 18, "Mastering New Forms of Intelligence" introduces Howard Gardner's theory of multiple intelligence. By reading about emotional intelligence and multiple intelligence you may recognize additional characteristics or strengths about yourself that you might want to mention in your personal narrative.

The Myth of the "Perfect Life"

How are you to structure your narrative? Simply put, there is no single way to tell your story. Often students have a difficult time selecting what to write. Some students may feel that their life lacked direction, and that to admit that their life was not focused from day one would be somehow held against them. Others may not want to disclose certain things about their lives, while others may dwell on events or activities that may not necessarily be looked upon favorably by the reader. Here are some rule of thumb guidelines:

- ✓ Assume a general reader who does not know you personally.
- ✓ Do not disclose anything of which you are ashamed.
- ✓ Do not disclose any illegal activities, even if they are limited to recreational drug use.
- ✓ Do not dwell on the negative.
- ✓ If you need to discuss some major negative event, such as an accident or illness, try to emphasize what you learned from the experience rather than on the disappointments or shortcomings it may have caused.

One way to structure your narrative is as a journey of self-discovery. In other words, your education has been a journey of self-discovery. During the course of your education you have discovered not only what you are good at, but also your passion—what you want to learn more about and spend the rest of your life pursuing.

Another way to structure your narrative is to write about your life in terms working on fulfilling a goal. Your identity as an interdisciplinarian could be considered as a goal that you are currently working on. Some other common autobiographical narrative structures include tales of survival, stories of overcoming adversities or oppression, and as Mary Catherine Bateson mentions in Reading 3, tales of conversion. Ultimately, your intellectual autobiography should be a success story, i.e., affirm your interdisciplinary path.

Readings 1 and 2

The readings for this chapter were selected to help you write your intellectual autobiography. They will also help you think about what you want to include in your narrative. Readings 1 and 2 are recent *New York Times* obituaries of two well-known and influential men: Isaiah Berlin and Fred Rogers. In Reading 1, "Isaiah Berlin, Philosopher and Pluralist, Is Dead at 88" by Marilyn Berger, we learn that Isaiah Berlin was a well renowned philosopher. In Reading 2, "Fred Rogers, Host of *Mister Rogers' Neighborhood*, Dies at 74" by Daniel Lewis, we read about how important Mr. Rogers was for generations of American children.

READING

ISAIAH BERLIN, PHILOSOPHER AND PLURALIST, IS DEAD AT 88

by

Marilyn Berger

Sir Isaiah Berlin, the philosopher and historian of ideas, revered for his intellect and cherished for his wit and his gift for friendship, died of a heart attack following a long illness Wednesday evening in Oxford, England. He was 88.

A staunch advocate of pluralism in a century in which totalitarians and utopians claimed title to the one, single truth, Sir Isaiah considered the very notion that there could be one final answer to organizing human society a dangerous illusion that would lead to nothing but bloodshed, coercion and the deprivation of liberty.

Sir Isaiah defied classification. A renowned scholar, he was also a bon vivant, a sought-after conversationalist, a serious opera buff and an ardent Zionist. He shattered the popular concept of the Oxford don surrounded by dusty books and dry tutorials. His was an exuberant life crowded with joys—the joy of thought, the joy of music, the joy of good friends. Sir Isaiah (pronounced eye-ZIE-uh) seemed to know almost everyone worth knowing in the 20th century, among them Freud, Nehru, Stravinsky, Boris Pasternak, T.S. Eliot, W.H. Auden, Chaim Weizmann, Virginia Woolf, Edmund Wilson, Aldous Huxley, Bertrand Russell and Felix Frankfurter.

Sir Isaiah liked to say that his reputation was built on a systematic overestimation of his abilities. In fact, his reputation rests securely on his lectures and essays—a cornucopia of Western philosophical and political thought involving inquiries into the nature of liberty, the search for utopia, the misconceptions of the Enlightenment, the innate human yearning for a homeland, the roots of nationalism, the underpinnings of Fascism.

"The Hedgehog and the Fox," the essay perhaps best known to American students of philosophy, is a study of Tolstoy's view of history as embodied in *War and Peace.* Written in 1953, it is regarded as a classic of political inquiry and literary criticism. Taking his title from the Greek poet Archilochus ("The fox knows many things, but the hedgehog knows one big thing"), Sir Isaiah's essay was a study of the mind and the work of Tolstoy but went beyond that to become an exploration of his own central themes about the place of the individual in the historical process and the struggle between monism and pluralism.

In this essay, which became part of a great body of work by Sir Isaiah on Russian thinkers of the 19th century, he drew a distinction between two human types: those, like the fox, who pursue many ends, often unrelated, even contradictory, and those, like the hedgehog, who relate everything to a single universal organizing principle. He saw Tolstoy as a fox who wanted to be a hedgehog. He considered Aristotle, Goethe, Pushkin, Balzac, Joyce and Turgenev foxes. Plato, Dante, Pascal, Proust and Dostoyevsky were counted among the hedgehogs.

Sir Isaiah's 1959 essay, "Two Concepts of Liberty," is considered a major contribution to political theory. In it, he made a distinction between negative liberty, that which the individual must be allowed to enjoy without state interference, and positive liberty, that which the state permits by imposing regulations that, by necessity, limit some freedoms in the name of greater liberty for all. He argued that both kinds of liberty were required for a just society.

Investing Philosophy with Personality

To his philosophical and historical work, Sir Isaiah added elegant profiles of great figures. For him, ideas could not be divorced from people and their psychological and cultural milieu. If thinking thoughts was his chosen line of work, people were what he called his "scenery."

Sir Noel Annan, who wrote the introduction to his 1980 book, *Personal Impressions,* observed: "Nobody in our time has invested ideas with such personality, given them a corporeal shape and breathed life into them more than Isaiah Berlin; and he succeeds in doing so because ideas for him are not mere abstractions. They live . . . in the minds of men and women, inspiring them, shaping their lives, influencing their actions and changing the course of history."

At each stage of his life, whether young or old, acquaintances remember him as having the look of "indeterminate middle age," bespectacled, baldish, of medium height. In his conversation as in his writing—which he mainly dictated so it carried the full flavor of his voice—Sir Isaiah's sentences were constructs of dazzling erudition, built clause upon clause, wisdom intermixed with anecdote, quotations, historical parallels and flashes of wit. Sir Isaiah was so beguiling a conversationalist that when Prime Minister Harold Macmillan nominated him in 1957 for the Queen's list he noted that the knighthood should be bestowed "for talking."

Not everyone understood what he was talking about, for he spoke with extraordinary rapidity, his tongue barely able to keep up with his thoughts. His English bore the traces of his native Russian, and, in his later years, he suffered from a paralyzed vocal cord that never slowed the flow of his words but rendered some of them indistinct.

But even before this affliction, when he met Harold Ross of *The New Yorker,* Mr. Ross told him, "I don't understand a word you've said, but if you have something to publish, I'll publish it."

Gathering Writings Left in a Basement

As for his writing, much of it might have been left lying in the basement of Headington House, his elegant Queen Anne residence in Oxford, had an enterprising young graduate student not come along to gather it together.

Sir Isaiah's lectures were often not published and his essays were scattered in so many magazines and journals that his body of work was inaccessible to most people. Henry Hardy, the graduate student, set out to collect it in four volumes that became five: *Russian Thinkers* (1978); *Concepts and Categories* (1978); *Against the Current* (1979); *Personal Impressions* (1980) and *The Crooked Timber of Humanity* (1990). In addition, Sir Isaiah was the author of five other books: *Karl Marx* (1939); *The Age of Enlightenment (*1956); *Four Essays on Liberty* (1969); *Vico and Herder* (1976) and *The Magus of the North: J.G. Hamann and the Origins of Modern Irrationalism* (1993). This year, another collection edited by Mr. Hardy, *The Sense of Reality,* was published by Farrar, Straus & Giroux in the United States. It will soon be followed by another book, *The Proper Study of Mankind: An Anthology of Essays.*

Until the publication of the Hardy collections, Sir Isaiah had been known as a man who talked much but wrote little and had, in fact, been taken to task for not producing a major opus, a failing attributed to his reluctance to sit at a desk in front of a blank piece of paper. But Sir Isaiah said he gave no thought to leaving a legacy and insisted that he had no interest whatsoever either in his reputation or in what people would say about him after he died. Sitting in his London flat for an interview last year he said: "I really am very unambitious. I'm underambitious, if anything. I've never, never aimed at anything. I didn't shape my life. I did simply one thing after another. When opportunities arose I took them. It's all unplanned life essentially." When it was suggested that he was known as a man who took great pleasure in intellectual life, he said, "I take pleasure in pleasure."

A Deep Commitment to Ideas' Importance

Among the opportunities he grasped that afforded him many pleasures were assignments in Washington during World War II. Moscow just after the war, and a long association with Oxford. But underlying whatever he did was his belief in the overriding importance of ideas. "When ideas are neglected by those who ought to attend to them—that is to say, those who have been trained to think critically about ideas—they often acquire an unchecked momentum and an irresistible power over multitudes of men that may grow too violent to be affected by rational criticism," he wrote in "Two Concepts of Liberty."

He added, "Over a hundred years ago, the German poet Heine warned the French not to underestimate the power of ideas: philosophical concepts nurtured in the stillness of a professor's study could destroy a civilization . . . if professors can truly wield this fatal power, may it not be that only other professors or, at least, other thinkers (and not governments or congressional committees) can alone disarm them? Our philosophers seem oddly unaware of these devastating effects of their activities."

Isaiah Berlin was born in Riga, Latvia, on June 6, 1909. His father was a successful timber merchant and land-owner and his grandfather on his mother's side was a Hasidic rabbi of the ecstatic Lubavitch tradition. His family moved to St. Petersburg where he was a witness to the two Russian revolutions of 1917. The family then immigrated in 1921 to London, where it had business interests.

As a boy, Isaiah, then known as Shaya, had some religious education, although he said he found the Talmud a "very, very boring book. I could never figure out why I should care why the bull gored the cow." Nevertheless, he continued his religious education in London, where he had his bar mitzvah.

Although he said he never felt the sting of anti-Semitism himself, he said he gave up the thought of going to Westminster School when a teacher suggested to him that with a name like Isaiah he wouldn't "be comfortable" there. He dealt with it simply by attending St. Paul's instead.

Second-Rate Student, and a Very Happy One

"I never was at the head of a single class," he remembered. "I was fourth, fifth, seventh or eighth. But this didn't bother me. Once, when I tried very, very hard, in my last year at St. Paul's, I was second. My parents thought I could do a little better, but they didn't bully me either. I was a very happy child." When he tried to get into Balliol at Oxford he was told he wasn't up to its level, but he managed to get a scholarship to Corpus Christi. He said he was not a top student at first, but found his strength in philosophy.

He said he had no idea what to do with himself when he finished school. He said he couldn't be a doctor because he knew no science. He couldn't be a civil servant because he wasn't born in England. He was turned down when he applied for a job at The Guardian of Manchester because he told the editor that he thought he wasn't much of a writer. His father wanted him to join him in the timber business, but he said that after one luncheon with him and his associates he decided he couldn't. "I couldn't laugh at their jokes and I thought, this is no good, this is a world I could never belong in," he said. "My father was very disappointed."

After that he considered law. He dined at the law temples, as he said he was supposed to, but "I never did the exam; I never opened a law book, because then I was offered a job in Oxford to teach philosophy. That's the end of my story."

It was, of course, the beginning of his story. He became a lecturer in philosophy at New College in 1932, and, a few years later, it was in his rooms at All Souls College that a circle of the leading analytic philosophers of the day gathered to hold regular meetings. They included J.L. Austin, A.J. Ayer, Stuart Hampshire, Donald MacKinnon and Donald Macnabb.

Wartime Dispatches Win Churchill's Notice

World War II pulled him out of the ivory tower. He was sent first to New York, where he worked for the British Information Service, and then to Washington, where his assignment was to report back weekly to London on the mood of wartime America. His brilliant dispatches soon came to the attention of Prime Minister Churchill, who instructed that he be invited to lunch one spring day in 1944.

As Sir Isaiah was fond of recounting, the invitation found its way to the wrong person. The conversation took an awkward turn that day at 10 Downing Street when Churchill asked his guest, "Berlin, what do you think is your most important piece you've done for us lately?" His guest replied hesitantly, "White Christmas." The invitation had been sent to Irving, not Isaiah, Berlin.

Sir Isaiah was sent to the British Embassy in Moscow just after the war. It was his first visit to Russia since he left with his family and it was to be a visit, he remembered, that "permanently changed my outlook." Warned that he would not be able to speak with anyone but officials assigned to him by the Communist regime, he wrote that he was able to meet a number of Russian writers, "at least two among them persons of outstanding genius."

They were Boris Pasternak and Anna Akhmatova. To each of them he brought news of the outside world. He later wrote in his essay "Meetings With Russian Writers" that "it was like speaking to the victims of a shipwreck on a desert island, cut off for decades from civilization."

Fifty years later he explained that what had so deeply moved him was "the fact that these people preserved their integrity, completely unflawed, through a miserable regime." He recalled them as people of great personal sweetness, moral integrity, even nobility. "I was struck," he said, "by the possibility of heroic behavior on the part of highly civilized, highly intelligent people of great sensibility."

Anna Akhmatova was under constant surveillance and paid heavily for her meeting with Isaiah Berlin. The very next day the Soviet authorities stepped up their harassment of her, so much so that some years later, when she visited Sir Isaiah in Oxford, she solemnly informed him of a terrible secret that had taken hold of her.

He wrote that Akhmatova told him that "she and I—inadvertently, by the mere fact of our meeting—had started the cold war and thereby changed the history of mankind. She meant this quite literally."

By the time he returned to Oxford after the war, Sir Isaiah had lost interest in the kind of analytic philosophy that had preoccupied him during the 1930's. To him, philosophy had come to seem sterile, disconnected from history and human lives. He said it was the work of the Russian philosopher and revolutionary Alexander Herzen that set history of social and political ideas. He said that when he picked up Herzen's autobiography, *My Past and Thoughts* he thought of him as "some kind of boring writer with a beard of the mid-19th century." But, he said, "it was one of the best books ever written by a human being. I was hooked."

Once set on a new course, his life became tremendously productive. From 1947 to 1958 he wrote and lectured at Oxford, in London and Washington, and at such American universities as Harvard, Princeton, Bryn Mawr and Chicago. Some of those lectures and essays were later included in his collections. He also published translations of Turgenev's *First Love* and *A Month in the Country*.

Evaluating Trade-Offs Inherent to Liberty

The theme that runs throughout his work is his concern with liberty and the dignity of human beings, and he sought to emphasize that at all times, difficult, even tragic tradeoffs had to be made. It was his view that man must forever choose among incommensurable and often incompatible values, that equality, for example, must at times be sacrificed to liberty. He told the philosopher Ramin Jahanbegloo in a conversation that was published as a book, *Conversations with Isaiah Berlin* (1992), "if you have maximum liberty, then the strong can destroy the weak, and if you have absolute equality, you cannot have absolute liberty, because you have to coerce the powerful . . . if they are not to devour the poor and the meek. . . . Total liberty can be dreadful, total equality can be equally frightful."

In "Two Concepts of Liberty," Sir Isaiah said that it is the question of who establishes the rules of positive liberty that is of crucial importance. "Paternalism is despotic," he wrote. "I may, in my bitter longing for status, prefer to be bullied and misgoverned by some member of my own race or social class, by whom I am, nevertheless, recognized as a man and a rival—that is as an equal—to being well and tolerantly treated by someone from some higher and remoter group." He added, "Although I may not get 'negative' liberty at the hands of the members of my own society, yet they are members of my own group; they understand me, as I understand them; and this understanding creates within me the sense of being somebody in the world."

Sir Isaiah insisted that there could be no single all-embracing solution to the central problems of society. He wrote, "any study of society shows that every solution creates a new situation which breeds its own new needs and problems, new demands." In "The Pursuit of the Ideal," he suggested that "Utopias have their value—nothing so wonderfully expands the imaginative horizons of human potentialities—but as guides to conduct they can prove literally fatal."

He wrote that the idea of a single solution "turns out to be an illusion: and a very dangerous one. For if one really believes that such a solution is possible, then surely no cost would be too high to obtain it: to make mankind just and happy and creative and harmonious forever—what could be too high a price to pay for that? To make such an omelet, there is surely no limit to the number of eggs that should be broken—that was the fate of Lenin, of Trotsky, of Mao, and for all I know of Pol Pot."

Prolific Writing, but No Masterpiece

Although Sir Isaiah had the gift for saying in 90 pages what it took others 900 pages to say less well, colleagues remembered that it took some time for him to come to grips with a nagging feeling that he was a fraud because he had not produced a weighty book-length philosophical work. "I never had it in me to do a great masterpiece on some big subject," Sir Isaiah said without apparent regret as he looked back over his life.

"There was a subject on which I had views. Romanticism. The Romantics made a greater difference to us than anything else since the Renaissance, more than Marx, more than Freud. Until the Romantics came along there was only one answer to any question. Truth was one; error was many. You might not know it, you may be too benighted to find it, but there must be one answer. The Romantics said the same question can have more than one answer. The Romantics were the first to say the answer was not something built into the universe."

Sir Isaiah did write and lecture extensively on Romanticism. He was also preoccupied with cultural nationalism, a concept that he felt was deeply misunderstood and overlooked during the 19th century with its appeal to universalism as a legacy of the Enlightenment. Hegel, he said, once wrote that "freedom consists in being at home." Everyone, he believed, needed to belong to a group. He wrote about Johann Gottfried Herder, the German philosopher and poet, who convinced him of the basic need of man to be part of a particular human community with its own traditions, language, art and imagination to shape his emotional and physical development.

Yet he said that Herder believed that if people were allowed to fulfill their yearning to belong, nations could live peacefully, side by side. "I'm afraid not," he concluded. "Perhaps in the 18th century you could believe that." Although he believed in the power of ideas, he said he had no solution for the excesses of nationalism. "I have no idea," he said, "how one stops one group, one race, from hating another. The hatred between human groups has never been cured, except by time."

From Schiller he borrowed the metaphor of the "bent twig," that was bound to snap if a society is oppressed or humiliated. And from Kant he took the title of his 1990 collection *The Crooked Timber of Humanity* ("Out of the crooked timber of humanity no straight thing was ever made"), to suggest that the utopian notion of one big answer that is knowable and self-contained must always be fallacious because it does not take into account the cultural pluralism and conflicting values that are part of "the crooked timber of humanity."

A Zionist Perspective Rooted in Pluralism

Sir Isaiah's fervent Zionism derived from his experience as much as from his philosophy. "I can tell you why I'm a Zionist," he said in a conversation in the year before his death. "Not because the Lord offered us the Holy Land as some people, religious Jews, believe. My reason for being a Zionist has nothing to do with preserving Jewish culture, Jewish values, wonderful things done by Jews. But the price is too high, the martyrdom too long. And if I were asked, 'Do you want to preserve this culture at all costs?' I'm not sure that I would say yes, because you can't condemn people to permanent persecution. Of course assimilation might be a quite good thing, but it doesn't work. Never has worked, never will. There isn't a Jew in the world known to me who somewhere inside him does not have a tiny drop of uneasiness vis-à-vis *them*, the majority among whom they live. They may be very friendly, they may be entirely happy, but one has to behave particularly well, because if they don't behave well *they* won't like us."

When it was suggested to him during that conversation in 1996 that he was surely the exception, that he had been knighted; awarded the Order of Merit, Britain's highest honor for intellectual achievement; that he was a renowned and beloved Oxford scholar, a president of the British Academy; that he had been saluted, cherished and accepted with pride in England, the recipient of innumerable honorary degrees, he had an immediate response: "Nevertheless, I'm not an Englishman, and if I behave badly. . . ."

In his scholarly work, Sir Isaiah had traced the origins of Zionism in a profile of the 19th-century German-Jewish revolutionary Moses Hess, one of his many portraits of political philosophers. Often, though, he was drawn to his opposites, like Karl Marx, the subject of his first book in 1939, and Joseph de Maistre, a French philosopher of the Napoleonic age whom he regarded as a proto-fascist. Michael Ignatieff, Sir Isaiah's biographer, said, "He is liberalism's greatest elucidator of the antiliberal . . . He is always drawn to his opponents. Here is a liberal, balanced, amusing, witty man drawn to lonely, eccentric, crazed characters. It is said he is a rationalist who visits the irrational by day and comes back to the rational stockade at night."

Faith in the 'Great Man' to Change History

A critic of the concept of historical inevitability, Sir Isaiah believed that the "great man" can bring about significant historical change. He saw Franklin D. Roosevelt as an example of such a man, and wrote of him "He was absolutely fearless . . . one of the few statesmen in the 20th century or any other century who seemed to have no fear at all of the future." Another was Chaim Weizmann, the scientist and statesman who became the first President of Israel. Weizmann, he wrote, "committed none of those enormities for which men of action, and later their biographers, claim justification on the ground of what is called raison d' état . . . Weizmann, despite his reputation as a master of realpolitik, forged no telegrams, massacred no minorities, executed and incarcerated no political opponents."

With the exception of his wartime diplomatic service and a number of visiting professorships, Sir Isaiah was associated with Oxford all his life. He began his career there in 1932 as a lecturer in philosophy at New College and spent seven years as a fellow of All Souls College. He was said to be very conscious that he was the first Jew to hold such a position at Oxford. From 1957 to 1967, Sir Isaiah held the prestigious Chichele Chair in Social and Political Theory. As the first president of Wolfson College from 1966 to 1975, he was instrumental in attracting a strong faculty to a new school at Oxford.

In the 1950's he fell in love with Aline d'Gunzbourg, a French woman who is the descendant of a noble Russian family. They were married in 1956 and enjoyed more than 40 years of what friends say was particularly felicitous life together. She and her three sons from previous marriages Michel Strauss and Peter Halban of London and Dr. Philippe Halban of Geneva, survived him.

No one who knew Sir Isaiah could remember him without remarking on his love of music and the long distances he traveled to hear concerts. He was particularly devoted to opera, an affection he attributed to his mother, who he said was a very good amateur who sang arias from all the great operas. He wrote about Verdi, numbered among his friends some of the leading musicians, and served on the board of the Royal Opera House, Covent Garden.

Sir Isaiah radiated well-being. "He gives everybody the unforgettable feeling of what it's like to be well in your own skin, of what sense of health one derives from the intellectual life," his biographer, Mr. Ignatieff said in 1996.

He was also a man of great equanimity even when talking about his own death. I don't mind death," he said, "I'm not afraid of it. I'm afraid of dying for it could be painful. But I find death a nuisance. I object to it. I'd rather it didn't happen . . . I'm terribly curious. I'd like to live forever."

READING

FRED ROGERS, HOST OF *MISTER ROGERS' NEIGHBORHOOD,* DIES AT 74

by

Daniel Lewis

Fred Rogers, the thoughtful television neighbor whose songs, stories and heart-to-heart talks taught generations of children how to get along in the world, died yesterday at his home in Pittsburgh. He was 74.

The cause was stomach cancer, said David Newell, a family spokesman who also portrayed Mr. McFeely, of the Speedy Delivery Messenger Service, one of the regulars on *Mister Rogers' Neighborhood.*

Mr. Rogers entered the realm of children's television with a local show in Pittsburgh in 1954. But it was the daily half-hour *Neighborhood* show, which began nationally on public television in 1968 with homemade puppets and a cardboard castle, that caught on as a haven from the hyperactivity of most children's television. Let morphing monsters rampage elsewhere, or educational programs jump up and down for attention; *Mister Rogers* stayed the same year after year, a low-key affair without animation or special effects. Fred Rogers was its producer, host and chief puppeteer. He wrote the scripts and songs. Above all he supplied wisdom; and such was the need for it that he became the longest-running attraction on public television and an enduring influence on America's everyday life.

For all its reassuring familiarity, *Mister Rogers' Neighborhood* was a revolutionary idea at the outset and it remained a thing apart through all its decades on television. Others would also entertain the young or give them a leg up on their studies. But it was Fred Rogers, the composer, Protestant minister and student of behavior who ventured to deal head-on with the emotional life of children.

"The world is not always a kind place," he said. "That's something all children learn for themselves, whether we want them to or not, but it's something they really need our help to understand." He believed that even the worst fears had to be "manageable and mentionable," one way or another, and because of this he did not shy away from topics like war, death, poverty and disability.

In one classic episode he sat down at the kitchen table, looked straight into the camera and calmly began talking about divorce: "Did you ever know any grown-ups who got married and then later they got a divorce?" he asked. And then, after pausing to let that sink in: "Well, it is something people can talk about, and it's something important. I know a little boy and a little girl whose mother and father got divorced, and those children cried and cried. And you know why? Well, one reason was that they thought it was all their fault. But, of course, it wasn't their fault."

When the Smithsonian Institution put one of Mr. Rogers's zippered sweaters on exhibit in 1984, no one who had grown up with American television would have needed an explanation. He had about two dozen of those cardigans. Many had been knitted by his mother. He wore one every day as part of the comforting ritual that opened the show: Mr. Rogers would come home to his living room—a set at WQED-TV in Pittsburgh—and change from a sports coat and loafers into sweater and sneakers as he sang the words of his theme, "It's a beauti-ful day in this neighborhood . . . won't you be my neighbor?"

This would be followed by a talk about something that Mr. Rogers wanted people to consider—maybe the obligations of friendship, or the pleasures of music, or how to handle jealousy. Then would come a trip into the Neighborhood of Make-Believe, where an odd little repertory company of human actors and hand puppets like King Friday XIII and Daniel Striped Tiger might dramatize the day's theme with a skit or occasionally stage an opera.

The show had guests, too, often musicians like Wynton Marsalis or Yo-Yo Ma, and field trips. Mr. Rogers would venture out to show what adults did for a living and the objects made in factories, passing along useful information along the way. Visiting a restaurant for a cheese, lettuce and tomato sandwich, he would stop to demonstrate the right way to set a table. And the sign that said restroom? It just meant bathroom, and most restaurants had them, "if you have to go."

Among his dozens of awards for excellence and public service, he won four daytime Emmys as a writer or performer between 1979 and 1999, as well as the lifetime achievement award of the National Academy of Television Arts and Sciences in 1997. Last year President George W. Bush gave him the Presidential Medal of Freedom.

No visit to the Neighborhood was complete without the counsel and comfort to be found in his easy-to-follow songs, which covered everything from the beauty of nature to the common childhood fear of being sucked down the bathtub drain with the water. He wrote about 200 songs and repeated many of them so regularly that his viewers, most of them between 2½ and 5½ years old, knew them by heart.

"What Do You Do," about controlling anger, began this way:
What do you do with the mad that you feel
When you feel so mad you could bite?
When the whole wide world seems oh, so wrong
And nothing you do seems very right?
What do you do? Do you punch a bag?
Do you pound some clay or some dough?
Do you round up friends for a game of tag?
Or see how fast you can go?
It's great to be able to stop
When you've planned a thing that's wrong.

Long ago, in the days before grown-ups learned how to say "mission statement," Mr. Rogers wrote down the things he wanted to encourage in his audience. Self-esteem, self-control, imagination, creativity, curiosity, appreciation of diversity, cooperation, tolerance for waiting, and persistence.

It was no coincidence that his list reflected the child-rearing principles gaining wide acceptance at the time; he worked closely with people like Margaret McFarland, a leading child psychologist, who was until her death in 1988 the principal adviser for *Mister Rogers' Neighborhood*.

Like any good storyteller, he believed in the power of make-believe to reveal truth, and he trusted children to sort out the obvious inconsistencies according to their own imaginations, as when the puppet X the Owl's cousin, for example, turned out to be the human Lady Aberlin in a bird suit.

His flights of fantasy probably reached their apex in his extended comic operas; "trippy productions," as the television critic Joyce Millman called them, that were "a cross between the innocently disjointed imaginings of a preschooler and some avant-garde opus by John Adams." At least one of these works, *Spoon Mountain,* was adapted for the stage. It was presented at the Vineyard Theater in New York in 1984.

Those who knew Mr. Rogers best, including his wife, said he was exactly the same man on-camera and off. That man had a much more complex personality than the mild, deliberate, somewhat stooped fellow in the zippered sweater might let on. One got glimpses of this in film clips of him behind the scenes, especially when working his hand puppets: here he wore a black shirt to blend into the background, became lithe and intense, and changed his voice and attitude like lightning as he switched back and forth between characters.

He was Henrietta Pussycat, who spoke mostly in meow-meows; the frequently clueless X the Owl; Queen Sara; the pompous and pedantic King Friday XIII; Lady Elaine Fairchilde, heavily rouged and evidently battle-tested in the theater of life; and others.

He inhabited his characters so artfully that Josie Carey, the host of an earlier children's series in which Mr. Rogers did not appear on camera, said that she would find herself confiding in his puppets and completely forgetting he was behind them.

He had known everything about puppets for a long time, since his solitary childhood in the 1930's. The story of how he and they came to appear together on television is a good one.

Fred McFeely Rogers was born in Latrobe, Pa., on March 20, 1928, the son of Nancy Rogers and James H. Rogers, a brick manufacturer. An only child until his parents adopted a baby girl when he was 11, and sometimes on the chubby side, he spent many hours inventing adventures for his puppets and finding emotional release in playing the piano. He could, he said, "laugh or cry or be very angry through the ends of my fingers."

He graduated from Latrobe High School, attended Dartmouth College for a year, and then transferred to Rollins College in Winter Park, Fla., graduating magna cum laude in 1951 with a music composition degree. From there he intended to study at a seminary. But his timetable changed in his senior year when he visited his parents at home and saw something new to him. It was television.

Something "horrible" was on, he remembered—people throwing pies at one another. Still, he understood at once that television was something important for better or worse, and he decided on the spot to be part of it. "You've never even seen television!" was his parents' reaction. But right after graduating from Rollins he got work at the NBC studios in New York, first as a gofer and eventually as a floor director for shows like *The Kate Smith Evening Hour* and *Your Hit Parade.*

In 1953 he was invited to help with programming at WQED in Pittsburgh, which was just starting up as this country's first community-supported public television station. The next year he began producing and writing *The Children's Corner,* the show with Ms. Carey, and he simply brought some puppets from home and put them on the air. In its seven-year run, the show won a Sylvania Award for the best locally produced children's program in the country, and NBC picked up and telecast 30 segments of it in 1955–56.

Meanwhile, Mr. Rogers had not given up his other big goal. Studying part-time, he earned a divinity degree from the Pittsburgh Theological Seminary in 1962. The Presbyterian Church ordained him and charged him with a special mission: in effect, to keep on doing what he was doing on television.

He first showed his own face as Mister Rogers in 1963 on a show called "Misterogers" when the Canadian Broadcasting Corporation asked him to start a show with himself as the on-camera host. The CBC-designed sets and other details became part of the permanent look of Rogers productions. But as for Canada, Mr. Rogers and his wife, Joanne, a pianist he had met while at Rollins, soon decided they should be raising their two young sons back in western Pennsylvania.

He is survived by his wife, their sons and two grandchildren.

Mr. Rogers returned to WQED where, in 1966, *Mister Rogers' Neighborhood* had its premiere in its fully developed form. It was distributed regionally in the East, and then, in 1968, what became PBS stations began showing it across the country.

In their own way, the shows and Mr. Rogers's production company, Family Communications, constituted one of the country's more stable little industries. Underwriting by the Sears, Roebuck Foundation provided long-term financial security. Technicians, collaborators and cast members like Mr. McFeely, the deliveryman, enjoyed virtual lifetime employment. (Did anyone not know that McFeely was Mr. Rogers's middle name, which came from his maternal grandfather?)

The unlikelihood of such an institution, along with Mr. Rogers's mannerisms—that gleaming straight-ahead stare, for instance, which could be a little unnerving if you really thought about it—made parody inevitable. Perhaps the most famous sendup was on *Saturday Night Live,* with Eddie Murphy as a black "Mr. Robinson" who lamented: "I hope I get to move into your neighborhood some day. The problem is that when I move in, y'all move away." When Mr. Murphy later met Mr. Rogers, it was reported, he did what most everyone else did. He gave him a hug.

Mr. Rogers was a vegetarian and a dedicated lap swimmer. He did not smoke or drink. He never carried more than about 150 pounds on his six-foot frame, and his good health permitted him to continue taping shows.

But two years ago he decided to leave the daily grind. "I really respect opera singers who stop when they feel that they're doing their best work," he said at the time, expressing relief. The last episode was taped in December 2000 and was shown in August 2001, though roughly 300 of the 1,700 shows that Mr. Rogers made will continue to be shown.

He took a few years off from production in the late 1970's, and later, toward the end of his long career, he cut back to taping 12 or 15 episodes a year. Although his show ran daily throughout those years, what his latter-day viewers saw was a mix of new material and reruns, the differences between them softened by a bit of black dye in Mr. Rogers's gray hair. As a spokesman for Mr. Rogers said, it didn't matter so much that the shows were repeated: the audience was always new.

Mr. Rogers kept a busy schedule outside the Neighborhood. He was the chairman of a White House forum on child development and the mass media in 1968, and from then on was frequently consulted as an expert or witness on such issues. He produced several specials for live television and videotape. Many of his regular show's themes and songs were worked into audiotapes. There were more than a dozen books, with titles like *You Are Special* and *How Families Grow.*

He was also one of the country's most sought-after commencement speakers, and if college seniors were not always bowled over by his pronouncements, they often cried tears of joy just to see him, an old friend of their childhood.

When he was inducted into the Television Hall of Fame in 1999, he began his formal acceptance speech by saying, "Fame is a four-letter word." And now that he had gotten the attention of a house full of the industry's most powerful and glamorous names, he asked them to think about their responsibilities as people "chosen to help meet the deeper needs of those who watch and listen, day and night." He instructed them to be silent for 10 seconds and think about someone who had had a good influence on them.

Yesterday, Mr. Rogers's Web site, www.misterrogers.org, provided a link to help parents discuss his death with their children.

"Children have always known Mister Rogers as their 'television friend,' and that relationship doesn't change with his death," the site says.

"Remember," it added, "that Fred Rogers has always helped children know that feelings are natural and normal, and that happy times and sad times are part of everyone's life."

 Questions on Readings 1 and 2

Were Isaiah Berlin and Fred Rogers successful in your humble opinion? Why or why not?

What is your definition of success?

What is your idea of a successful life?

Does the biography of either Isaiah Berlin or Fred Rogers represent "the myth of a perfect life"? Why or why not?

Would you consider Isaiah Berlin an interdisciplinarian? Why or why not?

Would you consider Fred Rogers an interdisciplinarian? Why or why not?

Discussion on Readings 1 and 2

Readings 1 and 2 were selected because both men share some interesting similarities. Both men did not start out knowing what exactly they would end up doing. Nevertheless, both men ended up accomplishing a great deal, even though both men did not achieve instant success.

Were both men successful? Berlin never did write the great book of philosophy. He was, according to Marilyn Berger, a *bon vivant*, meaning he was more interested in enjoying life than collecting and editing his essays into books. Perhaps a more contemporary term for Berlin instead of *bon vivant* would be *partier*, as he seemed to have valued his social life a great deal. Can you imagine how his biography could have been written differently, more negatively, by stressing what he did not accomplish but perhaps should have?

Berlin's obituary could have been written even more positively by minimizing what could be construed as his "shortcomings" rather than emphasizing how he succeeded in spite of them. Learn from this example and avoid emphasizing what could be regarded as shortcomings. For example, students sometimes will go into much detail in their intellectual autobiographies about all the wild things they may have done during high school. Instead of detailing all of your "bad girl" or "bad boy" behavior, you can summarize that period in your life by writing a sentence similar (but not exactly—avoid plagiarism!) to the following one sentence: "I had some wild times during high school, from which I learned the importance of accountability and responsibility."

You might want to emphasize those experiences in which you had significant learning experiences, even if they were short-term, such as during a summer job or internship. If it was a life-altering event, it is worth mentioning and describing how you changed, what you learned from the experience, and its continuing relevance in your life.

Some students may experience difficulties writing about their accomplishments. They may be modest. They may prefer to remain humble. They may have been taught that telling others about their accomplishments is tantamount to bragging and self-centeredness. Think of writing your autobiography, then, as an exercise in stating the facts, or even a preliminary exercise in personal marketing. If you do not tell others about the wonderful things you have done, who will? How will others learn about your accomplishments? Learning how to talk about your accomplishments is a necessary skill in today's workplace. Without this skill you may not get the job you want. You will be passed over in promotions, and you could even be fired as many positions require you to list your accomplishments for annual reviews or performance evaluations. Stating your accomplishments is not the same as exaggerating. Be proud of your accomplishments and of your identity as an interdisciplinarian!

Reading 3

Readings 1 and 2 are meant to be read with Reading 3, "Construing Continuity," by scholar Mary Catherine Bateson. Bateson's parents, Margaret Mead and Gregory Bateson were both famous anthropologists. Bateson in Reading 3 calls life stories such as Berlin's and Rogers' "discontinuous narratives." Nevertheless, Bateson believes that common threads or patterns can be found in the most discontinuous life story. For example, one continuity in Mr. Rogers' career would be his love of music. Can you find the continuities despite the discontinuities in your own life? What are those continuities? How do they relate to your academic and professional interests?

READING

CONSTRUING CONTINUITY

by

Mary Catherine Bateson

It was not until thirty years after the senior year of high school I spent in Israel that I returned in 1988 for an extended visit, accompanied by Vanni. We traveled around the country, and I told her stories of what that year had meant to me, even as I kept trying to understand the changes in the interval: three wars, expanded territories, and new waves of immigrants. Vanni's responses were different from mine at her age, more skeptical. Although she was only a year older than I had been, she filtered her perceptions through different experiences, including seven years of childhood in Iran. I was different too: whenever I tried to fathom how much things had changed, I was confounded by the problem of knowing whether the change was in myself or in the country.

In 1956 Israel matched my youth. It offered me, as an American teenager, a model of commitment that I took away with me and treasured, so I was startled at the ways individual plans had been redirected, how different my friends' lives had been from what they had firmly predicted. They still had the same intensity, but not the same innocent idealism. They commented constantly on the extent of changes, boasting and kvetching alternately, but that was a familiar pattern. I found that I responded to the same individuals I had liked thirty years before and to the familiar atmosphere of questioning and debate. It reassured me of a basic continuity across the years: that I was in some sense the same person I had been, and so were they.

Israel had also offered me a vision of equality for women, but returning with my perceptions changed by progress and debate in the interval, I was startled to realize that, by 1988, even with a backlash under way, the status of women looked better in the United States—but how to be certain that the status of women had not also changed in Israel, perhaps for the worse, because of increasing numbers of ultra-Orthodox? I was puzzled at things I had failed to see during my first stay and unsure whether I had been too busy or inattentive or simply blind. Why, for instance, had I never climbed up to the fortress of Masada as a teenager? Simply because the archaeological excavations that led to opening the site, where Jews had fought to the death to preserve their tradition, had not been completed. Why had I never been to Yad Vashem, the vast holocaust memorial? I had, but most of it was built later, and preoccupation with the holocaust has intensified since.

I returned again a year later and made a project of seeking out high school classmates from thirty years before, asking them to tell me the stories of their lives in the interval and pondering their experiences of continuity and change. Israel is not an easy site for research, for I found I had to answer five questions for every one I got a response to. Still, I was startled to realize how often, in this context where everyone spoke of change, families hunkered down, couples stayed together, and children settled close to their parents.

Both Iran and the Philippines have gone through revolutions since we lived there, yet continuities keep emerging under superficial change, sometimes a long time later, like the forms of nationalism that emerged in the former Soviet Union after seventy years of Communist rule. Revolutions sweep individuals from positions of power but rarely sweep away the old concepts of power and how to use it, so patterns reassert themselves. The search for change is almost always the assertion of some underlying value that has been there all along, for men and women who set out to build something new bring with them their ideas of what is possible as well as what is seemly and what is comely. Social visions come like brides, dressed in hand-me-down finery.

In Iran after the revolution, old themes resurfaced very rapidly. I had been with the students when they went through the buildings and took down all the portraits of the Pahlavi dynasty at our fledgling university on the Caspian, sharing their euphoria and sense of liberation. The removals left pale patches on the walls, but repainting was not necessary. Within weeks they were covered with portraits of Khomeini on the same scale. One common portrait of the ayatollah standing against the sky was virtually a remake of a favorite picture of the shah. From our first arrival in Iran, the prison at Evin had been pointed out to us as a symbol of the kind of political repression that must be changed, but once emptied it was quickly filled again with dissidents against the new regime. The rumors of corruption among the mullahs and even the members of Khomeini's family sounded suspiciously similar to rumors about the old elite, whether the actual continuity was in a pattern of corruption or a pattern of paranoia about the powerful—or both. The names of streets have changed, the women are veiled, the cabarets are gone, but at a deeper level I suspect that much is the same. The Islamic revolutionaries were seeking continuities with Iran's religious past and, at another level, reasserting an ancient longing for authenticity that recurs through Iranian history. But there is also a recurrence of familiar and unlovely ideas about power and the corrupting nature of social life.

In all learning, one is changed, becoming someone slightly—or profoundly—different; but learning is welcome when it affirms a continuing sense of self. What is learned then becomes a part of that system of self-definition that filters all future perceptions and possibilities of learning. It is only from a sense of continuing truths that we can draw the courage for change, even for the constant, day-to-day changes of growth and aging.

When Vanni was reaching her teens, already committed to a career in acting, she said one day, "Mommy, it must be awfully hard on you and Daddy that I don't want to do any of the same things you and Daddy do, or Grandma and Granddad." Well, how could I know whether the sense of continuity was critical at that moment or the sense of rebellion? Somehow both must be present. I crossed my fingers and said, "You can't be a good actress unless you're an observer of human behavior and unless you wonder about other people's motivations. Actually, what we do has a lot in common." I was lucky, since apparently what I said then was useful in setting up a relationship between continuity and change that fit her needs. American families have traditionally felt they were combining continuity and change when the sons of garage mechanics have become engineers and their sons have became physicists, but they might as easily have felt alienation across the differences in income and education.

In Israel I had repeated conversations with older members of kibbutzim bewailing the fact that their children do not want to "follow in their footsteps," choosing to leave the kibbutz, even to live abroad. "Did you grow up on a kibbutz?" I would ask. "Oh, no, my father was a shopkeeper in the city and very religious." The parents had left home to found the kibbutz, and now the children are following in their footsteps by leaving. Any social innovation, like the cooperative living of the kibbutz, is vulnerable to the fact that the next generation may be more interested in emulating the novelty of innovation than in continuing the parents' particular solutions. The pioneers of Israeli kibbutzim wanted to go back to the soil and to productive labor, but they tried to retain many aspects of urban life in their attitudes toward ideas and toward the arts, reading, questioning, and debating political ideals. If the kibbutz movement ever does fully settle into a pattern of biological recruitment—of one generation replacing the next—these older stylistic continuities may fade into country ways.

Several years ago I was invited to speak at a national conference of midlife members of a teaching order of nuns. They all belonged to the age cohort that had entered the order shortly before aggiornamento in the Catholic Church: when they entered, they came to live in large, routinized convents, eating and sleeping and praying on a strict schedule. They wore old-fashioned black and white habits, with wimples and veils, and they were taught to avoid friendships and personal conversation. Today they live in apartments, some alone and some with other sisters, developing friendships and dressing as they please. As high school and college teachers, they were all well-educated, but today they can choose their assignments, and many work in other social service professions. During the transition from the past to the present, a great many young women left the order—as many as four out of five of those entering in some years some because of too much change and others because of too little, whether in the order or in the church. The ones I met were forceful women who had been able to embrace a radical change in the pattern of their lives by recognizing continuity in discontinuity. They could assert that their commitment was still evolving, which helped them to be patient with the rigidities of the institution, to find discontinuity in continuity.

Even in our change-emphasizing culture, we often reconstruct and romanticize the past to emphasize continuity, and we retell the lives of great men and women as if their destinies were fixed from childhood. Henry Ford is said to have lost his heart to the first horseless carriage he saw as a child; Teresa of Avila is said to have tried to run away to be martyred by the Moors; mothers of musicians describe their children's response to the radio—you see, these stories suggest, this child was already on the path to this particular kind of greatness. Children are offered models of achievement that minimize discontinuity, proposing a single rising curve of development, marked with a rhythm of recognizable milestones: promise in childhood, preparation in youth, continuing progress in adulthood.

The traditional model of a successful life does not include radical new beginnings halfway through—these, by implication, are only necessary when a life has gotten onto the wrong track—but we do have an alternative story type in which the plot involves a major shift, repudiating a bad course and turning onto a good one. In his *Confessions*, St. Augustine emphasized the wickedness of his early ways, highlighting his conversion, and so did Malcolm X in his *Autobiography*. This way of construing the past is increasing through the development of twelve-step programs, which require that some moment be identified as touching bottom, after which ascent becomes possible. Narratives of discontinuity offer the chance to leave the past behind, the good as well as the bad, yet anyone who claims the liberating experience of being born again must also face again the groping learning of an infant. Some people handle a transition like the disintegration of a marriage by amplifying discontinuity: moving to a new town, growing a beard, getting a makeover, becoming a new person, erasing affection in legal fights. Others minimize the change: "We haven't gotten on for years," they say. "All we did was to make it official."

Often those who have made multiple fresh starts or who have chosen lives with multiple discontinuities are forced by the standard ideas of the shape of a successful career to regard their own lives as unsuccessful. I have had to retool so often I estimate I have had five careers. This does not produce the kind of résumé that we regard as reflecting a successful life, but it is true of more and more people, starting from the beginning again and again. Zigzag people. Learning to transfer experience from one cycle to the next, we only progress like a sailboat tacking into the wind.

A single rising curve is unlikely to reflect the lives of very many in a world where life expectancies approach and then pass seventy. Now the norm of a successful life more often involves repeated new beginnings and new learning. All those who become immigrants and refugees, displaced housewives and foreclosed farmers, workers whose skills are obsolete and entrepreneurs whose businesses are destroyed will have to learn new skills. Increasingly, returning to the classroom and sometimes totally shifting gears from one identity to another will be fundamental to adult development. We will become aware that a zigzag, seen from another angle, may be a rising spiral, so that readjustments are a record not of failure but of growth. Beyond a certain level of economic and technological development, any society must become a learning society, one in which many of the most talented and energetic members have more than one career, as athletes and military people do today. Learning is the new continuity for individuals, innovation the new continuity for business. Each requires a new kind of self definition.

The traditional tales of achievement or of conversion, whatever suspense and danger were built in along the way, were always cultural constructions, fabricated to make the confusing realities of life fit in with ideas like salvation or progress. People from different cultural traditions see the past differently, whether they are glorifying the industrial revolution or justifying their individual choices, but any cultural theory of the life cycle is likely to leave some people feeling that their own narratives do not measure up. Our narratives are becoming more complicated and ambiguous, and the culturally given plotlines are likely to mislead. The continuities of the future are invisible, horizons in shades of blue we have not learned to name.

In my recent work on the ways women combine commitments to career and family, I have been struck by how commonly women zigzag from stage to stage without a long-term plan, improvising along the way, building the future from "something old and something new." For men and women, résumés full of change show resiliency and creativity, the strength to welcome new learning, yet personnel directors often discriminate against anyone whose résumé does not show a clear progression. Quite a common question in job interviews is "What do you want to be doing in five years?" "Something I cannot now imagine" is not yet a winning answer. Accepting that logic, young people worry about getting "on track," yet their years of experimentation and short term jobs are becoming longer. If only to offer an alternative, we need to tell the other stories, the stories of shifting identities and interrupted paths, and to celebrate the triumphs of adaptation.

Recently I have been experimenting with asking adults to work with multiple interpretations of their life histories by composing two brief narratives, one focused on continuity, the other on discontinuity. "Everything I have ever done has been heading me for where I am today" is one version of the truth, but most adults can say as well, "It is only after many surprises and choices, interruptions and disappointments, that I have arrived somewhere I could never have anticipated." Most people have a preference, one way or the other, a version that is normally in focus for them, underlying and justifying their current choices, but almost everyone can discover the alternative version. Some solve the problem I have set them by focusing on different aspects of their lives: same spouse, different job; same job, different city. Some notice that the appearance of discontinuity is increased or reduced by the choice of words, so they can make the contrast by saying, "I have always been a writer" and "I used to write poetry, but now I am a journalist." A friend pointed out to me during a period when I was complaining of the discontinuities in my own life that although I had changed my major activity repeatedly, I had always shifted not to something new but to something prefigured peripherally, an earlier minor theme, so that discontinuity was an illusion created by too narrow a focus and continuity came from a diverse fabric and a broader vision.

Continuity discontinuity are not mutually exclusive. "Wherever I go it's important to me to work with new people." "I have always enjoyed tackling the unknown." "I have always wanted my work to provide new challenges." Some offer metaphors of continuous variation, like surfing, a life of encountering one wave after another. Some say, after years in the same profession or setting, that life is filled with wonder because each day is different. One person wrote, "After all, the laws of physics never change," but, in the words of another, "Sure, I've had the same job for thirty years, but meanwhile consider the turnover in my body's cells." All these approaches can be part of the same repertoire, for these are not exclusive truths. Tales of both continuity and discontinuity can be constructed from the same "facts," the dates and names and addresses of any life history. There is no single true interpretation that must be discovered and held to—on the contrary, each of these interpretations offers a different kind of strength and flexibility for fitting into a society of multiple systems of meaning.

Some dimension of continuity is essential to make change in other dimensions bearable. The evolution of the Great Atlantic and Pacific Tea Company into the modern A&P is said to have depended on affirming that the company had been and would continue to be a food company. When I was an infant, my mother ruled that it was all right to leave the baby in a strange place with a familiar person, or in a familiar place with a strange person, but too frightening if both were strange. Through most of my childhood, the sense of home was constant, but great numbers of people moved through the household. When Vanni was a child my husband and I moved frequently, but she had a much smaller number of caretakers than I did. Even today, after all those moves, Vanni worries about maintaining friendships across distance—a compensation for disruption? Or a learned appreciation of the value of continuity? Each of us can tell his or her story with alternative emphases.

At some deep level of the personality, perhaps, all change evokes the terrors of abandonment and dissolution, loss of those others who define self, or confrontation with a self become a stranger. During states of high vulnerability, panic is sometimes triggered by minute changes, so we arm ourselves with tokens of continuity. The wanderer or adventurer learns to finger a "lucky piece" along the way, and parents are sometimes advised to encourage an infant facing travel or multiple caretakers to cling to a blanket or a teddy bear, so the same tattered reassurance of the familiar can be carried from place to place. Immigrants and pioneers have always carried with them at least a few objects that provide a link with the past: Grandmother's photograph, a Bible, a pair of Sabbath candlesticks, a small blue china jug that, moved from mantel to mantel, converts a new house into a home. Devout Shiite Muslims carry a little molded block of clay from the site of the great martyrdoms, so that when they prostrate themselves for prayer their foreheads will touch the soil of Qarbala. The mementos I brought with me, reminders of multiple homes, converted an unfamiliar table at the MacDowell Colony into a desk where I could resume the task of composition: recalled in the text, the ammonite and the bluegreen globe, the carpet and the Passover plate connect the chapters and lines of reflection.

If I recognize my situation today as comparable to but not the same as my situation yesterday, I can translate yesterday's skills and benefit from yesterday's learning. I will make the mistake neither of trying to start from scratch nor of simply replicating previous patterns. Reinterpretation and translation, so useful in moving from one culture to another, turn out to be essential skills in moving from year to year even in the same setting. But if a situation is construed as totally new and different, earlier learning may be seen as irrelevant. The transfer of learning relies on some recognizable element of continuity—a woman describing her patchwork of careers for me recently remarked wryly on a continuity between work as a kindergarten teacher, a teacher of the deaf, and dean for "Greek life" (fraternities) on a university campus!

Gender stereotypes often suggest that females emphasize continuity (this is called "keeping the home fires burning"), while males venture forth on the new. Yet traditional female roles involve a high degree of unacknowledged adaptation to change, while many men have plied the same trade for a life-time with little new learning. Women often use labels to construe adaptation as continuity. When farmers lose their farms or men their jobs, their wives may be quicker to adapt, for while the men mourn their homes, their livelihoods, and their identities, the women, equally homeless and impoverished, hold on to their identities as wives, looking for new ways of caring for and supporting their husbands. Men sometimes use labels to assert continuity as well, as when sudden military adventures are justified as defense. The Vietnam War, which triggered profound change both in the United States and in Southeast Asia, was rationalized as a way of maintaining balance.

Along with the odd distortion, now much commented on, of women who used to say, "I don't work, I'm just a housewife," there is a second usually unremarked distortion when women say, "I've been doing the same thing for the last fifteen years, just looking after the kids and keeping house." If a corporate assignment changes, involving new skills and increased responsibility, the title often changes as well, and the discontinuity (and success in bridging it) is noted. But you rarely hear someone say, "I was getting pretty good at being the mother of an infant, but my new assignment, caring for a toddler, is still really challenging." Mother of one becomes mother of two? Mother of an adolescent? Mother-in-law? My suspicion is that although women may have been less likely to initiate significant change than men, they are highly resilient in finding ways to respond and adapt when change is thrust upon them.

The recognition and celebration of developmental change, season by season and year by year, underline the continuity of family life. Part of the agony of caring for a severely retarded child is the lack of change, the lack of milestones. The definition of any stage of the life cycle only as a plateau, without a dimension of growth, seems likely to lead to stagnation and discontent—living happily ever after is a swamp. The famous "midlife crisis" may be an artifact of such a misdefinition, so too much of the senility observed in the elderly.

Raising children does involve the transmission of continuities, but it also requires sustained and loving attention that welcomes particularity. It involves both providing a base of security and continuing identity, and freeing the individual for risk and experimentation. In a rapidly changing society, parents struggle to make tradition available and to affirm their own continuing convictions while affirming that a child who comes home with a new religion or sexual identity or a Mohawk haircut is still beloved.

The weave of continuity and creativity in the ways that individuals "compose" their lives is not unlike the way they put together sentences and other sequences of behavior. In speaking, we follow culturally transmitted rules of grammar, but these allow totally original utterances; most sentences we speak or hear have never before been spoken, and the most profoundly original insights are only intelligible because they are phrased in recognizable form. Even that family of art forms referred to as improvisatory, such as jazz or epic recitation, actually depend upon endless practice and the recombining of previously learned components so that each performance is both new and practiced. Children need to learn both kinds of skills. No list of appropriate behaviors, no finite set of skills is sufficient.

A story used to be told about the cyberneticist Norbert Wiener. Sometime in the fifties, they say, he was riding in a car driven slowly by a student through narrow streets, when they glancingly struck a child chasing a ball. The student pulled over, helped the child up, crying but unhurt, took her into a nearby pharmacy, got a Band-Aid for her scraped knee and a lollipop, called her mother on the pay phone, delivered her at home a few houses away, and eventually got back in the car with a sigh of relief. Wiener had not moved. "You have hit a little girl before with your car?" he said. The student: "My God, no, heaven forbid." "But then how did you know what to do?" In fact, in order to know what to do in a novel situation, he had to draw on a truly vast amount of existing knowledge: law, psychology, first aid, how to use a telephone. Even in completely new situations response depends on. recognizing continuity. Yet from year to year I have to make allowances, as I tell the story, for changes. Neighborhood drugstores disappear, lawsuits multiply, lollipops are branded bad for the teeth and become unwelcome favors.

All around the world we can find transitions under way in which the challenge to leadership is to make change tolerable by providing affirmations of underlying continuity, as Ethiopian Jews arriving in Israel are able to greet the most radical shift in their circumstances by saying they have come home. The nuns who outlasted the reforms were asserting, *Plus ça change, plus c'est la même chose* (the more it changes, the more it's the same).

Without such a sense of underlying continuity, change is so frightening that some are driven into reactionary identities. The pitfall of fundamentalism—whether it is Jewish, Christian, or Islamic, or cropping up in some other tradition—is that when some item is held constant while the context varies, constancy is an illusion, and those who resist change often suffer the reverse, *Plus c'est la même chose, plus ça change* (the more it's the same, the more it changes). The long coats and fur-trimmed hats worn by Hasidic Jews, like the habits of nuns, were only slightly different from general patterns of dress when they were adopted, but freezing these styles created later situations of extreme differentiation. Christian fundamentalists claim that they are practicing "that old time religion," but when they assert the literal truth of ancient words of scripture in the context of modern notions of truth and falsehood, they are in effect asserting something new. Translating the cosmology of the Old Testament into the format of "creation science" turns the insight of an ordered universe into a caricature. The return to tradition that fundamentalists promise, carried out in a new context, often results in radical change, just as, during the Reagan-Bush years, radical change was camouflaged with the label of conservatism.

Sameness and difference are a matter of context and point of view, change and continuity often two sides of the same coin. We can only make sense of the relationship between change and constancy by thinking of them in layers, one flowing under or over or within the other, at different levels of abstraction: superficial change within profound continuity, and superficial continuity within profound change. The deepest changes may take generations, with old attitudes concealed beneath efforts to adapt. My mother once commented that, when a woman who was herself breast-fed shifts to bottle feeding, she still holds her infant as she was held, as if the nourishment were coming from her body; but when her daughter bottle-feeds, the echo is lost. Sometimes the descendants of religious families retain their parents' ethical principles for a generation or more after abandoning the doctrines that supported them. Sometimes groups that have been persecuted act out patterns of self hate when the persecutor is long gone.

One day a senior colleague told me a joke with a typical mixture of the academic and the mildly salacious, ending with the assertion that physics is like copulation and mathematics like masturbation. He broke off suddenly with an air of contrition and said, "I shouldn't be telling that joke, that's a sexist joke." When I looked puzzled, he explained that it's only for the man that copulation is like physics, whereas, he said, for the woman, "sex doesn't have an object." I was chilled. He had learned that it was a mistake to be overtly sexist and was trying to watch his step, but he had no awareness whatsoever, under the effort at superficial change, of the profoundly sexist nature of the assumptions revealed in his explanation: that sex is something a man does to a woman, a process in which the woman is the object. This was for him self-evident fact.

Changes can be made quickly on the surface that take a generation or more to affect more basic structures, so both progress and degeneration are deceptively slow. In evolution, the very continuity of survival depends upon multiple superficial changes, many of them temporary. If temporary adaptations were to become permanent and genetic (this theory, the inheritance of acquired characteristics, is today associated with Lamarck; but Darwin believed it at one time as well), survival would become harder. Thus, dogs and horses grow thicker fur when exposed to cold, but if a thick coat is inherited, the capacity to adjust fur thickness has been replaced by fixed heavy fur thickness, and the animal can no longer adjust. Natural selection works more slowly, favoring traits that prove useful generation after generation. My father used to point out that a tightrope walker maintains balance by changing the angle of the balancing pole. Freeze the angle of the pole, and the tightrope walker will fall. Death and extinction are the discontinuities avoided by the capacity to change.

The pattern in which corrective feedback brings about the changes or adjustments that will maintain a deeper constancy is what defines a balanced cybernetic system. Human beings can respond more quickly than dogs and horses to messages of heat or cold, putting on or taking off a sweater to maintain a comfortable body temperature. But even among humans the needed adjustment is not available if, for instance, an outer garment is specified by religion. I have often felt sorry for Hasidic Jews in the furred hats and dark coats adopted generations ago in Northern Europe and carried with them to the Mediterranean climate of Israel. In the same way, when educational or political systems are frozen into some form that seems good to one generation, they may lose the flexibility to adapt in the next. Efforts to address social issues by amending the U.S. Constitution instead of learning to read it differently risk compromising the flexibility which is its greatest strength. Protecting the environment with more and more regulations may block the development of improved ways to handle wastes or conserve energy. Rigid standards can undermine thoughtful education, and sometimes overspecific codes of conduct can lead to the atrophy of ethical choice. Only children who are allowed to make mistakes can become responsible adults.

Many kinds of addiction can be seen as efforts to maintain some constancy that at another level brings about damaging change. Withdrawal from a drug is a little like an autoimmune disease, the self-estrangement of a system no longer recognizing itself, and the symptoms of some kinds of withdrawal look curiously like allergies. Alcoholics drink to feel right, to feel like themselves. Sober, they encounter uncomfortable strangers in their own skins, and pouring a drink feels like coming home; their bodies have learned to regard the presence of alcohol as a natural state and adjusted to it.

Chemical addiction is the result of a kind of bodily learning; the learning of ideas also produces a kind of addiction. All views of the world are acquired, and learning a way of seeing the world offers both insight and blindness, usually at the same time. Losing the certainty of a particular worldview can make you feel sick, bewildered, dizzy. From this point of view, culture shock is a withdrawal phenomenon; we reject the new because we have learned to be dependent on the old. In the same way, I may learn to trust someone, premising my life on that trust, and then be unable to reject it when I am betrayed. People will accept martyrdom in order to hold on to an idea.

Sometimes those who have learned to need a particular substance or behavior have learned to need a constant change in the supply, overcoming the adaptive effect of habituation. This need for a constant change develops in some forms of alcohol and heroin use, defining what feels normal. The American economy is addicted to increases in the gross national product, for growth has come to be regarded as the only stable state of a modern economy. Anorexics must get thinner and thinner in order to feel slim; more and more missiles are needed in order to feel secure; pornography must become progressively more horrendous to continue to titillate. Treatments of addiction like methadone or daily attendance at AA meetings are also in a way addictive, but they make sense if they involve replacing an escalating need with a stable one that carries a reduced cost. Perhaps all pleasures that do not bring a natural satiety have an addictive potential. Once money is invented, wealth seems to become addictive, for the wealthy are never rich enough. "Rich" is apparently not a continuity; "richer" is. The present leverages the future.

It is fashionable today to speak of behaviors that used to be regarded as good or evil as addictions: gambling, sex, work, all those behaviors that the person feels compelled to pursue and that may come to seem dysfunctional. No choice, no morality. Yet the moral judgment survives under the clinical veneer in that we do not often speak of couples contentedly and prosperously married as mutually addicted, and we are just beginning to speak of the more respectable substance addictions in those terms. Even those who are proudly free from addictions to morning coffee or afternoon tea are likely to be committed to such learned constancies as jogging or a morning shower or moving their bowels at a particular time, all behaviors that become virtually a part of self-definition by long conditioning. Where is one to draw the line in a thicket of metaphors that both illuminate and confuse? We might do better to see a relationship between addictions and commitments and teach children not so much to avoid addiction as to choose their addictions carefully. Dental floss yes, laxatives no.

The constancies of modern life are increasingly the products of technology: we depend on an information-rich environment, on constant entertainment, on air-conditioning. Some kinds of resistance have been lost, so we have come to require clean drinking water. In a real breakdown of technology, our withdrawal symptoms would kill us. In postwar Iraq, illness and death spread as the society struggled for self-regulation. Some of the constancies we have come to expect, like medical care and increased longevity, are dangerously cumulative. Sometimes, however, a constant in society affects the individual as a violent discontinuity—losing a job is no less painful when economists speak of acceptable levels of unemployment. Sometimes we blame individuals when society is the addict: Who after all really is addicted to crack cocaine? Where is the addiction in the system? What constancies does it maintain?

From the point of view of composing a life or managing an institution, the ability to recognize any situation as representing both continuity and change makes it possible to play that double recognition in tune with changing needs, to avoid the changes that reduce flexibility and the constancies that eat away at the necessities of survival. We know that keeping consumption at familiar levels is eventually going to deplete resources, yet patterns of consumption are oddly difficult to change. When change itself becomes addictive, it seems almost bound to lead to trouble, yet not all acquired habits of constant change are degenerative: constant learning, for instance, is not. A willingness to change in response to a new social environment can be a style of relating to the world throughout a lifetime. Yet the modern vulnerability to boredom may be the long-term result of an addiction to variation.

When I first lived in Israel, less than ten years after independence, military preparedness was a short-term adaptation, but over time, as new generations grew up under arms, it seemed to become intrinsic to the structure of the state. What looked impressive then is worrying today, potentially replacing other constancies of Jewish identity and becoming an end in itself. Thoughtful Israelis today make a distinction between being able to fight for survival, as many of those who died in the holocaust were not, and risking addiction to militarism. There are positive side effects of this drug, for it works to promote solidarity and the maturity of young people—I sometimes wish all my freshman students had spent two years in the military—but there are negative side effects too, such as secrecy and sexism. When I returned to visit Israel, I found I was as concerned about constancies as I was about changes. Yet I could see other processes of change growing into new constancies, like the long-lived forests slowly created of trees planted one by one.

Readings 4 and 5

The following two readings are sample intellectual autobiographies by interdisciplinarians like you. Reading 4, "Confessions of an Unconscious Interdisciplinarian," was written by Thomas H. Murray when he was already an accomplished scholar. Reading 5, "The Celtic Question," was written by Richard W. Jackson while he was a student in the author's spring 2004 Foundations of Interdisciplinary Studies class. These two intellectual autobiographies serve as examples to help students craft their own stories of how they are becoming interdisciplinary.

READING

CONFESSIONS OF AN UNCONSCIOUS INTERDISCIPLINARIAN

by

Thomas H. Murray

ABSTRACT

This is a cautionary tale, told by one whose venture into interdisciplinary work began with a social psychology experiment. Realizing there were moral dimensions to the experiment, be began following his interests across conventional boundaries. Ultimately, this led to studies of how people think about responsibility and, more recently, the ethical dilemmas faced by nurses and doctors who care for seriously ill newborns, an area that reaches far beyond the boundaries of moral philosophy into economics, sociology, and health policy. These experiences suggest that interdisciplinary theorists would do well to study what actually happens when people do interdisciplinary research. By creating and studying narratives about cases of interdisciplinary research, those who study interdisciplinarity will be able to temper abstract theory with experience.

I

I didn't start out that way; hardly anybody does. I was going to be like the rest, and walk the straight and narrow. I guess I just couldn't resist temptation.

You don't just one day decide to *be* one! In fact, you don't even realize it's happening until it gradually dawns on you. By then it's already too late to turn back. You're hooked, and there's nothing, nothing you can do to get loose;

no way to regain your lost innocence. The most you can hope for is to warn others about the perils of following along the same path that led you to this state. About the only way I know of doing that is to tell cautionary tales, and who can you talk about more authoritatively than yourself? So, for the sake of those who might otherwise naively have followed, I offer here the confessions of an unconscious interdisciplinarian.

I suppose it all began in graduate school, about the time I started on my MA research. I was doing this nice, innocent experiment in social psychology where we cleverly tricked undergraduates into thinking they were witnesses to someone accidentally receiving a severe electrical shock: a clever experiment with good results. One thing bothered me though: the subjects would tell me how interesting and ingenious the experiment was, how wonderful it was that I was doing it, how happy they were to have participated in it. But their eyes, and their voices, and their trembling bodies contradicted their words. Some of them—many of them, especially those who had not sought help for the phony shock "victim"—gave every indication of serious emotional distress, every indication except the words they used to assure me and praise the research.[1]

Eventually I remembered that subjects in other studies like this one, studies in which subjects were placed in potentially emotionally wrenching situations, and in which they sometimes did not react as we all know good, courageous folks are supposed to react, those subjects told their experimenters the same things mine were telling me. And the researchers doing those other studies reported their subjects' words as proof that the research wasn't having any bad effects on them.[2]

I couldn't be so sure. I began seeing things in the research in my field that unsettled me, things like the "self-esteem" manipulation where you give a supposed personality profile test to people, flip a coin (or consult a table of random numbers), and give them one of two already prepared profiles, one very flattering, the other speaking of shallowness and insincerity. You give one of these fake results, and then watch what effect the supposedly raised or lowered self-esteem has on what they do in a staged situation.

This made me uncomfortable, though I couldn't explain it very well. When I raised questions about the self-esteem ploy, questions like, "Is it right to do that to people, especially vulnerable adolescents?," I got a variety of responses. Some people thought I was simply daffy—a premature eccentric. Others reacted as if I had come to high tea in a dirty, torn shirt with "Born to Party" printed on the front, and then proceeded to talk of gross and unmentionable things to the other guests. In other words, I was committing a fairly serious breech of etiquette. But I think the third response was the most interesting. These folks seemed to regard me as we would someone from another culture where they used many of the same words we do, or at least the same word-sounds, but with different meanings. They saw me as some sort of an intellectual dyslexic.

But though this may have been the beginning of my fall from grace, I had not yet become a flaming, no-holds-barred interdisciplinarian. I was looking at one thing—psychological research—from a vastly different perspective—morality. But I had not yet committed the mortal sin of trying to (forgive me for using such language) *integrate* the two perspectives in any way. Still, I had begun my descent, and the remaining voyage down the slippery slope was prolonged but inexorable.

The next big step came with my doctoral dissertation. At that point, I wasn't fooling anybody. But I had become interested in how people think about responsibility. The specific problem was how people attribute responsibility for accidents. Earlier research gave conflicting results.[3] Generally, researchers had set out to prove that people made these judgments in a systematically irrational fashion. And the patterns they found were certainly irrational in that no one could explain them. It struck me that the way the questions were usually asked—"Is so-and-so *responsible* for this accident?"—was more than a little ambiguous. So then I took the plunge and started reading—oh, that first fatal article—philosophy.[4] Specifically, I read H.L.A. Hart, Patrick Devlin and others on the concept of responsibility in law and philosophy. And when I realized that people might be understanding the question quite differently, according to the circumstances of the particular case they were being given, I thought that maybe that might account for the otherwise inexplicable patterns—patterns that might not be at all irrational, but possibly quite sensible. I did the studies, and learned that indeed people took the question of responsibility to mean different things as I had expected.[5]

But of course, by now my ultimate capitulation was all but a *fait accompli*. I had dared to inject semantics, moral philosophy, and jurisprudence into the very heart of a social psychology experiment. And it had worked. And I had *enjoyed* it!

As everyone knows, the sure way to damnation is to keep bad company. Naturally, that's what I did, hanging around with faculty at colleges that openly permitted—sometimes even encouraged, if you can believe it!—interdisciplinary studies. I sealed my doom in a pair of fellowship years during which I consorted brazenly with philosophers and theologians. And, rather than overlook any possible detour from the abyss, I have for the past many years labored in not one, but two interdisciplinary research institutes.

But enough about the general lamentable trajectory I have followed since first tasting the forbidden fruit. I want to talk about a specific problem that will show to the unwary innocent how easily one can be enticed from the disciplinary path into the fires of interdisciplinarity. (The late John Gardner captured some of the flavor of this journey in his book *Mickelsson's Ghosts* about the misadventures of a philosopher named Mickelsson, who teaches, among other things, a course in medical ethics: "What a world, Mickelsson was thinking. Tillson and himself, arch-enemies, sheparding another poor innocent—fugitive from the clean, honest field of Engineering—into the treacherous, ego-bloated, murder-stained hovel of philosophy.")[6]

Ironically enough, the problem I want to talk about involves the most innocent of the innocent—babies; specifically, seriously ill newborns who find themselves exposed to the exigencies of the Neonatal Intensive Care Unit, a glaring, technology-dominated environment of lights, buzzers, bleeps, gauges, dials, and the odors of disinfectant.

My involvement began innocently as well. The director of a large NICU came to my Institute and asked for assistance in dealing with the grave ethical dilemmas the doctors and nurses in his unit confronted regularly. Not to be disagreeable, and because in part our bluff was being called, we agreed. But first we insisted that we be permitted to spend time in the unit, familiarizing ourselves with it, with the problems, and with the personnel. I became one of the key people in this effort, and made a number of visits to the unit. After several months, I had learned three things; one was expected, but two were surprises. The expected one was that, yes, there were grave moral dilemmas in that unit. After all many of the babies there were on the brink of death. Some would live lives of gross impairment, even if treated with everything modern medicine would offer them. Some would die, no matter what, and perhaps merely have their brief life extended only at the cost of great pain and suffering for them, their families, and their nurses and physicians. The ethical issues raised there continue to absorb me to this day, and will probably do so for some time.[7]

But the second discovery was interesting as well. You should know that to the experienced nurses who work in these units are often masterful, and frequently have a better understanding of what will help a particular infant than many of the physicians. This is especially true if the physician is junior and inexperienced. Yet, units like this are usually organized hierarchically, with the physician giving orders to the nurse. Most units bow to reality, and despite the formal hierarchy, instruct the young MDs to pay careful attention to the advice of the nurses. This unit reflected the hierarchical bent of its director, and put even naive physicians in charge. Nurses, knowing they knew better than the junior physicians, nonetheless were not permitted to argue medicine. So they argued ethics. In significant measure the agitation in that unit that focused on ethical dilemmas was actually displaced from a genuine sore point—nurse-physician relationships. Had we accepted the director's definition of the problem, worn our philosopher's robes and blinders, we would have missed an important element of the problem.[8] Fortunately we did not, and in the subsequent retreat with the unit staff, we did discuss the ethical dilemmas, but we also pointed out tactfully some of the sociological and organizational factors the exacerbating tensions in that unit.

Someone might correctly object that this was not an instance of genuinely interdisciplinary scholarship, but rather a response to a practical, non-scholarly problem, namely dissension in an organization. There may be no deep linkage between the moral problems surrounding the care of seriously ill newborns, and the questions about the psychological and social dynamics of the NICU. At a practical level though, we cannot expect to make any realistic recommendations for policies or practices without a grasp of both the moral and the organizational issues. So such recommendations may be in that sense interdisciplinary, but are they scholarship?

We can do scholarship in moral philosophy or in the sociology of organizations without reference to the other discipline. But if the vineyard in which you labor is something called medical ethics or bioethics, then perhaps we have learned something of scholarly value by observing the discrepancies between how moral problems are formulated by health professionals, and the actual appearance and significance of those problems to an observer trained in moral philosophy.

The third discovery, which was later to become much more important, was that contrary to the impression given by the then sparse literature on moral dilemmas in newborn care, the most common and morally complicated problems in NICUs were not what would later be called "Baby Doe" or "Baby Jane Doe" cases. These two unfortunate infants were born with congenital anomalies, and questions were raised about the appropriateness of treating them aggressively in light of their other disabilities, especially the fact that they would be retarded to some degree.[9] While these cases have dominated the public debate, and have been extremely influential in shaping the response by federal and state governments, they are relatively uncommon, and usually unproblematic from a moral point of view, though some hard cases appear. But by far the most common cases in the NICU, often very morally problematic, are the very premature infants who, even with the most skilled and aggressive care, have slim odds of living, and a significant probability of mental or physical disabilities if they should survive. To complicate matters further, the proportion of infants born so prematurely in the U.S. appears to be much higher than in other industrialized nations, and probably reflects decisions about health policy.[10] In short, we give little weight to prenatal health care, prenatal nutrition; education of pregnant women, and—not least—prevention of teenage pregnancies.

So, it turns out that in order to understand "ethical issues in the care of newborns," we must reach far beyond the boundaries of moral philosophy into the fields of economics, sociology, health policy. Furthermore, if we want to understand something about the sources of our responses—moral and otherwise—to seriously ill newborns, we must make use of a wide range of humanities disciplines. We arranged a conference, just now published with additional material as a book, that called on the disciplines of history, literature, religion, jurisprudence, and medicine as well as philosophy. The individual articles are mostly disciplinary.[11] The cumulative impact, though, is clearly multidisciplinary, at least.

In my own writing on this and other issues, I now routinely find myself relying on the insights of several disciplines, including the biomedical sciences, sociology, psychology, literature, history, and of course law and ethics. The focus is ethics and public policy, but, I believe the approach is thoroughly interdisciplinary, not from any a priori ideological commitment to the alleged superiority of interdisciplinary work, but because the nature of the questions I find interesting and my own inclinations leave me no choice.

"Unconscious" is probably the wrong adjective. But so would be "unwitting" or "unwilling" or any of the others I can think of at this time. Perhaps the way to conceive of my route down the interdisciplinary garden path is that I was drawn there by the nature of the problems I chose to find interesting. Like the scientist who does not set out to become a theorist of this or that, I simply followed my questions, which turned out to have a logic of their own, or at least to compel the use of certain methods and theories in order to give passably valid answers.

On the relation of interdisciplinary studies to the disciplines, I see no natural or necessary conflict between the two. Indeed, interdisciplinary work, like all scholarship, builds on what has come before, and that includes disciplinary as well as interdisciplinary work. In my own case, I discovered the enormous value of good legal scholarship as well as the importance of a range of humanities disciplines for illuminating the problems that obsess me. And I continue to find that my training in science and statistics serves me very well in understanding and analyzing ethical issues in science and medicine.

II

What purpose might be served by telling such "stories" as this one? In the midst of theoretical debates about the nature and justification of interdisciplinary studies, it is all too easy to lose sight of the complex actualities of interdisciplinary research. Take, for example, the accusation by Thomas L. Benson that interdisciplinary studies "rests upon serious conceptual confusion."[12] Benson is certainly right in saying that advocates of interdisciplinary studies have typically been less than clear or consistent about their methods or purposes. William H. Newell's defense of interdisciplinary studies meets Benson on the same, relatively abstract ground.[13] Such theoretical debates are important and necessary to clarify the intellectual foundation for interdisciplinary studies. But they are not sufficient.

Abstract discussions too easily lose sight of the thing-in-itself—the rich array of interdisciplinary scholarship. This creates at least two difficulties. First, they allow us to construct elaborate models of what interdisciplinary research must be, undisciplined by the realities of how it actually does proceed. Second, it may lead us into agnosticism about the very *existence* of interdisciplinary research.

The novel *The Master and Margarita* by the Russian writer Mikhail Bulgakov opens in a park where two men are discussing a poem ridiculing belief in the existence of Jesus. Agreeing that Aquinas' five arguments for the existence of God all fail, as does Kant's sixth proof, a third man joins the discussion and offers a seventh: he recounts the story of Jesus' meeting with Pontius Pilate, and then proceeds to demonstrate the supernatural in action. (This fellow is, in fact, the devil.)[14] Let this "confession"—this story—be a "seventh argument for the existence of interdisciplinary studies": I, like many others, have committed them.

My hope is that this narrative, along with many others, will serve as the raw material for analyses that will tell us much better than mere speculation ever can what interdisciplinary studies really is. What I am suggesting is that patient study of what actually happens when people do interdisciplinary research will yield insights into the process that together with theorizing about it in the abstract will enhance our understanding of it. Within the past couple of decades, the philosophy of science was rescued from an abyss of irrelevant abstraction by the attention some individuals paid to what scientists actually did, rather than devising logical reconstructions of what they supposed scientists must have been doing. Probably the most famous product of this movement to infuse historical narratives into the philosophy of science is Thomas Kuhn's *The Structure of Scientific Revolutions.*[15] But the change in method—forcing speculation to confront historical particularity—is at least as important as the specifics of Kuhn's own theory. Even critics of Kuhn's work recognize that one must show respect for the actualities of scientific practice. In that sense, Kuhn has wrought his own "revolution" in paradigm. And I see no reason in principle why the same methods and the same concepts could not be applied fruitfully to the study of change in non-scientific disciplines, or to the evolution of interdisciplinary studies.

III

Let me offer a modest beginning to this effort by returning to the incident that began my own "career" in bioethics—the research project that led me to have grave misgivings about deception in social psychological research. It seemed clear to me that the research subjects who had negative reactions to the research (more than half) often showed quite profound indications of their discomfort. The messages they gave with their tenseness, pained faces and choked voices contrasted starkly with what they said to me. They spoke calm words of admiration for my cleverness, and assurances that they were not the least bothered by it all; everything but their words gave precisely the opposite message.

Only much later did perspective and a general increase in knowledge about human behavior and motivation permit me to see that those people who had just let themselves down precipitously by failing to help a fellow in apparently great danger had, at that moment, no one else to lean on to prop up their imperiled sense of self-worth. No one except me, whom they could not afford to offend, no matter how awful or angry they felt.

I also realized then how vacuous was the comfort taken by other deceptive researchers who reported that their subjects "approved" of what the researchers had done. If the dynamics were anything like what I had observed, the subjects had little choice, and the justifications little meaning.

In what sense is this argument "interdisciplinary"? It is not merely an argument in moral philosophy that deceptive research is wrong per se; nor is it merely an empirical observation or theory. It requires as necessary components *both* moral arguments *and* insights from psychological theories (dealing with discrepancies between verbal and non-verbal behavior, factors affecting interpersonal interactions, the need for and methods by which self-esteem may be sustained, and the potential for self-deception in the service of avoiding internal conflict) as well as the privileged empirical observations I was able to make in my role as experimenter.

I believe a similar account can be given of my work on issues in neonatal intensive care. And within the field of bioethics I am by no means alone. In a not yet published paper, David H. Smith, a leading scholar in bioethics whose disciplinary training was in religious studies, argues convincingly that there are at least three species of important work in bioethics: scholarship that essentially plies a single discipline, particularly moral philosophy or religious ethics; scholarship that has a principal home in one discipline, but that incorporates other elements to the degree that it can no longer be said to be merely work in that discipline nor can or ought it to be judged solely by the criteria normally applied to purely disciplinary work; and scholarship that defies any efforts to "place" it within a particular discipline.[16] David goes on to argue that all three types of work are valuable.

To a considerable degree, work at the second and third level utilizes work at the first or "foundational" level. But I am convinced that calling it "applied philosophy" is grossly misleading. The image of a mechanical application of principles derived elsewhere could not be further from the truth as a description of excellent work in bioethics at the second or third levels. If anything, such mechanistic writing is frowned upon as unimaginative, uninformed, useless, and even subversive to the larger goals of the field—which include the desire to encourage dialogue among disciplines.

Another problem with the "foundational" metaphor is the implication that influence moves in only one direction—from the disciplines outwards or upwards. But an equally forceful argument has been made that bioethics has made substantial contributions to moral philosophy: as one article by a renowned philosopher put it: "How Medical Ethics Saved the Life of Philosophy."[17] The jist of this argument is that moral philosophy had become so detached and intellectually arid that it virtually ceased having anything interesting to say to the world; that it was not merely less practically useful, but even less intellectually rich and exciting. Talking once again about substantive moral problems has had a tonic effect on the entire discipline. The relationship between disciplinary and interdisciplinary inquiry is not that of foundation to application, but of two parallel and mutually influential enterprises, with related but by no means identical standards of excellence and overlapping but not identical "communities of interest" or "epistemic communities"—terms employed by Julie Thompson Klein to describe those groups of scholars who share interests, commitments, and mastery of a literature which qualify them to judge each other's work.[18] These scholarly mini-communities exist in all disciplines and all intellectually respectable "interdisciplines." Indeed, they supply the small-d "discipline" that is often confused with the larger organizational entities we call misleadingly "Disciplines."

The point, after all, of a Discipline is to impose discipline—orderliness, standards, etc.—and to avoid undisciplined efforts—that is, disorder, chaos, that which cannot be judged. That goal is in all cases accomplished by the very small community of scholars interested in that particular sort of research. There are two noteworthy exceptions to this generalization. First, critiques from outside the mini-community are sometimes very helpful in illuminating what important things are not being taken into account theoretically or practically. Second, new forms of work sometimes fail to find a home in any existent community of interest. This makes judging such work especially difficult. It makes doing it perilous. And indeed, much of it is of little enduring worth. But occasionally, work of this type can transform a current community of interests, or even perhaps establish a new one.

IV

All that I said speaks directly to interdisciplinary research, and not to interdisciplinary education. I have always argued that, politically, the case for interdisciplinary education will be greatly strengthened by a showing of vigorous interdisciplinary scholarship. I still believe that is true as a fact about academic politics. Reflection, though, has led me to doubt whether there is such a close coupling between the case for interdisciplinary research and interdisciplinary education, at least at the undergraduate level.

For one thing, the best argument in favor of interdisciplinary education emphasizes its potential for fostering intellectual flexibility and problem solving, including, not least, practice at learning to see the interests and world views that often determine the way a problem is framed, so that one may reframe it. This *is* a point that gives interdisciplinary education a leg up on strictly disciplinary studies. In competent hands, it can even show measurable results.[19] For life skills, it is valuable training. Whether it makes for better scholarship later on than disciplinary training is an open question. My point here is that it counts unequivocally in favor of interdisciplinary education.

A second consideration is suggested by Raymond C. Miller's apt remarks about those programs of study on college campuses that are already interdisciplinary—nursing, social work, engineering, and journalism among others.[20] These are all of course openly vocational. The message would seem to be that interdisciplinary education is the best job training. As in the first consideration; however, there is no clear lesson for interdisciplinary scholarship. To state my point simply, the cases for and conditions of interdisciplinary undergraduate education and interdisciplinary scholarship may not be as closely conjoined as I once thought.

V

It is time for observers of interdisciplinary research to tie their theories of interdisciplinarity down to the realities of its practice. Probably the best way to do that is to tell "stories"—to create narratives—about cases of interdisciplinary research. By studying these narratives, we can temper our theories of interdisciplinarity in the forge of experience. My hope is that this "confession" will be a small contribution to that purpose. As for the characters in Bulgakov's novel, and as it was for my Apostolic namesake, seeing is believing—and perhaps the beginning of understanding as well.

Notes

1. T. H. Murray, "Learning to Deceive: The Education of a Social Psychologist," *Hastings Center Report* (April 1980), 11–14.
2. S. Milgram, "Subject Reaction: The Neglected Factor in the Ethics of Experimentation," *Hastings Center Report* 7:5, (1977), 19–23.
3. The leading articles at that time included K. G. Shaver, "Defensive Attribution: Effects of Severity and Relevance on the Responsibility Assigned for an Accident," *Journal of Personality and Social Psychology*, 14, (1970), 101–113; J. I. Shaw and P. Skolnick, "Attribution of Responsibility for a Happy Accident," *Journal of Personality and Social Psychology*, 18 (1971), 380–383; and E. Walster, "Assignment of Responsibility for an Accident," *Journal of Personality and Social Psychology*, 3 (1966), 73–79.
4. P. Devlin, *The Enforcement of Morals* (New York: Oxford, 1965); H. L. A. Hart, *Liberty and Morality* (New York: Vintage, 1963).
5. T. H. Murray, "Attributing Responsibility for an Accident: Defensive Attribution in the Light of a Conceptual Analysis of Responsibility." Ph.D. Dissertation in the Department of Psychology, Princeton University, 1975.

6. J. Gardner, *Mickelsson's Ghosts* (New York: Knopf, 1982), p. 11.

7. See, e.g., A. Fleischman and T. H. Murray, "Ethics Committees and Infants Doe," *Hastings Center Report* (December, 1983), 5–9; T. H. Murray, "The Final, Anticlimactic Rule on Baby Doe," *Hastings Center Report* (June 1985), 5–9: T. H. Murray, "Why Solutions Continue to Elude Us," *Social Science and Medicine,* 20: 11 (1985), 1103–1107; T. H. Murray, "'Suffer the Little Children': Suffering and Neonatal Intensive Care," In T. H. Murray and A. L. Caplan (eds.) *Which Babies Shall Live?: Humanistic Dimensions of the Care of Imperiled Newborns* (Clifton, N.J.: Humana Press, 1985).

8. A. Caplan, "Can Applied Ethics Be Effective in Health Care and Should It Strive to Be?" *Ethics,* 93 (1983), 311–319.

9. For a good description of the facts in the best known cases, see J. Lyon, *Playing God in the Nursery* (New York: Norton, 1985).

10. T. H. Murray, "Ethics and Health Care Allocation." *Public Law Forum* 4 1, (1984), 41–50.

11. *Which Babies Shall Live,* op. cit.

12. T. L Benson, "Five Arguments Against Interdisciplinary Studies" *Issues in Integrative Studies,* 1, (1982), 38–48.

13. Three responses to Benson's article appeared in *Issues in Integrative Studies* 2, (1983) along with Benson's reply. They are, with respective page numbers, W. H. Newell, "The Case for Interdisciplinary Studies: Response to Professor Benson's Five Arguments," 1–19; J. L. Petr, "The Case For/Against Interdisciplinary Studies: A Comment on the Debate," 20–24; R. C. Miller, "What Do You Say to a Devil's Advocate?," 25–30; and T. L. Benson, "Response," 31–34.

14. Mikhail Bulgakov, *The Master and Margarita* (New York: Harper and Row, 1967.)

15. T. Kuhn, *The Structure of Scientific Revolutions* 2nd ed. (Chicago: U. of Chicago Press, 1970.)

16. D. H. Smith, "Quality Not Mercy: Some Reflections on Recent Work in Medical Ethics." Paper presented at a conference on "Bioethics as an Intellectual Field" held at the Institute for the Medical Humanities, U. of Texas Medical Branch, Galveston, Texas on Nov. 13-14, 1985.

17. S. Toulmin, "How Medicine Saved the Life of Ethics," *Perspectives in Biology and Medicine,* 25 (1982), 736–750.

18. J. T. Klein, "The Dialectic and Rhetoric of Disciplinarity and Interdisciplinarity," *Issues in Integrative Studies,* 2 (1983) 35–74.

19. See e.g., W. H. Newell and W. Green, "Defining and Teaching Interdisicplinary Studies" *Improving College and University Teaching* 30:1 (Winter 1982), 23–30.

20. Miller, op. cit, p. 27.

READING

THE CELTIC QUESTION

by

Richard W. Jackson

When I was in the seventh grade my social studies teacher went around the room asking each of us who our hero was. My answers were Julius Caesar, Hannibal, and Alexander the Great. I am not sure why I named those three gentlemen who had been dead for over two thousand years. There might have been something romantic about the idea of taking elephants over the mountains into Italy like Hannibal or changing the world by the force of your will like Caesar and Alexander. I daydreamed for hours about what it must have been like to match wits with an opposing general on the battlefield like Caesar did with Vercingetorix. What would I do in that situation? What abilities and situations arose that allowed these men to convince thousands of soldiers to die for them? Why did the Celts always lose?

The idea of studying history or anthropology never occurred to me when I finished high school. I allowed my parents to convince me to study mathematics at the University of Syracuse. The decision to study mathematics was the first instance of a recurring theme in my life of not listening to my heart, although when you are eighteen years old you do not always realize your heart is trying to tell you something. It quickly became apparent that while I was good at math I was not interested in it. Anyone can tell you that if you are not interested in something there is very little chance you will succeed. Soon this disinterest became reflected in my studies and I transferred to Corning Community College to study electrical technology after two and half years.

This move was the second instance of not listening to my heart. I enrolled in the electrical technology program because my grandfather got me a job at the cable television company in Corning and I enjoyed working with the technicians. The work was interesting and the pay was good. The manager said a degree in electrical technology would help me get a permanent job with the cable company so that is what I took. I enrolled in a degree for the sake of getting employment, not for the love of what I was studying. My parents reinforced this choice because getting a job and supporting myself was an important part of success to them. Our family had always scraped by so doing something you truly enjoyed did not necessarily go together with doing what it takes to survive.

I was more mature by the time I was at Corning and learned how to study and apply myself to my studies. One thing I had learned from my experiences at Syracuse was to ignore the truly unimportant things that sidetrack someone from achieving their goals and focus on the task at hand. I graduated on time with an Associate of Applied Science in Electrical Technology. A few months before I graduated the manager of the cable company had hired his son to work there and my grandfather had retired, so the reason for getting the degree was gone. Reality never loses its sense of humor.

If I had listened to my heart at either of these two junctures I would have studied history or anthropology as my major instead of using all of my electives on these two subjects. It mystifies me that I did not come to this conclusion at the time because I had earned more credits at Syracuse in history, geography, sociology, and religion than I did in my major of mathematics. When I was at Corning Community College and did not have to take any social sciences because I had transferred in enough classes to cover those requirements, I still took some geography and history courses because they were interesting to me. It is not too hard to see I truly want to study people. I might have been better off growing up in California where the idea of spending ten years to discover your true self is acceptable. Instead, I grew up in New York where people seem too busy to bother with that type of nonsense.

I have worked in electrical design for ten years since I graduated from college. I have learned more from on the job training than I ever did in school and have become good at what I do. I have become specialized in designing electrical and communication systems for process-specific specialty systems in the semiconductor industry. I have never lost my love for ancient history and continued to read Plato, Caesar, Homer, and others on my own. My questions had changed some since I had read what tactics Hannibal or Caesar used or what technological advance took place that enabled those men to conquer the known world. My questions now moved more towards the logistics of moving men around and why various tribes migrated across Europe. How did an area as harsh as Scandinavia produce wave after wave of Germanic migrations? How did they ever grow enough food to do that? Why were there continuous migrations across the Russian steppes?

A strange twist of fate took place last fall that brought this love to the forefront once again and gave me an opportunity to listen to my heart. My company won a contract just outside of Dublin, Ireland while I was reading *The Conquest of Gaul* by Julius Caesar. The book raised old questions again. How do you coordinate an attack of forty thousand people? Why do the Celts always lose? How can a culture known for its warlike nature win only one major battle in nearly two thousand years and still be known for its warlike nature?

These questions were fresh in my mind as I visited Ireland over the next ten months. There is a certain fascination you get when you read about an event or an idea and there is quite a different fascination you get when you put your hands on it. I had read about Celtic crosses, Newgrange, Stonehenge, and the Roman baths at Bath. Now I had the opportunity to put my hands on them and see them up close.

It occurred to me that I have been continuously flirting with the path through the woods that history and anthropology were to me, and now it was time to seriously walk down the path and see where it went. It was time to listen to my heart and do what it told me. The need to have my questions answered outweighed the work needed to find out the answers. I need to find out why the Celts always lost instead of just thinking about it.

I had originally wanted to just take classes without enrolling in a specific degree program. I wanted to take some history classes, some anthropology classes, and possibly some literature or sociology classes that pertain to ancient European history. My goal was to learn about the Greeks, Romans, and Celts. Interdisciplinary studies allowed me to make a major out of the classes I wanted to take. I could take any history classes that fell under the heading of ancient history and take a mixture of cultural and social anthropology classes.

I chose history and anthropology because I believe neither tells you the full story of what has happened and why it happened. You can read about Caesar's conquest and manipulation of the Celts, but why was he able to accomplish such things? Was Caesar just a great military leader who outmaneuvered the Celts at every turn or was there something in the Celtic culture that was working against them? I feel these two disciplines will allow me to look at the situation from different angles and perspectives. It has been my experience as an electrical designer that a truly good design cannot be accomplished without involving the mechanical and process designers.

History will tell you what happened and some of the why. It may not always tell you the true driving force behind the actions that were recorded. It misses the reasons why cultures accept actions such as continuously waging war for four hundred years. Anthropology will help you figure out the possible reasons for behavior. There could be a reason in the kinship structures of the Celts that kept them from uniting and fighting the Romans together instead of allowing Caesar to pick them off one by one. There could be religious rituals that kept the Celts from defending their lands. Anthropology delves into the reasoning of human behavior. It offers theories to explain rituals and social interactions that are present in every culture.

I believe a clearer answer for historical events will emerge if you combine these two disciplines together. I think one day you will be able to gain insight into present day events and possible future events by studying historical events with an anthropological eye. Major themes in human society or culture do not seem to change. People always want the same things in life—food, housing, freedom, a better life for their children. The methods they use to obtain these things change.

I feel very fortunate because I can pursue this degree for what I feel are the right reasons. I do not need this degree to get a job nor am I getting it because someone wants me to. I am getting the degree either to satisfy my curiosity or to gain the tools that will allow me to satisfy my curiosity. It is easier being a student when you truly want to be there and learn. The motivational problems that existed at Syracuse and the stress of getting a degree that will get me a job no longer exist. I can enjoy the experience.

One of my future goals is to go to Europe someday and study the ancient history of Europe. I would like to see what clues are still hidden on the banks of the Po River and the Black Sea. I would like to return to Ireland and study the last Celtic nation on earth. There could be evidence in the people living there now that could give insight into what transpired two thousand years ago. There could be evidence in France as to why the Celtic tribes never united to drive a numerically inferior foe back across the Alps. That same evidence could also help explain why Europe is still suffering through a nation-building stage. Why can a large multi-ethnic nation work here but not there? Why is Europe actually breaking down into smaller nations?

I would also like to teach. I believe after finishing this degree and then working in anthropology or historical research I would be able to present information and ideas to people in a new perspective. There is a reason people dread history classes. The format tends to be read this book, memorize these events, and write a paper about them. The classes are hours of listening to lectures. There is no need for it. If you can present some insight into why humans do what they do, then I believe history would be more interesting to study. There is no reason why a class cannot talk about the Greek hoplites by showing you how the formation actually worked and also go into how the Spartan culture of equality combined with the landscape around Sparta went hand in hand with this style of fighting.

Interdisciplinary studies are the tools that will allow me finally to study what I have always wanted to study but never have. By allowing me to choose two disciplines I am interested in, I feel I am getting a better education. I do not have to take course A followed by course B or take courses that other people think would be important to a history degree or anthropology degree but have no interest to me such as a foreign language. My degree in interdisciplinary studies is set up to let me decide which classes best help me answer why the Celts always lost.

Reading 6

The following reading is not a reading *per se* but an assignment. The assignment, "Autobiographical Map," was created by G. Layne Gneiting, lecturer in Interdisiciplinary Studies at Arizona State University. Gneiting showed me several of his students' autobiographical maps, and I was impressed by the innovative ways the students conceptualized what Gneiting refers to as their "interdisciplinary journeys" by creating innovative visual metaphors. The ability to communicate visually your identity as an interdisciplinarian is a very useful skill, especially for those who have their own personal web pages. The more you can draw in viewers visually, the more interested they will be in learning more about your identity as an interdisciplinarian.

READING

AUTOBIOGRAPHICAL MAP

Assignment Created by

G. Layne Gneiting

OVERVIEW

PURPOSE

The primary purpose of the autobiographical map is three-fold: to (1) assess the effect of past experiences on your life's current trajectory, (2) explore those life episodes that have shaped your value system, and (3) identify specific steps you must take to reach your professional goals.

SECTION I—INTELLECTUAL AUTOBIOGRAPHY (NARRATIVE)

Following the guidelines of your textbook, *Becoming Interdisciplinary*, write an intellectual autobiography. Then create a visual map that illustrates your journey of discovery. Your narrative and map should depict *continuity within discontinuity* (see Reading 3) and demonstrate *shifting or evolving identities*.

SECTION II—VISUAL AUTOBIOGRAPHY (MAP)

Create a visual depiction of your interdisciplinary journey in the form of a map. Creating and seeing a visual representation of your life will reveal continuity within discontinuity, and help gauge your progress toward your ultimate dreams and goals.

This map should include topographical and political elements, boundaries, roads, sites of significance, cities and towns. Each map should convey the following elements:

- Territory you visited
- Territory you chose not to visit
- Territory you have yet to visit

Additionally, your map should reveal the development of your *value system,* convey an interdisciplinary blend of your concentration areas in the creation of your map, and demonstrate how all of the *areas* or disciplines you are studying fit into your life.

The map should be *metaphorical* (see Chapter Three) rather than geographical. Avoid the urge to narrate the *geographical* movements of your life (e.g. In Idaho . . . then when moving to Arkansas . . . and upon coming to Arizona . . .). Instead, create your own metaphorical place. Then use metaphors to depict the significance of that place. For instance, someone with a musical background may say, "My life is an orchestra." Your map would then show an orchestra pit, complete with different sections (brass, woodwind, bass, percussion) to represent developments in your life.

Organize your map around your narrative. Follow the same structure as your narrative so that the map becomes a *visual* depiction of your *written* intellectual autobiography.

Inscribe your journey upon the map. Demonstrate the path you've followed. Show continuity within discontinuities. Here are some suggestions to get your started.

1. **Symbolism**—What elements do you use to symbolize your life, why did you choose these elements, and what do they mean?

2. **Life's Path**—What direction(s) does your path take, over what terrain, through what settlements/towns/cities/star systems?

3. **Terrain**—Why do you choose certain terrain at specific points during your life? Explain both the terrain along your path, and the terrain *not* on your path. Why did you not choose a life's path that followed into such territory?

4. **Defining Moments**—Identify four or five defining moments (sites of interest) on the map and explain both the context surrounding each moment and how the defining moment shaped you.

5. **Evolving Identity(ies)**—When did your identity shift? What influenced that shift, and with what effect(s)?

6. **Undiscovered Terrain**—What lies in your projected future? Explain how your map unveils your future. Identify meaningful elements in this "undiscovered terrain" and explain their symbolic significance.

7. **Value System**—How and where does the map illustrate your value system? What particular values does it illustrate?

8. **Study Areas**—How does the map integrate your areas of study? Where do we see the development of your interest in each area? How do they impact your life?

FAQ

Q: Should I show where I've moved around in my life (grew up in Idaho, moved to California, ended up in Arizona)?

A: No. The road should not be a literal geographic illustration of where you have lived. Your map is metaphorical, not literal. Your roads should show the development of your identity, values, and ascent into interdisciplinarity.

Q: Do I have to write anything?

A: Yes. Your intellectual autobiography is the written version of your map.

Q: I don't know what lies in my future. Can I show the various options I could pursue?

A: No. Forecast the continuities and discontinuities you think will occur in your life.

Selected Readings

Bateson, M. C. (1994). Constructing continuity. *Peripheral visions: Learning along the way* (pp. 77–94). New York: Harper Collins. [See Reading 3 in this volume.]

Berger, M. (1977, Nov. 9). Isaiah Berlin, philosopher and pluralist, is dead at 88. *The New York Times*, p. A1. [See Reading 1 in this volume.]

Ibarra, H. & Lineback, K. (2005). What's your story? *Harvard Business Review*, 83 (1), 64–71.

Klein, J. T. (1996). *Crossing boundaries: Knowledge, disciplinarities, and interdisciplinarities.* Charlottesville and London: University of Virginia Press.

Lejeune, P. (1975). *Le pacte autobiographique.* Paris: Éditions du Seuil.

Lewis, D. (2003, February 28). Fred Rogers, host of *Mister Rogers' Neighborhood*, dies at 74. *The New York Times*, p. A1. [See Reading 2 in this volume.]

McAdams, D. P. (1993). *The stories we live by: Personal myths and the making of the self.* New York and London: The Guilford Press.

Murray, T. H. (1986). Confessions of an unconscious interdisciplinarian. *Issues in Integrative Studies*, 4, 57–69. [See Reading 4 in this volume.]

Petr, J. L. (1983). The case for/against interdisciplinary studies: A comment on the debate. *Issues in Integrative Studies*, 2, 20–24.

ADVANTAGES AND DISADVANTAGES OF INTERDISCIPLINARY STUDIES

There is no defense like a good offense.

Thomas C. Benson (1982, p. 38)

Learning Objectives

After reading Chapter Six of *Becoming Interdisciplinary* you should be able to:

1. List and understand the criticisms lodged against interdisciplinary studies.
2. "Defend" your degree persuasively.
3. List some of the advantages of interdisciplinary studies.
4. Understand how interdisciplinary projects begin.
5. Understand how disciplines can have differing and even conflicting disciplinary insights on a given problem or topic.
6. Understand the necessity of planning your college career carefully.
7. Know what employers like about interdisciplinary studies majors.

Understanding the Disadvantages of Studying Interdisciplinary Studies

It is important to be positive and to feel confident about your decision to major in interdisciplinary studies. If you are not confident and positive about your degree, how do you expect others to be so? You will feel more positive and confident about your degree if you familiarize yourself with the major criticisms lodged against interdisciplinary studies *well in advance* of any situation that could arise in which you have to defend either yourself or your degree. You will also feel more assured if you can understand the rationales behind such criticisms. As Benson (1982) points out in Reading 7, "Five Arguments Against Interdisciplinary Studies," "it is not without its consequences" to be inattentive to the criticisms of interdisciplinary studies (p. 38). According to Benson (1982), by not paying attention to these criticisms we end up doing the following two things: first, "we squander opportunities to respond effectively to arguments that rest upon correctable misperceptions of interdisciplinary studies," and second, "we also neglect potentially valuable instruction concerning our weaknesses" (p. 38). In Reading 8, "The Case for Interdisciplinary Studies: Response to Professor Benson's Five Arguments," we will consider some of the more common criticisms of interdisciplinary studies as well as the rebuttals to five of these criticisms by one of the leading scholars of interdisciplinary studies, William H. Newell. By the end of this chapter you should be prepared to respond to any criticisms regarding your major by being able to explain clearly in a non-defensive manner the advantages of having an interdisciplinary studies degree.

Reading 7

In the following reading, "Five Arguments Against Interdisciplinary Studies," Thomas C. Benson considers five arguments against interdisciplinary studies for the purpose of better understanding interdisciplinary studies and how interdisciplinary studies can be further developed.

READING

FIVE ARGUMENTS AGAINST INTERDISCIPLINARY STUDIES

by

Thomas C. Benson

In our enthusiasm and occasional defensiveness concerning interdisciplinary studies, we sometimes fail to listen carefully to the arguments of its numerous opponents. Instead of attending to the diverse charges and criticisms, it is tempting to concentrate on the strengths and merits of interdisciplinary studies—presumably on the assumption that well-articulated pluses will cancel the alleged minuses. After all, there is no defense like a good offense. This inattentiveness to the substance of the criticisms of interdisciplinary studies is not without its consequences. Not only do we squander opportunities to respond effectively to arguments that rest upon correctable misperceptions of interdisciplinary studies, but we also neglect potentially valuable instruction concerning our weaknesses.

In this brief paper, I shall identify five of the most popular arguments against a substantial role for interdisciplinary studies in the undergraduate curriculum. Each argument will be sketched in broad terms, with no attempt made to defend interdisciplinary studies from the respective charges. Call this, if you will, a bit of enlightened devil's advocacy. The temptation to respond to the diverse arguments has been checked, not for want of inspiration, but in keeping with the stated purpose of the paper: to focus attention on the nature of the arguments against interdisciplinary studies. It is clear that there are some important arguments against interdisciplinary studies neglected in my brief inventory. Those that I have included, however, strike me as being at or near the top of the list in popularity and forcefulness.

The first argument against interdisciplinary studies is that it rests upon *serious conceptual confusion*. Quite simply, the practitioners of interdisciplinary studies lack a coherent, defensible sense of their purposes. Interdisciplinary studies purports to be concerned with examining and developing significant lines of connection between two or more disciplines. It is not at all clear, however, just what it means to connect the disciplines nor what the value of such activity might be. Most of the discussion of interdisciplinary or integrative studies assumes clarity in these matters and moves on to other concerns. Part of the difficulty here might be thought to derive from the notorious uncertainties surrounding the nature of the disciplines themselves. Seen in the worst light, integrative studies is a fool's project, propounding equations where *all* the terms are unknown. Things are not quite this bad, however, and although the arbitrary hands of chance and politics have played important roles in the definition of the disciplines,[1] their latter-day contours and boundaries turn out, on the whole, to make surprisingly good sense. Each of the disciplines offers us some general criteria for locating questions inside or outside of its boundaries. For the most part, the boundary lines among the disciplines are drawn by means of appeal either to a distinctive subject matter or to a distinctive method of inquiry. There is, of course, nothing perfectly neat or grayless in such boundary demarcations; but most of the problems are confined to marginal cases and relatively minor "turf" disputes. The lack of clarity associated with integrative studies cannot be excused, then, as derivative from the underlying vagueness of the concept of the disciplines.

If the connection among the disciplines contemplated by integrative studies is nothing more than a matter of borrowing insights or methods from one or more disciplines to illuminate problems in another, it seems fair to ask why such extra-curricular borrowing is called "integration." The concept of integration suggests a more substantial and enduring bond than that involved in the paradigms of integrative studies. Indeed, the proponents of integrative studies seem unwilling to regard the envisioned connections among the disciplines as forming a permanent bond. The disciplines are not dissolved in the transactions of integrative studies. Moreover, the kind of borrowing suggested in the proposed account of integrative studies already occurs routinely within the framework of most disciplinary activity. The physicist is lost without the tools of mathematics; the political scientist borrows insights from sociology, history and economics; the literary studies scholar makes use of the methods of linguistics and analytic philosophy. There is nothing special about this import/export business across disciplinary lines; and it hasn't occurred to anyone to call the process integrative or interdisciplinary. Clearly, the proponent of integrative studies owes us a better account of the nature of the integration he contemplates, one that is, at once, coherent and non-trivial.

In addition to demystifying the nature of the disciplinary connections he seeks, the proponent of integrative studies should be prepared to articulate more fully the principle or principles that determine when these connections are to be sought. The disciplines, as we have noted, are guided by broad, internal standards of relevance, whether that of distinctive subject matter or of method. But what principles guide the integrative studies practitioner in choosing to make these connections rather than those? Is he responding to some larger teleological sense of the natural connectedness of things or is his motivation essentially pragmatic, stimulated by what he sees as theoretical or practical impasses within specific disciplines? There appears to be no agreement among integrative studies advocates in this matter. Some talk about a grand holistic scheme and the unity of knowledge, while others speak more modestly about the practical value of interdisciplinary projects in the solving of specific problems. Still others see the applications of integrative studies as primarily centered in instruction rather than research. However sharp the contrasts here, the diverse options tend to be discussed with a characteristic air of romance and all too little rigor and specificity. For all of their worried criticism concerning the dominance of the disciplinary model in higher education and their curative ambitions, the proponents of integrative, studies have given surprisingly little attention to the important work of defining their goals and their methods clearly. The consequences of this neglect can be seen both in the lack of reliable traditions and literature concerning interdisciplinary studies teaching and in the widespread doubts about the intellectual foundations and value of integrative studies.

A second argument against interdisciplinary studies holds that it is a *pedagogically doubtful business to spend time in interdisciplinary learning projects when the student lacks a mature base in any of the contributing disciplines.* Sound educational development requires proper background and critical participation on the part of the student. Having no firm hold on any of the associated disciplinary traditions, the student in an interdisciplinary studies course or curriculum can be little more than a spectator to the marshalling of arguments, methods, and insights from the diverse contributing disciplines, with their voluminous literature and often highly technical research traditions. However exhilarating the discussion, the interdisciplinary studies course promises little in the way of long-term benefits for the student. If integrative studies are to be pursued properly and have lasting value, the student must first acquire a strong foundation in at least one of the contributing disciplines. This suggests that substantial involvement in integrative studies should be deferred to a point relatively late in the undergraduate career. And, even at this point, given the demands associated with the acquisition of disciplinary competence, it is likely to be of doubtful value.

Undergraduate programs in interdisciplinary studies appear fated to wander between two unattractive poles—either they assume disciplinary sophistication in the students, in which case most, if not all, of the students are left in the dark, unable to manipulate the central issues at stake or—and this is much more frequently the case—they assume little, and the program of study is diluted and homogenized to the point where it is almost totally devoid of a critical base. Under the guise of an invitation to wrestle with what are frequently fascinating and important issues, the student is cheated of a precious opportunity to develop the skills and background required for mounting a proper attack on the issues. As Robert Paul Wolff has noted in *The Ideal of the University*, undergraduate courses in theoretical economics and logic may well do more to prepare students for grappling with the socio-political crises of their time than interdisciplinary seminars on poverty and the philosophy of war.[2]

We are facing a growing crisis in the planning and politics of the undergraduate curriculum. The explosion of knowledge in the disciplines is leaving less and less time for study outside the student's major disciplinary program. On many campuses, the requirements for major programs in mathematics and the natural sciences constitute as much as two-thirds of the student's academic program. Although a backlash in favor of stronger liberal arts distribution requirements has appeared on some campuses, it is difficult to see how the tide of early and intensive specialization in a disciplinary area can be resisted. Adequate preparation for graduate and professional study and for careers in the disciplinary area requires increasing amounts of course work in the major program.

On this account, a third argument against interdisciplinary studies has acquired heightened importance. It is argued that *a substantial commitment to integrative studies in the undergraduate program will impede the student's development of an essential disciplinary competence.*

However attractive the ideal may be in the abstract, there simply is not enough time within the traditional four year, 120 credit framework of undergraduate education to do all of the things that our educational ideals suggest. We are being forced with increasing urgency to cut corners, to choose the lesser from among a number of curricular evils. Whatever sacrifices we make, it seems clear that we cannot forfeit the development of sound, critically based disciplinary competence. Such competence is best fostered in the rigorous and orderly pursuit of a well-designed sequence of disciplinary courses. The idea that disciplinary competence can be acquired in the midst of a substantial commitment to a program of integrative studies is so much wishful thinking—given the time, energy, and learning abilities of most undergraduate students. Of course, a proper regard for the liberal arts ideal requires some learning experiences beyond the disciplinary concentration. Here it seems preferable to introduce the undergraduate to the foundations, the essential concepts, methods and traditions of a range of disciplines through undiluted, introductory level courses. Rather than teasing a student with fragmentary exposure to philosophy and literary studies in an interdisciplinary course in philosophy and literature, let him take a rigorous course in the classics of Western literature and/or a challenging introductory course in philosophy.

The primary responsibility of the university, given the premium on time and study opportunities, is to equip the student with adequate foundations for future growth and development. Although a course here and there along the way in interdisciplinary studies may make sense for some students, such activity should be kept to a minimum and pushed to the margins of the college agenda. Interdisciplinary studies opportunities on a more substantial scale are best left to extracurricular agencies, e.g., community forums, topical conferences and institutes, and continuing education programs.

The cultivation of competence in a particular discipline is not just a matter of educational ideals, it is also, increasingly, a matter of practical importance. Students seeking admission to graduate school and entry to highly competitive career areas are faced with requirements and expectations that stress close identification with and substantial development in a particular disciplinary tradition. However arbitrary and unfair such standards may be, they are part of the post-graduate world to which the student must adapt. Students must be advised of these expectations and assisted in finding a sensible pattern of response. It is unconscionable for interdisciplinary studies faculty to use students as unwitting flag bearers for their dreams of educational reform. To be sure, there are student aspirations and career plans that can be adequately served by undergraduate programs concentrating in integrative studies. For most students, however, the price of concentration in integrative studies with the attending neglect of a disciplinary base, will be the risk of disqualification from coveted graduate school and job opportunities.

Among the more popular arguments directed against interdisciplinary studies programs none is as widely subscribed as the charge that *integrative studies courses are characteristically shallow, trading intellectual rigor for topical excitement.*[3] This fourth argument has special currency among academic traditionalists who are instinctively suspicious of any course that sounds remotely "relevant" or of popular interest, and among rivals in the disciplinary departments who are sensitive to what they see as naked marketing ploys in the escalating competition for student registration. Some of it, however, issues from a genuine concern for academic integrity and what might be called truth-in-teaching standards. Student enrollment response to an appealing seminar theme and even favorable student course evaluations are not necessarily the best measures of the worth of a course. The emphasis in contemporary mass media on "big picture" treatment of broad themes has stimulated a demand in the academic market for comparably wide-angled course offerings. Some integrative studies faculty play to this vogue with results that can only reinforce the hostile stereotypes of the interdisciplinary studies course. Although there are, to be sure, many demanding and intellectually rich programs and courses focusing on attractive topical issues, there are simply too many interdisciplinary studies faculty driving curricular ice cream trucks down the academic alleys.

Not only are many of the "big picture" integrative seminars ill-conceived, but there is also a disturbing tendency for such courses to be taught in a sloppy, chat-in-the-round fashion that does little to cultivate either critical skills or a systematic grasp of the issues under review. The pedagogical deficiencies in these courses are frequently compounded by a heavy reliance on splashy special events: guest speakers, films, video-cassettes, and other classroom equivalents of easy-listening radio. Instead of a carefully planned, intellectually demanding mix of lectures, sharply focused discussions, exams, and papers, the student is exposed to a semester long variety show, doubtless interesting, but of very little long term educational value. Moreover, even where there are adequate measures of order, method, and rigor in the integrative studies seminar, the theme often fails to "pan out." The anticipated synthesis fails to materialize. In such cases, some may wish to write the seminar off as a noble experiment that failed. Such failures are so common, however, as to raise serious questions about the judgment and, still worse, the integrity of many interdisciplinary studies teachers. It is irresponsible to use students as semester-long guinea pigs in the testing of what are frequently half-baked notions of curricular value. As the popular television spots for the Black colleges insist: "A mind is a terrible thing to waste."

A fifth argument against interdisciplinary studies programs focuses on the *relatively high cost of the typical integrative studies course.* In a time of embattled budgets and overburdened academic resources, it is argued that the interdisciplinary studies programs, with their heavy reliance on team-teaching methods, special events, independent study, and relatively low faculty-student ratios, are extravagant and cost ineffective. It is assumed that the interdisciplinary studies programs cannot accomplish their goals without substantial resort to such expensive practices. The integrative studies programs are not charged with profligacy, but rather with a lack of redeeming educational value, sufficient to offset their hefty price tags. Proponents of this argument also note that many interdisciplinary studies programs place further burdens on severely limited academic budgets by either borrowing adjunct teachers from the disciplinary departments, creating thereby a need for part-time replacements, or by hiring their own psychologist or sociologist or historian, etc., and thus duplicating albeit with dubious quality control—the faculty resources already available in the department.

There are additional complaints about interdisciplinary studies worth examining; e.g., there is the claim that integrative studies faculty are, for the most part, second-class scholars, exiles and refugees from the disciplinary departments, where they either failed to measure-up or found themselves incapable of sustaining the kind of rigor and focus required for success in disciplinary scholarship. However painful the project, it would be a useful service to integrative studies to identify these additional arguments. It would also be helpful to examine the criticisms of interdisciplinary studies in an historical light and with a view toward the discover of both patterns of frequency and the correlations between particular arguments and the disciplinary base of their proponents.

Beyond the extension of the list of significant criticisms of interdisciplinary studies and the varieties of analysis suggested above lies the important and difficult work of responding to the arguments, both intellectually and politically. In meeting this challenge, it will not suffice simply to impart what we already know. Clearly, we need to know more. We need to think more fully and critically about the logical foundations of integrative studies. We need to develop more compelling justifications for including substantial integrative studies work in the ever more crowded undergraduate curriculum. We need to articulate more fully the connections between disciplinary work and interdisciplinary studies in the realization of the liberal arts ideal. We must cultivate and give increased attention to post-graduate study and career opportunities for students concentrating in integrative studies. We must place a greater emphasis on rigor and learning that lasts in the design and teaching of interdisciplinary studies courses; and finally, we must give more urgent attention to program economies that will allow integrative studies work to continue, while not sacrificing the unique values and traditions that have distinguished our work.

Notes

1. Cf. Frederick Rudolph, *The American College and University* (New York, 1962), pp. 399–400.
2. Robert Paul Wolff, *The Ideal of the University* (Boston, 1969), pp. 78–79.
3. CI. Christopher Jencks and David Riesman, *The Academic Revolution* (New York, 1968), p. 498.

❓ Reading 7 Discussion Questions

1. What do you think of Benson's article?

2. Which of the arguments if any do you find the most convincing? Why?

3. What does Benson mean by "conceptual confusion"?

4. What does it mean to have a "mature base" in a discipline?

5. Think about the courses you have taken in college. Which were the ones you learned the most in? What did you study in those classes? Would you characterize the class or classes as interdisciplinary?

6. Have you had any classes that Benson would describe as "shallow" and lacking intellectual rigor? What kind of course or courses were they, and did they fit his description of courses that focus on "attractive topical issues"? Did you enjoy taking those courses? Why or why not?

Table 6-1 **Summary of Benson's Five Arguments Against Interdisciplinary Studies**

1. Interdisciplinary studies rest upon serious conceptual confusion.
2. Interdisciplinary studies students lack a mature base in any discipline.
3. The commitment to undergraduate interdisciplinary studies programs impedes students' development of disciplinary competence.
4. Interdisciplinary studies courses are shallow and lack intellectual rigor.
5. Typical interdisciplinary studies courses are expensive for universities.

Other Criticisms of Interdisciplinary Studies

You should be aware of other criticisms of interdisciplinary studies. In Reading 10, "Do You See What I See?," which can be found in Chapter Seven, Petrie (1976) makes three additional criticisms of interdisciplinary projects:

1. Interdisciplinary projects never get off the ground.
2. The level of scholarship seldom exceeds that of "a glorified bull session."
3. Interdisciplinary studies are the dumping ground for the less than disciplinarily competent. (This criticism is along the same lines of Benson's third argument.) (p. 30)

Responding to Criticisms

In the following selection, William H. Newell clarifies many leading misconceptions about interdisciplinary studies. He addresses Benson's charges, but not always in the same order that Benson makes them. Newell counters the accusation of "conceptual confusion" by describing his conception of interdisciplinary study as the process of solving interdisciplinary problems. He corrects common misconceptions about integration by asserting that what interdisciplinarians integrate are disciplinary insights. In effect, Newell explains that "conceptual confusion" derives in part from a general misunderstanding of how interdisciplinary studies are done, in other words, the interdisciplinary studies process.

READING

THE CASE FOR INTERDISCIPLINARY STUDIES
RESPONSE TO PROFESSOR BENSON'S FIVE ARGUMENTS

by

William H. Newell

The objective of this paper is to respond serially to Professor Benson's five arguments by setting forth a conception of interdisciplinary study, not necessarily as it is practiced but as it should be, which largely meets his criticisms.[1] The final section of the paper offers suggestions for steps that the interdisciplinary studies profession should take to respond fully and effectively to its critics.

A. Responses to the Five Arguments

1. Interdisciplinary Studies Rest on Serious Conceptual Confusion

While single interdisciplinary courses may have a clear sense of purpose and method, it is undeniable that the practitioners of interdisciplinary or integrative studies share no such clear sense. This is apparent in the very analysis used by Professor Benson. While he assumes that interdisciplinary studies are concerned with "connections . . . between disciplines,"[2] he recognizes that some interdisciplinarians are more concerned with connections in the real world ("the natural connectedness of things"[3]), others with connections in ("the unity of") our knowledge of that real world, while still others emphasize the "practical value of interdisciplinary projects in the solving of specific problems"[4] where it is unclear that any of the above connections are of direct concern. In my view this last problem-solving conception of interdisciplinary studies is the most fruitful. It has the greatest capability of meeting the five arguments against interdisciplinary studies, and the connections that it requires are different from any of the above.

Interdisciplinary study should be understood to start with the confrontation of the interdisci- plinarian with the world, be it a problem, an event, or even a painting. Out of that phenomenological confrontation comes a question, one which is too broad to be answered by any single discipline. The strategy of the interdisciplinarian is to bring the relevant disciplines (or schools of thought) to bear upon the question, one at a time, letting each illuminate that aspect of the question which is amenable to treatment by the characteristic concepts, theories, and methods of the respective disciplines. Out of the resulting disciplinary insights, the interdisciplinarian fashions a response to the question that would ideally be a complete answer but which at the least leads to a greater appreciation of the nature and complexity of the question. What distinguishes interdisciplinary study from simple eclecticism is that disciplines provide much more than pieces of a jigsaw puzzle that the interdisciplinarian need merely arrange in proper order. Disciplinary insights are often conflicting, and when the disciplines are chosen from more than one area, such as the natural sciences and the humanities, their insights are typically of a qualitatively different nature as well. As Professor Miller stresses,[5] disciplines each have their distinctive world view or way of looking at the world, and it is these world views with their often contradictory underlying assumptions and diverse value judgments that lead to conflicting or incommensurate insights. The interdisciplinarian, then, may not simply combine disciplinary insights; rather, each world view and its assumptions underlying those insights must be illuminated and then evaluated in the context of the question at hand, before any interdisciplinary answer can be attempted. Out of this process comes a richness of insight not available to the adherent of any one disciplinary orthodoxy, as the interdisciplinarian comes to appreciate the value and legitimacy of alternative perspectives.

Professor Benson asks that we construct a "coherent, defensible sense of (our) purposes," that we be clear on "what it means to connect the disciplines" and on "what the value of such activity might be,"[6] and that we refrain from excusing our lack of clarity on the purported vagueness of the disciplines themselves. He is correct in his contention that none of the notions of "connecting disciplines" which he presents meets these requirements, but I submit that the conception set out above does meet them. The disciplines can give only partial answers to questions that go beyond their bounds, and when seen from the perspective of certain other disciplines their answers seem flawed as well as incomplete.

The purpose of interdisciplinary study is to address questions that transcend disciplinary boundaries. Only the interdisciplinarian, who is familiar with and receptive to those contrasting world views, can deal adequately with such questions. Further, interdisciplinary study does not directly involve the connection of disciplines, which would constitute a colossal intellectual task and a politically hopeless one in times of turf protection. Instead the interdisciplinarian connects disciplinary insights. This task is formidable but limited to the one question at hand, and it admits of the possibility for specialization, so that, for example, an interdisciplinarian might specialize in questions related to the modernization process. Professor Weaver has argued quite convincingly, I believe, that interdisciplinarians can only achieve intellectual respectability when they specialize.[7] Further, the value of interdisciplinary study lies in the fact that many important questions transcend the disciplines.[8] Finally, this conception of interdisciplinary studies in no way depends on well-defined boundaries between disciplines, only on clarity in their insights and in the world view underlying those insights.

Professor Benson goes on to criticize interdisciplinary studies which are nothing more than "a matter of borrowing insights or methods from one or more disciplines to illuminate problems in another." He also insists that we "should be prepared to articulate more fully the principle or principles that determine when these connections are to be sought." He asks, "What principles guide the integrative studies practitioner in choosing to make these connections rather than those?"[9] Finally, he requests that we define our methods more clearly. The conception of interdisciplinary study presented in this paper involves questions transcending any one discipline, thus avoiding the first criticism. The second one is not so easily addressed. Certainly it can be argued that the interdisciplinarian chooses disciplines that purport to address at least some aspect of the question, and the interdisciplinary specialist may only ask questions which require a certain set of disciplines for an answer. But it is not so clear what principles guide the interdisciplinarian in constructing a coherent response to the question out of mutually incoherent disciplinary insights. How does the interdisciplinarian, for example, connect the ethical insights of the philosopher, the technical insights of the natural scientist and the behavioral insights of the economist and political scientist into a coherent proposal for U.S. energy policy? Developing sensitivity to the world views and underlying assumptions of each discipline points out the direction, at least, which the interdisciplinarian must take to look for connections, but we are still far from meeting the last requirement that we spell out our method with some precision.

2. Interdisciplinary Study Requires a Mature Base in the Disciplines

Professor Benson presents the argument that until a student has a "firm hold" on "at least one of the contributing disciplines," that student can be "little more than a spectator" in interdisciplinary studies because of the "voluminous literature and often highly technical research traditions" of the disciplines. He goes on to note that if students are assumed to have little disciplinary sophistication, the course will be "almost totally void of a critical base."[10]

The appropriate relationship between the disciplines and interdisciplinary study is a divisive issue among interdisciplinarians too. Even those who accept the notion of interdisciplinary study presented in this paper might well argue that it takes time to learn the world view and assumptions of various disciplines, to say nothing of their characteristic concepts, theories, and methods. If interdisciplinary study builds on all these, then perhaps graduate school is the earliest we can expect students to be prepared to undertake serious interdisciplinary study.

I believe, however, that there is an essential complementarity between the disciplines and interdisciplinary study that makes it desirable for students to learn them together, from first semester freshman year on if not in high school. An academic discipline is a challenging intellectual game at best, and a sterile and meaningless exercise at worst, when it is taken out of the context of human experience, which is always too broad and complex to be captured fully by any one discipline. The disciplines need interdisciplinary studies to come alive to the students, to connect meaningfully to their lives, fully as much as interdisciplinary study needs the disciplines. Moreover, when students are thoroughly grounded in a discipline before becoming exposed to interdisciplinary studies, they tend to become indoctrinated into its world view, uncritically accepting its often implicit assumptions.[11] This indoctrination makes even more difficult the task of developing in students the openness to alternative ways of looking at the world which lies at the heart of the interdisciplinary method.

Interdisciplinary studies should, and can, be taught alongside the disciplines. A typical freshman takes four or five courses at a time, each in a different discipline. An early and continuing task in each of these introductory courses is to get the student to think like an economist, a physicist, or whatever, to imbue her or him with the world view of that discipline. Moreover, students are usually given problem sets or writing assignments in each course, in which they are asked to apply what they arc learning. No one expects the freshman so bring the sophistication of the graduate student to these tasks, to address the assignments in their full complexity, or to select from the full range of concepts and theories in the technical literature of the disciplines. Why should we think any differently about the freshman student undertaking an interdisciplinary analysis?

A freshman could reasonably take a load of three or four disciplinary courses and an interdisciplinary one that builds on those disciplines. As the student learns the world views of each discipline, she or he can learn to contrast them and scrutinize their assumptions in the interdisciplinary course. The assignments in the interdisciplinary course can start out as simple as those in the disciplinary course, leading the student to draw rudimentary connections between the insights of those disciplines. In fact, the problem can be chosen so that the student need draw only on those disciplinary insights taught so far in the disciplinary courses. Were we to construct such a freshman year, our students would not only learn solid disciplinary material, but they would also learn an interdisciplinary appreciation for those disciplines as limited but useful tools in their own lives.

When the curricular relationship between the disciplines and interdisciplinary studies is viewed in this light, it becomes possible to appreciate the educational merit of a well-conceived interdisciplinary program for freshmen. Instead of the administratively cumbersome freshman year sketched out above, why not set up a program where students are taught the relevant disciplinary materials in the same course where they learn to think about problems from an interdisciplinary perspective? Interdisciplinarians can select and teach the relevant disciplinary materials in the context of analyzing an interdisciplinary question. Disciplinary world views can be contrasted as they are learned and their strengths and limitations revealed as they are applied to an interdisciplinary question that grows out of the experience of the students. For example, I teach a first semester freshman social science course that examines what kind of control the students have over their own lives. They learn a portion of each social science discipline dealing with individual freedom, which means they learn everything from the theory of consumer behavior in economics, to operant conditioning in psychology, to the socialization process in sociology. The theories are treated in their full academic rigor, right down to problem sets with graphs; and their underlying assumptions are examined and explicitly compared. In the concluding section of the course entitled "Freedom within Social Controls," we pull together these disciplinary insights into a discussion of how much freedom students have and how that freedom can be expanded. Students come away from the course with a critical appreciation of a representative portion or two of each discipline, an appreciation for its analytical power and for its limited but genuine applicability to the world of their experience, and the beginnings of an awareness of the interdisciplinary process. Over a series of such courses, students become familiar with a considerable body of disciplinary material as they develop increasing sophistication in the interdisciplinary method.

While I believe that students can and should learn interdisciplinary studies alongside the disciplines, the difficulty of teaching the interdisciplinary approach should not be underestimated. The kinds of thinking involved in interdisciplinary study are more difficult and require more intellectual maturity than do the disciplines. Scholars studying the process of intellectual development of college students, from Bloom to Piaget to Perry to Kohlberg,[12] have argued that there is a hierarchy of intellectual skills or a series of stages of intellectual development through which students must pass on their way to full intellectual maturity. The integrative thinking required in interdisciplinary study which involves pulling together and synthesizing disparate disciplinary insights into a coherent whole is at the top of the hierarchy. The ability so embrace tentatively she use of one disciplinary world view and then switch to using another, possibly opposing, world view, and take that equally seriously requires some of the more advanced stages of intellectual development. Most freshmen I have taught find these skills difficult to develop, and a few never do; but the majority have risen to the occasion. In spite of the intellectual challenge of interdisciplinary studies, I conclude that they can and should be caught in conjunction with the disciplines instead of waiting for students to develop disciplinary competence first.

3. Interdisciplinary Study Impedes Essential Disciplinary Competence

The substance of Professor Benson's third argument is that time is scarce in the undergraduate curriculum, time that is required to provide adequate training in the more important disciplines rather than in possibly desirable but clearly less important interdisciplinary study. Disciplines are not only more rigorous and their study an orderly progression into more sophisticated thinking, but they are also practical preparation for graduate schools and competitive careers that expect and require disciplinary training. Time spent outside a disciplinary major in general education, so the argument goes, is best spent in disciplinary introductory courses because they are "rigorous" and "challenging" (nor "fragmentary" like interdisciplinary courses) introductions to the "concepts, methods, and traditions" which form the foundations of the disciplines.[13]

The first part of this argument strikes me as having the most force. Certainty some students should major in disciplines, specializing in one intellectual tradition in preparation for a career as a specialist. After all, division of labor based on specialization is essential to an industrialized society. But many, if not a majority, of the jobs in our society bear scant correspondence to any one liberal arts discipline: retail salesmen and administrators are more common than industrial chemists. For such positions, the abilities to understand and critically evaluate the work of experts and to make decisions based on that evaluation seem more important than a specialized knowledge of any one discipline. Furthermore, increasing numbers of careers require specialized backgrounds that are interdisciplinary. Dealing with environmental problems, urban problems, energy problems, and many others requires training in synthetic thinking, in weighing arguments from diverse narrow disciplinary perspectives, and in placing them in the larger context. The narrow vision and piecemeal approaches of disciplinary specialists have only exacerbated these problems.

While the expectations of employers are that college graduates applying for jobs will have a disciplinary major, most employees have no particular loyalty to the academic disciplines, especially when they are hiring for jobs that do not build directly on disciplinary competence. Employers are particularly attracted to interdisciplinary majors because of the abilities of the students "to think conceptually, to identify and solve problems, to understand other value systems, to evaluate alternatives and decide on a course of action, and to change one's opinion in the light of facts."[14] Employers also cite traditional liberal arts skills of effective written and oral communication when they explain why they hired graduates of interdisciplinary programs, as well as affective skills like effective group participation, ethical sensitivity, and constructive response to criticism which reflect the experimental college setting of many interdisciplinary programs. According to available data, placement rates of graduates from interdisciplinary programs are quite high.[15]

The charge that the disciplines are more rigorous and ordered than interdisciplinary studies has some limited validity as well. Because the disciplines have been around longer than formal interdisciplinary study, they have evolved further, become more codified and articulated, and have developed more systematic methods. But if one accepts the conception of interdisciplinary study as based on the disciplines, then serious interdisciplinary studying involves these disciplines in their full intellectual rigor. In addition, it is not at all clear that interdisciplinary study is inherently less rigorous than a discipline at the same point in its evolution. After all, rather rigorous and technical fields like bio- chemistry can be argued to have grown out of interdisciplinary efforts. Few scholars today would wish to claim that oceanography, for example is non-rigorous. Surely the intellectual skill of synthesis is as challenging as any required by the disciplines. There is an element of art in the interdisciplinary process of synthesis or integration which may never prove amenable to systematization, but many disciplines in the humanities contain similar room for creativity in their method without charges of nonrigor, and there is no basis in principle why interdisciplinary study should face that charge as well.

The argument for a general education composed of introductory disciplinary courses is curious indeed. What can be more fragmented than a series of disciplinary courses that are completely insulated from one another? What can be less fragmented than a well-constructed interdisciplinary course? Nor is it clear, that rigor in general education is best served by more of the same disciplinary training. After all, the real claim to rigor by the disciplines is based on their highly developed literatures and technical methods which are inaccessible to students in the introductory course. It may be that the charge here is fundamentally one of poor quality, not fragmentation or lack of rigor. In part, however, I suspect the basis for the charge lies in the implicit premise that the disciplines are sufficient as well as necessary to the world of the intellect, and consequently that introductory courses should have as their primary goal the introduction of a discipline, and only secondarily the introduction of knowledge or intellectual skills. This logic clearly relegates interdisciplinary study to secondary importance at best, but it also begs the question.

On the other hand, if one believes that most use of the disciplines by non-specialists requires the judicious weighing of the contributions of several disciplines to the analysis of a problem and the eventual formulation of a means of dealing with the problem that goes beyond any of the disciplines while being informed by them, then interdisciplinary study forms a necessary component of general education alongside the disciplines. Certainly the trend in higher education over the last few years has been to increase substantially the role of interdisciplinary study in general education. Klein and Gaff found that 69% of the colleges they surveyed include an interdisciplinary component in their new general education programs; 55% requite a core of interdisciplinary courses.[16] The motivation for including interdisciplinary study in general education appears similar, at least, to the argument presented here: 53% cite the ability to synthesize as a major objective of their new general education programs.[17]

4. Interdisciplinary Courses Are Shallow

Professor Benson's fourth argument against including interdisciplinary courses in an undergraduate liberal arts education is that they trade "intellectual rigor for topical excitement."[18] Three criticisms are leveled under this heading. First, too many interdisciplinary courses are big-picture counterparts of the trendy, relevant and superficial treatments of important issues by the mass media: "There are simply too many interdisciplinary faculty driving curricular ice cream trucks down the academic alleys."[19] Second, such courses are "taught in a sloppy, chat-in-the-round fashion that does little to cultivate either critical skills or a systematic grasp of the issues. . . . compounded by a heavy reliance on splashy special events . . ." such as films and guest speakers.[20] Third, too often "the anticipated synthesis fails so materialize," leaving students as guinea pigs for irresponsible faculty who have not thought out the course with sufficient care.[21] Each of these charges is serious, in my opinion, because each contains a substantial element of truth, and my discussion of each is aimed at understanding why, inasmuch as it is defending interdisciplinary studies.

One can reasonably point out, in response to the first point, that interdisciplinary study is ideally suited to address the relevant issues of the day crying out for analysis, that there is educational merit in enhancing student motivation to learn through the use of interesting examples, and that disciplinary criticism comes from sour grapes tasted by faculty whose fields have less innate interest and less direct applicability to the world we all live in than does interdisciplinary study. Nonetheless, I saw many so-called interdisciplinary courses taught in the late 60s and early 70s that were little more than academic froth, and I still run into such courses today on occasion. These courses lack substance, in my opinion, because they ignore the disciplines, preaching instead an ideology or simplistic solution—say the 'soft-path' approach to energy—which draws selectively upon disciplinary findings without giving students any feel for how each discipline arrives at those findings or how each has a different perspective on the issue that might contribute to a richer analysis. I call this approach 'adisciplinary' because it tries to operate in an intellectual vacuum, drawing facts from the disciplines while pretending that their extensive intellectual traditions and well-developed perspectives are nonexistent or worthless.[22] In some cases this approach stems from the faculty member's adherence to any of several partisan ideologies, but in others it simply reflects a lack of clear notion of the nature of interdisciplinary study.

It is not surprising that faculty who are curricularly innovative will be pedagogically innovative as well. Indeed it must take a moss-backed traditionalist to argue that films and guest lectures lead to lack of rigor. But too often self-styled interdisciplinary courses are little more than a sequence of "splashy special events" which replace critical student thinking more than they excite it. Too often discussion groups in interdisciplinary courses slide from recognizing the limited validity of alternative disciplinary perspectives into accepting each participant's perspective as equally valid, without examining either the limitations or interrelationships of those perspectives, and certainly without attempting to synthesize them into a more comprehensive approach to the issue under discussion.

One consequence of innovation is that well-established norms are left behind. Faculty attempting to put together and teach interdisciplinary courses can draw upon no clear curricular and pedagogical guidelines, any more than interdisciplinary researchers can be guided by the canons of interdisciplinary scholarship. Until the interdisciplinary studies profession reaches some agreement on what it means to put together and teach an interdisciplinary course, and do it well, we will continue to find nonrigorous and uncritical interdisciplinary courses designed in good faith by faculty in pursuit of the elusive goal of interdisciplinarity.

The third point especially hits home to me, since most interdisciplinary courses I have taught failed to result in a clear-cut synthesis. My observation is that most other interdisciplinary faculty encounter similar difficulties even though there is widespread agreement that a synthesis at the end of the course is desirable. In some cases, synthesis is attempted by assigning a paper at the end of the course in which the student is asked to integrate the course material into a coherent position or policy or personal statement. I have used this device myself on several occasions. When a paper assignment replaces an integrative unit in the course, however, faculty are simply asking the students to do what they, themselves cannot or will not. Synthesis is a skill that requires training and practice and feedback like any other skill: assigning the task of synthesis and grading the result does little to foster the development of this skill. Especially with a higher order skill like synthesis, students need exposure to several alternative attempts at synthesis which are analyzed and critically evaluated before attempting their own. They need guidelines, or helpful hints at least, to get them started, and they need standards by which to judge their own progress. Unfortunately guidelines and standards are hard to come by in our profession. The process of integration or synthesis is poorly understood and little studied by professional interdisciplinarians. It is no wonder that we achieve synthesis so seldom in our courses.

There is a sense, however, in which it is unnecessary as well as unreasonable to expect that each interdisciplinary course should end with a synthesis. Perhaps interdisciplinary courses, like disciplinary ones, should not be expected to present definitive answers to the important questions they raise. Perhaps synthesis should be an ideal, nor a goal. It seems more realistic to ask that interdisciplinary study illuminate the question, pointing up the limitations and strengths of competing disciplinary approaches, exploring the full scope and implications of the question, clarifying the nature of the question, and devising standards which an answer must meet, rather than insisting that the question be answered. After all, the pedagogical value comes from getting the students to see the richness of the question and what would be involved in answering it, more than from learning the answer itself.

5. Interdisciplinary Courses Are Relatively Expensive

The final argument that Professor Benson raises against interdisciplinary studies is that their heavy reliance on "team-teaching methods, special events, independent study, and relatively low student-faculty ratios" makes them too "cost-ineffective," at least during the era of fiscal austerity faced by higher education during the next decade. In addition, he points out, many interdisciplinary programs compound this waste by "borrowing adjunct faculty from the disciplinary departments, creating thereby a need for part-time replacements, or by hiring their own psychologist . . . etc., and thus duplicating . . . the faculty resources already available in the departments."[23] Even if one grants the validity of the responses in this paper to the other four criticisms of interdisciplinary studies, one might still oppose them on the basis of this argument alone—such is the power of economic arguments today in educational decision-making.

Two of the four examples on which this argument is based are simply inappropriate. Special events and independent study can enrich any course, interdisciplinary or disciplinary, but they play no inherent part in interdisciplinary study as it is conceived in this paper. Innovative faculty can be expected to include them in their courses, and if such innovators are found in disproportionately large numbers in interdisciplinary programs, then it is easy to see why faculty unacquainted with the nature of interdisciplinary study might leap to the conclusion that such features are necessary to it.

The example of low student-faculty ratios is equally inappropriate, but for different reasons. High student-faculty ratios are achieved largely through lectures, which have come to gain acceptance in most disciplines, but which seem to me to serve the same limited functions in the disciplines as in interdisciplinary study, namely to summarize large bodies of literature by placing the issue in its intellectual context, to impart facts, or to explain a technical process. While such background information is necessary to any intellectual process, the heart of that process begins later as we critically evaluate, proffer alternative hypotheses or interpretations, and move towards an appreciation of the issue and towards our own position. This process can be done on one's own, with sufficient feedback from the instructor, or it can be done rather more expeditiously in a well-conducted seminar or discussion section where the group as a whole explores the issue and feedback is more frequent; but it cannot be done in a lecture, where the student is passive recipient not active learner. It is unclear to me that disciplinary inquiry needs active student participation and interaction any less than does interdisciplinary study, or that discussion groups need be smaller in interdisciplinary courses. The problem of student-faculty ratios is not that interdisciplinary courses require lower ones, but that the disciplines have come—perhaps through previous encounters with financial exigency—to accept uncritically a predominantly lecture format for their lower division high-enrollment courses. Because the interdisciplinary programs are the "new kids on the block," and their faculty more idealistic perhaps, they may understandably insist on lower student-faculty ratios; but as they and their faculty grow more worldly in the face of economic pressures, there is no reason inherent in the nature of the interdisciplinary process why they cannot come to tolerate ratios fully as high as those of disciplinary departments.

The example of team-teaching, on the other hand, points up a serious economic problem facing interdisciplinary studies. Team-teaching, meaning two or more faculty in the same classroom at once and hence greater expense, has become a common feature of interdisciplinary programs because it is the simplest way to ensure that different disciplinary perspectives are accurately and convincingly presented to the students, and that any synthesis take full account of each discipline involved. Advocates of team-teaching for interdisciplinary courses argue that a faculty member alone in the classroom is likely to present the strongest case for the discipline of her or his graduate training because it is most familiar, and more likely to accept its implicit presumptions uncritically. Since most faculty in interdisciplinary programs do not have interdisciplinary graduate degrees (and chose that do seldom have the kind of grounding in several disciplines needed for interdisciplinary study as conceived in this paper), this argument appears to have considerable force.

Where interdisciplinary courses can attract sufficient enrollment to justify multiple sections, however, team-teaching can profitably be replaced by team-curriculum development. In the Western College Program at Miami University, for example, we rely on team-curriculum development in all our lower division core courses: faculty teach separate sections of a multisection course but they plan the course together and, most importantly, they cover the same material in their respective sections and evaluate their students with the same examinations and paper topics.[24] In my experience, this approach has educational as well as economic advantages over team-teaching. Because faculty must confront the students alone when they lead discussions that prepare students for common course examinations, the faculty are motivated to take seriously the disciplines outside their expertise and to learn them carefully. Faculty colleagues become important educational resources, and weekly staff meetings of the course become cooperative learning experiences as well as an opportunity to debate conflicting disciplinary perspectives. While this approach loses the spontaneous fireworks in the classroom from untrammeled debate between team-teachers, through which the relative merits of each disciplinary perspective are sorted out in front of the students, I believe it more than compensates by forcing the faculty to appreciate the strengths of opposing perspectives before they come into the classroom. Students become more active in the process of exploring the relative merits and weaknesses of competing disciplinary perspectives when they are not observing faculty argue among themselves, and faculty can better guide them through the process because the faculty have been through it themselves and need not concentrate on defending their discipline. Team-curriculum development is no more expensive than traditional teaching since only one faculty member is in the classroom at a time. Its staff meetings may appear to cost more faculty time, but the difference lies more in the manner of course preparation, where individual contemplation of a text is partly replaced by group discussion.

In courses where multiple sections are simply not feasible, the additional expense of team-teaching is more difficult to get around. Most interdisciplinary programs I have visited hold regular faculty seminars that are designed to break down the disciplinary parochialism of faculty. Sometimes these seminars are tied to courses where faculty teach their own sections as they wish; other times, they are unrelated to any course, moving from topic to topic of mutual interest to the participants. Stockton State College, New Jersey, has developed a peer curriculum review process which provides an alternative other than team-teaching to ensure that individually taught courses are in fact interdisciplinary. Their general education curriculum committees review course proposals and talk with the faculty submitting them while the courses are still in the planning stage. They offer suggestions for readings and topics and for ways to make the course more interdisciplinary, much as faculty do in our program during the early stages of team-teaching curriculum development. The proposals are reviewed again before they can appear in the catalog. These examples point up the feasibility of alternative means to team-teaching for promoting the full interdisciplinarity of courses that wish to be interdisciplinary. In my view they are not as effective as team-teaching, but they are possible compromises. Much more effective is to train faculty in interdisciplinary studies through team-curriculum development or team-teaching and then wean them to individually taught interdisciplinary courses after they have demonstrated sufficient command of and sensitivity to the other relevant disciplines and sufficient familiarity with the interdisciplinary method. This lest approach is effective, as I can testify from personal experience, and while it is expensive at first, it holds the promise of future costs more in line with disciplinary teaching.

The final charge under Professor Benson's fifth argument is that interdisciplinary programs are expensive because they borrow or duplicate faculty in disciplinary departments. The preceding discussion has already shown that many interdisciplinary courses can be staffed at a full cost quite comparable to that of disciplinary ones. In these cases, faculty may be borrowed to expand the disciplinary perspectives available in the interdisciplinary program or to make professional development opportunities available to faculty in disciplinary departments, but the program would be well served politically to compensate departments fully for borrowed faculty in order to make it dear that it is not hiding excessive costs in the process.

The duplication argument, on the other hand, reflects a confusion caused by the lack of Ph.D. programs in interdisciplinary studies. When a interdisciplinary program hires a new faculty member with a Ph.D. in psychology and a specialty in social psychology, the department of psychology sees that person duplicating the social psychologist in their department, while the interdisciplinary program believes it has hired someone with interest in and commitment to interdisciplinary studies who will bring the perspective of psychology to the program. What appears by virtue of formal training to be an overlapping specialty in social psychology is by virtue of interest a nonoverlapping specialty in interdisciplinary studies. This confusion would be reduced, but not eliminated, by establishing Ph.D. programs for those wishing formal credentials in interdisciplinary studies. Some disciplinary faculty will still be attracted to interdisciplinary study, however, as part of the process of normal intellectual growth after graduate school. Neither the borrowing not the apparent duplication of faculty, however, constitutes support for the criticism that interdisciplinary programs are too expensive. Such criticism need only be well-grounded when interdisciplinary programs cannot attract the enrollment to justify multiple section courses and when they are also too young to have trained their faculty on-the-job in interdisciplinary teaching. Even then, the root cause of the expense is the lack of graduate training in interdisciplinary study and not its nature.

B. Where Do We Go From Here?

The model set our above of what interdisciplinary studies should be seems to meet all five criticisms identified by Professor Benson. If our profession were to agree on a conception of interdisciplinary studies similar to it, we would be in a position to argue that, in principle at least, interdisciplinary studies can answer its critics. Until such agreement is reached, however, we are quite vulnerable to attack at the very time in American higher education when weak or ill-defined programs are being cut back or eliminated. The traditional means for reaching such accord is debate at professional conferences and in professional journals. The annual meetings of the Association for Integrative Studies provide such a forum, and with the advent of this publication we now have the other one in embryonic form at least. I hope that this exchange between Professor Benson and myself turns out to be the opening of a debate that will move our profession towards consensus on the nature of interdisciplinary study.

Even if that consensus is achieved, we then face the further challenge of bringing our practice in line with our rhetoric before our courses can meet the arguments against interdisciplinary studies. The preceding analysis of these arguments identifies two major tasks essential to meeting that challenge. We need to see standards of excellence in the conduct of interdisciplinary study, and we need to train faculty who teach interdisciplinary study in its method.

We need to agree, in particular, on what it means to teach interdisciplinary studies well. We need to exchange information on individual interdisciplinary courses from a variety of institutions in order to identify models of the most effective ways of introducing students to the interdisciplinary approach or to essential interdisciplinary skills. We need to examine sequences of interdisciplinary courses at various interdisciplinary programs to explore the most fruitful ways of developing interdisciplinary competence in our students; the sequence for introducing disciplinary concepts, theories, and methods; the timing of the introduction of models for bridging disciplines such as a structuralism, general systems, etc. And we need to examine the process of teaching itself, not just of curriculum development. Are there special pedagogical or classroom techniques which are particularly appropriate to teaching interdisciplinary studies?

Finally, we need to train faculty in interdisciplinary study. In part, this means training them in the interdisciplinary method, but probably more importantly it means developing in them an appreciation for the world views of the disciplines in which they have not been trained but which are relevant to the kinds of interdisciplinary problems they address. Of course, that appreciation comes only with command of the concepts arid theories of at least one portion of the discipline, making the task of training rather substantial. We need so retrain faculty already teaching in interdisciplinary programs as well as training those about to enter the profession. For the latter, we will eventually require a solid graduate program in generic interdisciplinary studies, or at least core courses of such strategies in graduate programs in interdisciplinary topics like urban or women's studies. Retraining of existing faculty, both to sharpen interdisciplinary competence and to provide them with the formal interdisciplinary credentials most lack, can be accomplished in a variety of ways—faculty seminars on individual campuses leading to summer workshops,[25] national summer institutes, summer courses offered by new interdisciplinary graduate programs, leading perhaps to formal certification. The tasks are formidable, as is that of securing consensus, but I am confident that we will accomplish them, and that we will be able to meet the arguments of our critics, both in Principle and in practice. I hope that Professor Benson's article plays a key role towards the achievement of that goal.

Notes

1. This conception is presented in my article with William Green, "Defining and Teaching Interdisciplinary Studies," *Improving College and University Teaching* 30:1 (Winter 1982), pp. 23–30.
2. Thomas C. Benson, "Five Arguments Against Interdisciplinary Studies," *Issues in Integrative Studies* 1 (1982), pp. 39.
3. Benson, p. 40.
4. Benson, p. 41.
5. Raymond C. Miller, "Varieties of Interdisciplinary Approaches in the Social Sciences," *Issues in Integrative Studies* 1 (1982), pp. 4–8.
6. Benson, p. 39.
7. Frederick S. Weaver. "A Study of Interdisciplinary Learning and Teaching at Hampshire College" (Amherst, MA Hampshire College, 1981).
8. Ralph Ross. "The Nature of the Interdisciplinary: An Elementary Statement," in Alvin White (ed.) *Interdisciplinary Teaching* (San Francisco: JosseyBass 1981), p. 23.
9. Benson, p. 40.
10. Benson, pp. 41–42.
11. Charles B. Fethe "A Philosophical Model for Interdisciplinary Programs," *Liberal Education* 4 (1973), pp. 490–497.
12. B. S. Bloom (ed.), *Taxonomy of Educational Objectives, Handbook In Cognitive Domain* (New York: Longmans, Green, 1965). Jean Piaget, "Intellectual Evolution from Adolescence to Adulthood," *Human Development* 15 (1972), pp. 1–12. William Perry, *Forms of Intellectual and Ethical Development in the College Years: A Scheme* (New York: Holt, Rinehart & Winston, 1970). Lawrence Kohlberg and E. Turiel, *Recent Research in Moral Development* (New York: Holt, Rinehart & Winston, 1973).
13. Benson, pp. 43–44.
14. William H. Newell, "Interdisciplinary Studies Are Alive and Well," *AJS Newsletter* 10:1 (March, 1988). pp. I, 6–8; reprinted in *AAHE Bulletin* 40:8 (1988), pp 10–12; also reprinted in *The National Honors Report* 9:2 (Summer, 1988), pp. 5–6.
15. Newell, "Interdisciplinary Studies," p. 2.
16. Thomas Klein and Jerry Gaff, "Reforming Higher Education: A Survey" (Washington, D.C.: Association of American Colleges, 1982), p. 4.
17. Klein and Gaff, p. 6.
18. Benson, p. 45.
19. Benson, p. 45.
20. Benson, p. 45.
21. Benson, p. 46.
22. Newell and Green, p. 24.
23. Benson, pp. 46–47.
24. William H. Newell. "Interdisciplinary Curriculum Development in the 1970s: The Paracollege at St. Olaf and the Western College Program at Miami University," in Richard Jones and Barbara Smith (eds.). *Alternative Higher Education* (Cambridge, MA: Schenkman, 1984, 127–147).
25. Alvin M. White "Developing and Challenging Faculty Through Interdisciplinary Teaching-Learning," in William C. Nelson and Michael F. Siegel (eds.), *Effective Approaches to Faculty Developments* (Washington, D.C.: Association of American Colleges, 1980), pp. 71–76.

Reading 8 Discussion Questions

1. What do you think of Newell's response to Benson's article?

2. Which of Newell's responses if any do you find the most convincing? Why?

3. Which of Newell's responses if any do you find the least convincing? Why?

4. What does Newell mean by "a conception of interdisciplinary study"?

Advantages of Interdisciplinary Studies

Newell (1983) provides some persuasive responses to Benson's arguments that emphasize many of the advantages of studying interdisciplinary studies. Newell responds in Reading 8 to Benson's arguments in Reading 7 one at a time. Within each response Newell, at times, responds indirectly, tangentially, implicitly, or in another sequence than Benson's. In the following sections each of Newell's responses to Benson's criticisms is reviewed with some commentary.

NEWELL'S FIRST RESPONSE

There is no conceptual confusion: Interdisciplinary studies are about complex problem solving.

Newell (1983) responds to Benson's charge that interdisciplinary studies rest on serious conceptual confusion. Newell points out that Benson (1982) is not clear (in other words, Benson can be viewed as confused) about the nature of the conceptual confusion because Benson describes interdisciplinary studies in several ways. With which of the following, Newell (1983) asks of Benson, are interdisciplinary studies concerned?

- ▪ Are interdisciplinary studies concerned with connections in the real world?
- ▪ Are interdisciplinary studies concerned with links between different knowledges of that world?
- ▪ Are interdisciplinary studies concerned with the "practical value of interdisciplinary projects in the solving of specific problems"? (p. 1)

Newell (1983) asserts that interdisciplinary studies are concerned with the last of these views, claiming that the "problem-solving conception of interdisciplinary studies is the most fruitful" (p. 1).

Newell (1983) then argues that if interdisciplinary studies are about problem solving, then as interdisciplinarians we have to understand better the interdisciplinary problem solving process. But before we can even attempt to understand the interdisciplinary problem solving process, we have to comprehend how interdisciplinary projects begin.

How Do Interdisciplinary Projects Begin?

Interdisciplinary projects begin with one's experience or "confrontation" with the world, i.e., with "a problem, an event, or even a painting" (Newell 1983, p. 1). What makes interdisciplinary projects different than other projects is *complexity*: projects that are not interdisciplinary can be addressed comprehensively from a single disciplinary perspective. As Newell (2002) writes elsewhere, "if the world around us were not complex, there would be no need for interdisciplinary studies" (p. 122). For example, you are at the gas station and are surprised to see a spike in gas prices. For Newell (1983), such a confrontation is the first step in the process of interdisciplinary study.

The second step is formulating a question, *one that is too complex to be answered by any discipline*. We must be careful to make certain first that the question is a complex one. For example, you are gazing at the stars one night and suddenly you see a shooting star. You wonder what is a shooting star. While this situation qualifies as a confrontation, is it a complex one? How can you know? You can know by articulating the following question: What is a shooting star? Then ask yourself whether or not the question that arises from the confrontation can be satisfactorily answered by a single disciplinary perspective or not. The answer to the question regarding the nature of shooting stars, while very complicated, is not complex as it can be answered by learning more about a single discipline—astronomy. Thus, the ability to formulate a question does not guarantee that your project will be interdisciplinary. In other words, *a question must be complex in order to be considered interdisciplinary*.

Complex questions are broad in scope, although not all questions that are broad in scope are complex and thus interdisciplinary. According to Newell,

> *a question about all the stock markets in the world—which is presumably broad —may still be answered satisfactorily by the discipline of economics alone. So not all broad questions are interdisciplinary. Furthermore a question can be very narrow—regarding the motivation of a single individual behind a single decision —and still require several disciplines to answer it. So some narrow questions are interdisciplinary.* (W. H. Newell, personal communication, July 22, 2004)

The previous example of the spike in gas prices raises the question: Why are gas prices suddenly so high? It is both a complex and a broad question as it necessitates the perspectives of multiple disciplines such as economics, politics, geology, Middle Eastern Studies, among others. Take another example that most if not all of us experienced: the tragic events of 9/11. The events led to the question asked all over the world: Why was the United States attacked?

The third step is to gather all the relevant disciplines. In the case of 9/11, what would those relevant disciplines be?

EXERCISE 6-1 Write down all the relevant disciplines you think are needed to understand the events of 9/11 and explain why here:

Fourth, consider the problem through the perspective of each discipline, one at a time. In the example of 9/11, looking at the history of al-Qaida will lead to an understanding that the events of 9/11 had precursor events, including the 1993 bombing of the Twin Towers. Learning more about fundamentalist Islam in religious studies will give a better understanding of why America is so hated by al-Qaida. Looking at politics can give a better understanding of why 9/11 was such an unexpected event even though there were apparently some concerns that a terrorist attack was imminent. Obviously this list is only a partial one, which makes sense since single disciplines can only provide partial answers to complex problems.

The fifth step is to gather together all the insights gained from each discipline. Make a list of all the disciplines you have consulted. For each discipline you write down, be sure to include a summary of its insights to the problem.

The sixth step is most challenging: evaluate the insights. This step is most challenging because different disciplinary insights to a particular phenomenon can conflict. A very dramatic example of how different disciplines can "see" or interpret a situation differently is the case of Andrea Yates, the Texas housewife who drowned her five children on June 20, 2001.

A Case of Conflicting Disciplinary Insights and Differing Perspectives

Andrea Yates had a history of mental illness after the birth of her fourth child in 1999. She attempted suicide twice within two months in 1999, was hospitalized twice and continued outpatient medical treatment, which included taking antidepressant and antipsychotic drugs. After her second suicide attempt she was thought to have postpartum psychosis, which is considered a medical emergency, and was advised not to have any more children (O'Mallery 2004, pp. 39–41). Within a year she became pregnant with her fifth child, Mary, who was born on November 30, 2000.

A few weeks after her father's death in March 2001, she was hospitalized again. She was hospitalized a month later in May 2001 and again put on the antipsychotic drug Haldol. On June 4th, 2001 her psychiatrist ordered Yates to taper Haldol even though it had helped her previously. On June 18th, Andrea and her husband Russell Yates visited her psychiatrist. Her psychiatrist decided not to put her back on Haldol despite her husband's view that she was declining (O'Mallery 2004, pp. 56–57). In effect, according to O'Mallery (2004), not only was she off antipsychotic medicine for two weeks, she "was on straight 'rocket fuel,' the term some psychiatrists give to the combination of antidepressants Effexor and Remeron" (p. 57).

Two days later, on June 20, 2001 Yates believed Satan was in her presence, and in order to save her children for heaven, she drowned them in the tub in the guest bathroom one at a time. Her children ranged in ages from seven years to six months. Her husband had left for work at 9 a.m. and his mother was on her way to the home to help Andrea with the children.

At 9:48 a.m. Andrea called 911 and asked for a police officer but declined to say exactly why. When a police officer arrived at the home and asked Yates why she needed a police officer, she replied that she had killed her children (O'Mallery 2004, p. 4).

Only the bare bones of the evidently complex case are presented here, enough for you to see how different disciplinary perspectives might usefully be at work and in conflict. Andrea attributed the disturbances of her thinking, her visions, and voices, to Satan. In other words, she had a religious explanation for her behavior and actions. Psychiatry viewed Yates in terms of illness. Her psychiatrists believed she was severely mentally ill—psychotic and delusional—and thus not responsible for her actions since she could not differentiate from right from wrong. Nevertheless, within psychiatry there were differences in perspectives. Several doctors diagnosed Yates differently, which may or may not have led to the murders: the "rocket fuel" medication may have incited in her a manic state at the time of the murders. She received inadequate treatment during her last two hospitalizations, and was sent to group therapy for chemical dependencies when she neither took recreational drugs nor drank alcohol. Her last hospitalization lasted only twelve days, which was as long as her insurance company allowed.

The law viewed Yates' actions in terms of crime. Yates had murdered five innocent children. The legal definition of criminal insanity is the inability to know the difference between right and wrong. The prosecution agreed with psychiatrists and the defense team that Yates was mentally ill. On this point there was common ground shared by these otherwise differing disciplinary perspectives. The prosecution argued that if Andrea knew the difference between right and wrong enough to call 911 after she murdered her own children, then she is not criminally insane regardless of any extenuating circumstances, such as the defendant had been released from a hospital from being treated for psychosis only weeks before committing murder. The jury members, while sympathetic to Yates, ultimately decided that she knew what she did was wrong at the time of the murders because she called 911 and immediately confessed afterwards to the police that she had done something for which she should be punished (O'Mallery 2004, pp. 19–20). In April 2002 Yates was convicted of murder of three of the children and sentenced to life in prison.

The story of Andrea Yates does not end with her prison sentence. Her murder conviction was overturned by the Texas 1st District Court of Appeals in January 2005 because of false testimony. An expert witness for the prosecution, a forensic psychiatrist, stated during the 2002 trial that he was a consultant for the television show *Law and Order* and that Yates killed her children after watching a certain episode (Williams & Associates 2005). O'Mallery (2004), who was covering the trial, discovered that the episode never existed and notified the court. Jurors were not informed of the false testimony until after they convicted Yates while they were deliberating on her sentencing. The jury then decided against the death penalty. Despite her conviction being overturned, Yates remains at a psychiatric prison for her own safety.

The example of Andrea Yates was an interdisciplinary "phenomenon" that the author's summer 2001 introductory interdisciplinary studies students sought to understand. Students asked two related questions: "How could a mother kill her own children?" "Was Andrea Yates guilty of murdering her children?" In so doing they attempted to understand how and why such a tragedy could have occurred by using interdisciplinary methods such as the one currently being described.

Forming an Interdisciplinary Response

The seventh step is to come up with an interdisciplinary response that is the result of your evaluation of all the disciplinary insights. According to Newell, "the response may or may not provide a definitive or fully satisfactory answer, though it will certainly provide a 'more' comprehensive or coherent or satisfactory answer" (W. H. Newell, personal communication, July 22, 2004). It should also, as Newell (1983) puts it, lead "to a greater appreciation of the nature and complexity of the question" (p. 2). This greater appreciation is the goal of interdisciplinary studies.

Newell's 1983 conception of interdisciplinary study can be understood as a way of doing interdisciplinary studies—in other words, a method of doing interdisciplinary studies. As Newell (1983) points out, the heart of the interdisciplinary studies method is "the openness to alternative ways of looking at the world" (p. 4). In the example of Andrea Yates, students who initially supported the death penalty for Yates reconsidered once they learned about the severity of her mental illness and the history of her flawed medical treatment. Some students blamed religion, some blamed her very traditional and religious husband, and most were appalled by both the inadequacies of her medical treatment and the actions of her medical insurance company. Nevertheless, most students after evaluating all the different disciplinary insights concluded that Yates was guilty of murdering her children even though they had a better understanding and appreciation of the complexities of the decision the jury had to make.

Table 6-2 Conflicting Disciplinary Insights: Was Andrea Yates Guilty of Killing Her Children?

Andrea Yates	Doctors	Prosecutors/Jury
"Religious" Insights	Psychiatry	Criminal Law
Yates believed that Satan spoke to her. Yates killed the children so they would go to heaven.	Severe depression; delusional; postpartum psychosis; attempted suicide twice in 1999; was hospitalized a month before the murders; recently off her antipsychotic medicine.	Mentally ill but competent to stand trial. Not criminally insane as she knew the difference between right and wrong; she called 911 immediately after the murders.
In eyes of God and the law it was wrong; in my thought it was right. Not guilty.	She thought what she was doing would save her children; she thought she was not a good mother; she didn't realize what she was doing. Not guilty by reason of insanity.	Yates was found guilty of capital murder; she was spared the death penalty by the jury when it was revealed after their verdict that an expert witness gave false testimony that implied premeditation. (O' Mallery, 2004). Her conviction was overturned in January 2005 because of this false testimony. Yates remains in prison for her own safety.

Table 6-3 Newell's 1983 Conception of Interdisciplinary Study

1. Become struck by a "confrontation" with a complex phenomenon.
2. Formulate an interdisciplinary question.
3. Gather all relevant disciplines.
4. Consider the problem/question through the perspectives of each discipline, one at a time.
5. Gather together all the insights gained from each discipline.
6. Evaluate all the insights.
7. Fashion an interdisciplinary response to the question.

Newell's conception of the interdisciplinary process discussed in Reading 8 is an early attempt at describing the interdisciplinary problem solving process. Others, including Newell (2001, in press), have subsequently modified and/or elaborated upon the process (see Hursh, Haas & Moore 1983; Klein 1990, 1996; Szostak 2002).

NEWELL'S SECOND RESPONSE

Interdisciplinary Study Avoids Indoctrination in Any Single Perspective World View and Teaches the Value of Considering Alternative Viewpoints.

Newell (1983) finds positive what Benson (1982) criticizes about undergraduate interdisciplinary education. For example, Newell refutes Benson's second argument that interdisciplinary studies students lack a "mature base" in their chosen disciplines in two ways. First he claims that as a matter of course interdisciplinary studies students learn the basics about disciplines, which does take time and research. In learning about disciplines students learn the following about any discipline:

- Its world views
- Its assumptions
- Its concepts
- Its theories
- Its methods (Newell 1983, pp. 3–4)

Second, taking interdisciplinary studies courses along with traditional courses within disciplines, according to Newell, avoids indoctrination to one world view. More specifically, Newell (1983) writes that "when students are thoroughly grounded in a discipline before becoming exposed to interdisciplinary studies, they tend to become indoctrinated to its world view, uncritically accepting its often implicit assumptions" (p. 4).

Newell (1983) believes that college students should learn about "the essential complementarity between the disciplines and interdisciplinary study" during their freshman year if not already in high school (p. 4). Newell does not go into much depth about the reasons why. One distinct advantage to learning about the relation between disciplines and interdisciplinary study is that students can understand better how knowledge is organized and the reasons why so much knowledge is organized by disciplines. Newell suggests that along with disciplinary courses students should take interdisciplinary courses that allow students to contrast and compare the views they are learning in their disciplinary courses. For example, if a freshman is taking geology and economics, the student can contrast and compare how the geologist's world view may be similar to or different from the economist's. Are there any overlaps in what the geologist and economist study? The allocation and composition of natural resources such as oil may be one area. Can you think of any others?

NEWELL'S THIRD RESPONSE

Interdisciplinary study facilitates students to be more pro-active in their education, and their interdisciplinary degrees are increasingly desirable for positions in the 21st century workplace.

Newell (1983) agrees with Benson (1982) that some students need to study one discipline in college, especially those who want to specialize in one area, such as accounting. Benson claims that such specialized study is extremely important for those pursuing graduate degrees. Newell (1983) does not go in much depth in answering such charges, suggesting that the culprit may be in poor quality of introductory courses (p. 7). His point is that students need to learn the foundations of any discipline they may pursue. To rephrase Newell (1983) a bit differently, one could say that rather than blaming the poor quality of introductory courses, students interested in attending graduate school would be better served by having clear plans.

Planning Is Crucial for Interdisciplinary Studies Students

Interdisciplinary studies students who want to attend graduate school need to plan their college careers carefully. They should do research and find out what are the minimum requirements for graduate school admission, and be sure to take the necessary courses that fulfill those requirements. A well-rounded education is regarded quite favorably in even very specialized graduate programs, such as medical or dental school, provided that the minimum admission requirements are met. For example, a former student of the author's introductory inter-disciplinary studies class expressed the strong desire to attend dental school and become a dentist. The student was in the process of completing the necessary science courses, and was a research assistant in a university labo-ratory. The student was combining biology and religion, for the purposes of better understanding the complex ethical questions in biotechnology and medicine such as cloning and abortion.

Two semesters later the student took a senior seminar in "Interdisciplinary Approaches to Contemporary Art" in which he did a presentation on *Genesis* (1999) and *The Eighth Day* (2001), two art works by the artist Eduardo Kac that by their very titles raise religious questions concerning the creation of transgenetic bacteria and animals. The student wrote about his interdisciplinary research in his admissions application and was not only accepted to the dental school of his choice, but was commended upon his acceptance on the strength of his essay and the relevant, interdisciplinary questions it raised. (For more information about Eduardo Kac and his interdisciplinary transgenetic art, see <http://www.ekac.org>.)

What Employers Like about Interdisciplinary Studies Majors

What Newell (1983) does mention is that most jobs are not so specialized that only the knowledge of one disci-pline is required. What they do require is the following:

- Abilities to understand and critically evaluate the work of experts and to make decisions based on that evaluation
- Specialized backgrounds that are interdisciplinary
- Training in synthetic thinking, in weighing arguments from diverse narrow disciplinary perspectives, and in placing them in the larger context. (p. 6)

According to Newell (1983), employers are interested in hiring interdisciplinary studies majors because of the following:

- Ability of students to think conceptually
- Ability to identify and solve problems
- Ability to understand other value systems
- Ability to evaluate alternatives
- Ability to decide on a course of action
- Ability to change one's opinion in the light of facts
- Effective written communication skills
- Effective oral communication
- Effective group participation (team work)
- Ethical sensitivity
- Constructive response to criticism (pp. 6–7)

NEWELL'S FOURTH RESPONSE

Interdisciplinary studies courses can be thoroughly relevant and innovative, enhancing student motivation to learn, which can make them highly effective.

While Newell (1983) agrees with Benson (1982) that sometimes courses that are deemed "interdiscipli-nary" rely on "splashy special events" and flashy multimedia rather than on substance or content (Benson 1982, p. 8), most are quite innovative when they address timely issues and use examples that are both interesting and relevant to students (Newell 1983, p. 8). The challenge for interdisciplinary studies instructors is to provide adequate guidelines and create assignments that can help students learn how to integrate.

NEWELL'S FIFTH RESPONSE

Interdisciplinary courses and programs can be relatively inexpensive and cost saving to universities.

Benson's fifth argument about the cost of interdisciplinary courses and programs is the one of least interest and concern to students and their parents, for it is an argument that primarily concerns university administrators. Universities have become notorious for raising tuition while undergraduates are increasingly being taught by teaching assistants and adjuncts. To say that interdisciplinary courses are relatively expensive because many are team-taught, requiring two instructors who have their Ph.D.s, or that such courses require low teacher-student ratios, will be generally regarded as positives to most students. As Newell points out, such arguments attest to "the power of economic arguments today in educational decision-making" (p. 10).

EXERCISE 6-2

INTERDISCIPLINARY STUDIES ON TRIAL

How well can you argue the case for interdisciplinary studies? How well can you defend your degree? As a class activity, the class will break down into two groups. One group will put interdisciplinary studies on trial, with the charge that interdisciplinary studies should no longer be a major. The other group will be known as "the great defenders of interdisciplinary studies," making the case for interdisciplinary studies. The prosecutors of interdisciplinary studies will rely on Reading 7, utilizing Benson's arguments against interdisciplinary studies as well as coming up with their own charges. The prosecution can utilize examples of "disadvantages" from personal experiences with their own major if there are any. The defenders will certainly rely on Newell's responses as well as coming up with their own examples of advantages for studying interdisciplinary studies.

Procedure

1. Every student will have read Reading 7 and Reading 8.
2. Every student will have taken notes from their reading.
3. Each student will decide if he or she wants to be a member of the prosecution or be a "great defender." Each student must take a position. The instructor will decide for the indecisive student which side he or she will be on.
4. Each group will meet and decide on a group recorder. The group recorder will write down all the points the group wants to make during its arguments.
5. Each group will decide on a group leader. The prosecution group leader will be the lead prosecutor; the defender group will be the lead defender. The leads will be the ones who make the initial arguments and defenses. The leads should be chosen for their oratory and argumentation abilities. Those who like to "put on a show" and add some dramatic flair to the debate will make the exercise all the more interesting.
6. The prosecution goes first, and makes its first charge. The defense will respond to the charge, to which the prosecution will answer back. The trial or debate will continue until either side can no longer respond to a point. In that case, the group that makes the last point will be considered to have "won" their point. The prosecution then will continue to their next charge.
7. Once a lead makes an initial charge, others in the group may "second" or "third," i.e., follow up and contribute to the discussion. Everyone in each group should participate in the debate.
8. The instructor will write down the charges and responses on the blackboard if possible. The instructor will be the trial judge, adjudicating whenever necessary.
9. After the trial, discuss among yourselves which side "won" and why.
10. An alternative approach to the class activity is to allow the undecided about interdisciplinary studies to play collectively the role of the jury. The jury will listen to the trial, and afterwards, deliberate and deliver a verdict to the judge. No hung juries please!

EXERCISE 6-3 — WORKSHEET ON NEWELL'S 1983 MODEL OF THE INTEGRATIVE PROCESS

In Chapter Six Newell's 1983 model of the integrative process was introduced. Using Newell's conception of interdisciplinarity, first identify an interdisciplinary problem. Then follow the sequence provided to address how the problem can be addressed or studied. Be sure to identify the complex phenomenon as an interdisciplinary problem, appropriate disciplinary perspectives to be used, complete list of disciplinary insights, areas of overlaps and areas of incongruity/conflict, your interdisciplinary response, and an evaluation/reflection on the process.

Example:

1. Description of Interdisciplinary Situation that Strikes You
2. Statement of Problem: Interdisciplinary Problem IP (name the problem)
3. Disciplines that study Interdisciplinary Problem IP: X, Y, and Z.
4. Discipline X views Interdisciplinary Problem IP as Orange. Discipline Y views Interdisciplinary Problem IP as Yellow, and Discipline Z views Interdisciplinary Problem IP as Pink. Discipline X's view of Interdisciplinary Problem IP is incommensurate with Discipline Z's, while it shares some common ground with Discipline Y, etc.
5. Insights from Discipline A:

   Insights from Discipline B:

   Insights from Discipline C:
6. Ask yourself which disciplinary insights conflict/overlap? Note any common ground among the disciplinary insights. Ask yourself how these insights can be integrated . . . or cannot be integrated.
7. Sample response: "Using an interdisciplinary approach, I can see that Interdisciplinary Problem IP can/cannot be solved unless . . ." (or something to that effect).
8. [Added Step] Review your process: do you need to go back to a step and expand upon it (Example: Oops! I see now that I should have included another concept/another discipline. Or, I spent a lot of time researching one discipline's approach to the problem only to find out it was not very useful. Darn!)

INTEGRATIVE PROCESS WORKSHEET

Step One: Become struck by a "confrontation" with a complex phenomenon.

[Make a list of possible complex (interdisciplinary) phenomena you are interested in learning more about/doing research on/studying further.]

Complex Phenomenon #1: _____

Why is it complex?

Why are you interested in this phenomenon/problem?

What future professional relevance does studying this problem have for you?

Complex Phenomenon #2: _____

Why is it complex?

Why are you interested in this phenomenon/problem?

What future professional relevance does studying this problem have for you?

Complex Phenomenon #3: _____

Why is it complex?

Why are you interested in this phenomenon/problem?

What future professional relevance does studying this problem have for you?

Decision Time! Now that you have identified three possible phenomena/problems, choose one that fulfills the following criteria: a) is of interest to you, b) pertains to your education, and c) has future professional relevance for you. In other words, you should choose a complex interdisciplinary phenomenon/problem that can be studied in at least one of the disciplines you are currently studying.

The complex problem I want to study further is Complex Phenomenon # _____

Step Two: Formulate an Interdisciplinary Question.

In step one you may have described a situation. Now try to give the situation a name or turn it into a question.

Examples:

How can sexual harassment be avoided?

How can we improve primary education?

Step Three: Gather all relevant disciplines.

List the relevant disciplines needed to study the problem further.

Step Four: Consider the problem/question through the perspectives of each discipline, one at a time.

Disciplinary Perspective #1:

Disciplinary Perspective #2:

Disciplinary Perspective #3:

[list as many as are necessary]

Step Five: Gather together all the insights gained from each discipline.

List all the insights by disciplines:

Discipline #1 Insights:

Discipline #2 Insights:

Discipline #3 Insights

[list as many as are necessary]

Step Six: Evaluate all the insights.

Which insights overlap? Note any common ground between disciplinary insights. Is there any conflict? Which insights are helpful? Not so helpful? Decide which ones are essential for solving the interdisciplinary problem. Example: both psychiatry and the prosecution viewed Andrea Yates as severely mentally ill, yet since she admitted guilt she did not meet the legal definition of insanity according to both the prosecution and the jury.

Step Seven: Fashion an Interdisciplinary Response to the Question.

Try to integrate the different responses into an interdisciplinary response.

Step Eight: Confirm or disconfirm the proposed response/solution (Evaluate Process).

You may have to repeat the entire process again. You may have to go back and fine-tune one or more of the steps. The process is not intended to be one way, nor is it "clean" or "simple." It is often a messy, convoluted process. You may not like that, thinking that it is unorganized. Then again, think of all the messy, interdisciplinary problems out there . . . this is real life problem solving and decision making!

READING

SAMPLE INTEGRATIVE PROCESS WORKSHEET

by

Joseph Allred

Step One:

Complex Phenomenon: Poor Oral Health in Latin America

- *Why is it complex?* The phenomenon is complex because it would take more than a truckload of toothbrushes to solve the problem.
- *Why are you interested in this phenomenon/problem?* This problem interests me because of my concern for oral health in general.
- *What future relevance does studying this problem have for me?* I plan on becoming a Spanish-speaking dentist and there might be a lot that I could do to help.

Step Two:

How can the oral health of Latin Americans be improved?

Step Three:

Relevant Disciplines:

- Dentistry
    - ☐ General
    - ☐ Periodontal
    - ☐ Surgical
    - ☐ Public health
    - ☐ Oral pathology
- Medicine
- Government
- Law
- International Affairs
- Business
- Education
- Communication
- Languages
- History
- Sociology
- Psychology

Steps Four and Five:

DISCIPLINE	DISCIPLINARY PERSPECTIVE
Dentistry	Dentistry is concerned with the oral health of the individual, the community and the world. There are sub-disciplines which are more concerned with large spread oral diseases such as oral pathology and periodontal dentistry.
Medicine	Oral health may be only part of a bigger health problem. Certain medical specialties such as epidemiology and virology may be most suitable to handle this problem.
Government	The problem exists in many different countries each with their own distinct government.
Law	Along with each government, all countries abide by different laws. These must be taken into consideration when attempting to solve this problem.
International Affairs	It may be difficult for foreigners to help in some countries. A form of diplomacy may be needed to smooth things over.
Business	Large corporations may be needed to sponsor or support any effort to correct the problem. Allowing certain dental products to be sold in underserved locations or reducing prices of products already being sold could help.
Education	The problem may be preventable for future generations if proper oral health education becomes a priority.
Communication	Organizing a relief effort requires excellent communication skills.
Languages	Latin America speaks several different languages. Spanish and Portuguese are the most prominent. However, there are many Indians who speak their native tongue.
History	Knowing the past gives a deeper understanding of current events and helps prevent future mistakes.
Sociology	The Latin American culture may give clues to how the problem may be addressed.
Psychology	What is going on inside their heads?

Step Six:

Dentistry and medicine are probably the most important disciplines to address this interdisciplinary problem. Those who have been trained in those areas are probably educated in many of the other disciplines such as communications, history, and psychology. A firm grasp of the languages would be very important but a translator could do the job. Business stands alone but could be the means of supporting any attempted efforts.

Step Seven:

Oral health in Latin America can be improved by a massive campaign to reach out to the uneducated and underprivileged. Government leaders would have to cooperate with volunteer dentists and doctors in a coordinated effort. Organizations would join forces with the support of large corporations and many but not all could be helped. With proper education it can be prevented altogether in future generations.

Step Eight:

The solution stated in Step Seven sounds good but may be difficult to undertake. While it is true that the relief effort is underway on a small scale, it should be taken to a higher level. It may need the help of specialists in organization and transportation as well as other disciplines that have not been mentioned. These insights are limited to one person's point of view and should be reviewed and added to by many other people.

Suggested Readings

Benson, T. C. (1982). Five arguments against interdisciplinary studies. *Issues in Integrative Studies*, 1, 38–48. [See Reading 7 in this volume].

Hursh, B., Haas, P., & Moore, M. (1983). An interdisciplinary model to implement general education." *Journal of Higher Education*, 54 (1), 42–49.

Klein, J. T. (1990). *Interdisciplinarity: History, theory and practice*. Detroit: Wayne State University Press.

Klein, J. T. (1996). *Crossing boundaries: Knowledge, disciplinarities, and interdisciplinarities*. Charlottesville and London: University of Virginia Press.

Newell, W. H. (1983). The case for interdisciplinary studies: Response to professor Benson's five arguments. *Issues in Integrative Studies*, 2, 1–19. [See Reading 8 in this volume].

Newell, W.H. (2001). A theory of interdisciplinary studies. *Issues in Integrative Studies*, 19, 1–25.

Newell, W. H. (2002). Integrating the college curriculum. In J. T. Klein, *Interdisciplinary education in K–12 and college* (pp. 117–38). N.Y.: The College Board.

Newell, W. H. (in press). Decision-making in interdisciplinary studies. In G. Morçol (Ed.), *Handbook of decision making*. New York: Marcel Dekker.

O'Mallery, S. (2004). *"Are you there alone?" The unspeakable crime of Andrea Yates*. N.Y.: Simon and Schuster.

Petrie, H. G. (1976). Do you see what I see? The epistemology of interdisciplinary inquiry. *Journal of Aesthetic Education*, 10, 29–43. [See Reading 8 in this volume.]

Szostak, R. (2002). How to do interdisciplinarity: Integrating the debate. *Issues in Integrative Studies*, 20, 103–122.

Williams, P. & Associates. (2005, Jan. 6). Conviction overturned for mom who drowned 5 kids. [Electronic version]. MSNBC News. Retrieved January 7, 2005 at <http://www.msnbc.msn.com/id/6794098>

DOING INTERDISCIPLINARY STUDIES

UNDERSTANDING AND DOING RESEARCH ON DISCIPLINES

The disciplines represent our best efforts to think systematically about the world, and they are prerequisite to competent disciplinary work.

Howard Gardner (2000, p. 54)

Learning Objectives

By reading Chapter Seven of *Becoming Interdisciplinary*, you should be able to:

1. Understand that each discipline has its own "disciplinary culture."
2. Be familiar with cognitive maps of disciplines, i.e., the basic elements of any discipline.
3. Understand what is meant by a *concept*.
4. Understand what is meant by a *theory*.
5. Do research on any given discipline.

Learning How to Do Interdisciplinary Studies

By now you may be asking the following question: How does one actually do interdisciplinary studies? You already have started to do interdisciplinary studies by reading Part One of this book. In Part One you learned some important information about interdisciplinary studies and were encouraged to reflect on your life as an interdisciplinarian. You were asked to determine the reasons why you chose interdisciplinary studies as a major, and to identify possible interdisciplinary issues or problems you may want to pursue studying. In effect, you focused on the more personal dimensions of interdisciplinary studies to prepare you for personal mastery and what psychologist Robert Kegan (1994) calls *self-authorship*, i.e., the ability to make up one's mind. Another way of describing self-authorship is the ability to write the script of one's own life.

You are now ready to move on and to concentrate on the more academic aspects of interdisciplinary studies. In Part Two you will investigate how to become interdisciplinary by learning how to do interdisciplinary research. In this chapter you will begin to learn how to do interdisciplinary studies by learning first how to do research on disciplines. By doing research on disciplines you will be able to gain insight on a given discipline's perspectives.

Why is a familiarity with disciplinary perspectives so important? In Reading 10, "Do You See What I See? The Epistemology of Interdisciplinary Inquiry," Petrie (1976) makes a powerful case for doing research on disciplines in his discussion of how and why interdisciplinary projects are done. This chapter will examine some of Petrie's main points before focusing and expanding upon his ideas concerning the epistemology of disciplines. Finally, in this chapter you will receive guidelines on how to do research on any given disciplines of interest and will be provided with a sample worksheet to do your research.

Reading 10

In "Do You See What I See? The Epistemology of Interdisciplinary Inquiry," Hugh G. Petrie examines the factors that he considers critical for the success or failure of interdisciplinary inquiry.

READING 10

DO YOU SEE WHAT I SEE?
The Epistemology of Interdisciplinary Inquiry

by

Hugh G. Petrie

It seems to me that since the answer to the question in the title of my paper is, for members of interdisciplinary groups, not always and obviously, yes, an examination of why this is so and how it might be overcome is in order. The impetus, and, indeed, part of the content for this investigation arose out of my participation in the Sloan Program of the College of Engineering at the University of Illinois over the past two years. That program was in large part designed as an interdisciplinary effort to examine the role of the social sciences and humanities in an engineering curriculum. The method was interdisciplinary faculty seminars, and my particular interest was in the processes which occurred in those seminars. I was a general participant in the meetings which brought in a series of speaker-discussants on the topics, "How does X View the World." "X" was each week replaced by the name of the discipline of the speaker. In addition, I chaired an interdisciplinary subgroup whose topic was the interdisciplinary research and teaching process. Much of what I will say in the following is a result of these experiences, and although a philosopher, I will be making some non-philosophical claims in what follows. That I dare to do this is part of what must result, I think, if interdisciplinary work is ever to be successful.

Harry Broudy has surely been one of the most persistent advocates, at least of late, for the importance, not to say the necessity, of interdisciplinary work.[1] Basically the argument is that a complex technological society requires interdisciplinary solutions to its problems. And I think the argument requires little restating. One need only consider the problems of pollution, world-wide inflation, energy production and conservation, and so on to get the flavor. In addition if one adds the increased sensitivity of professional schools to their broader social roles as evidenced by other papers, the importance of interdisciplinary work becomes apparent.

Unfortunately, the importance of interdisciplinary work has seldom been matched by its fruitfulness. All too often grandly conceived interdisciplinary projects never get off the ground and the level of scholarship seldom exceeds that of a glorified bull session. All too frequently, people look upon interdisciplinary projects as a dumping ground for the less than disciplinarily competent—and justifiably so. Yet, as I shall argue, it is only from among the most competent disciplinarians that an interdisciplinary group can draw its members if it hopes for success. It is in hopes of contributing to a higher rate of success for interdisciplinary projects that I offer the following "profile" of interdisciplinary inquiry—research or teaching.

First, however, a few preliminary distinctions need to be noted. I distinguish between interdisciplinary and multidisciplinary efforts. The line is not hard and fast, but roughly it is that multidisciplinary projects simply require everyone to do their own thing together with little or no necessity for any one participant to be aware of any other participant's work. Perhaps a project director or manager is needed to glue the final product together, but the pieces are fairly clearly of

From *Educational Researcher*, 5:2 1976 by Hugh Petrie. Copyright © 1976 by American Educational Research Association. Reprinted by permission.

disciplinary size and shape. Interdisciplinary efforts, on the other hand, require more or less integration and even modification of the disciplinary subcontributions while the inquiry is proceeding. Different participants need to take into account the contributions of their fellows in order to make their own contribution.

Take the energy crisis, for example. If the heating engineer as a member of a group looking at energy consumption in housing is simply asked to design houses which are more thermally efficient, he can do that in an almost wholly disciplinary way. He needn't worry about energy cost structures or legal restriction, etc. On the other hand, if the group is considering significant changes in social organization and life-style to meet the energy crisis, the same engineer will have to take projected altered living styles and arrangements, different patterns of energy consumption, and so on into account in order to do even his disciplinary work. And, of course, conversely with respect to the nonengineering participants. It is the interdisciplinary as opposed to the multidisciplinary process with which I shall be concerned in this paper.

The other distinction I want to make here is that I shall not be concerned with the single person who acquires more than one disciplinary competence. In the first place, such a person's problems will be mirrored, I think, in what I shall say about the workings of interdisciplinary groups. But second, such a solution, given the demands of time and energy placed on attaining even one disciplinary competence, is simply out of the question for most people. If we cannot stop short of making Renaissance persons out of a good deal of our population, then the interdisciplinary mode will *not* be able to contribute to the solutions of our pressing societal problems. Thus, I shall talk about groups instead of individuals.

With these preliminaries out of the way, let me indicate briefly what I shall be doing in the remainder of my paper. First I shall note several very important nonepistemological factors which seem to be particularly relevant to the success or failure of interdisciplinary inquiry. These include the notion of idea dominance, psychological considerations, and the institutional setting in which interdisciplinary work is carried on. Next, I shall turn to the epistemological and methodological constraints on interdisciplinary work. Here I shall concentrate on the problems raised by the apparent fact that different disciplines utilize different observational categories and occasionally mean quite different things by the same linguistic terms. I shall suggest that the kind of knowledge exhibited by knowing the observational categories and meanings of the key terms of any discipline is fairly close to what Broudy calls the interpretive use of knowledge. I shall then expand on this notion of interpretive knowledge as a universally necessary condition for successful interdisciplinary inquiry. I shall indicate how one can, in principle, tell when it has been obtained, and I shall conclude by noting the key pedagogical concept necessary for coming to understand the language of a wholly different discipline, viz., metaphor.

Nonepistemological Considerations

Idea Dominance. One of the central considerations necessary for interdisciplinary success seems to be what I will call the dominance of an idea. That is, there must be a clear and recognizable idea which can serve as a central focus for the work. It can be embodied in a single individual who leads the project through force of personality or importance of the perceived mission. The dominant idea may be imposed by some external necessity clearly perceived by all participants. Certain kinds of mission-oriented projects fit here. Finally, it may be an idea embodied in a new and powerful theoretical concept or model—a concept which does not find a natural home in an established discipline.

Closely associated with the idea dominance is the necessity for some kind of achievement. The need for achievement also appears under the heading of psychological characteristics, but here it is primarily directed toward the logical requirement of some kind of feedback to confirm the clarity and force of the idea originally conceived. Thus a dominant personality begins to lose dominance if the group cannot be led to some sort of achievement. A mission unachieved raises doubts as to whether it was properly defined. And a powerful new theoretical idea will ultimately be shelved if it fails to achieve results.

The notion of idea dominance seems to admit of degrees—there can be more or less of it. I would predict that, other things being equal, the stronger the idea, the more chance of success. A caveat must be entered here. In some cases it may be extremely difficult, if not impossible, to judge the strength and dominance of an idea independently of whether it turns out to be successful or not. However, at least a gross empirical handle does seem possible here in that this criterion would seem to rule out interdisciplinary projects undertaken simply for the sake of being interdisciplinary.

Psychological Characteristics of Participants. The second major category of nonepistemological factors is the psychological characteristics of the participants in a successful interdisciplinary effort. Of course, successful people here are very much like successful people in any endeavor, but several characteristics, attitudes, and motivations stand out. The person must, first of all, be secure in his or her original endeavors. Interdisciplinary efforts seldom work if the participants are not fully competent in their own fields. Second, the participants must have a taste for adventure into the unknown and unfamiliar, i.e., they must not be tied too closely to their secure home base. Of course, there is a sense in which a really good disciplinarian is, ipso facto, adventurous. It is a taste for *new* adventure that I am talking about here. Third, their interests must be fairly broad, if not in terms of their spheres of competence, at least in terms of what they feel is of importance.

It should be noted that disciplinary competence and security are sometimes at odds with broad interests and imaginative speculation. Given the current pattern of graduate education, the kind of people attracted to any discipline will tend to be those who are good at a fairly narrow thing. Furthermore, the rewards to a successful academic tend to reinforce the narrow, albeit incisive, disciplinary focus. Thus, on the whole one tends to see good disciplinarians uninterested in interdisciplinary efforts and many who are interested seem to have marginal disciplinary competence. A useful blend of competence and broad interest is rare.

The need for achievement enters into the psychological realm as well. Not only must there be achievement in the sense of the development and confirmation of the dominant idea as already mentioned, the participants must also feel that they are achieving something. This need magnifies the difficulties of combining in one person security of disciplinary competence and broad interest, for the external signs of achievement upon which people depend generally do not go to the person interested in interdisciplinary work. Thus the ability to get internal satisfaction and a sense of achievement are crucial in the early stages of interdisciplinary work. Providing signs of achievement might also be a very effective way for administrators and those concerned with the social setting of the effort to protect the very fragile nature of interdisciplinary projects in their early stages. (See the discussion of the sociological setting below.)

The precise mix of disciplinary competence, adventurous spirit, and broad interests may be very difficult to determine. What does seem clear is that no one of these can be allowed to predominate. By this I do not mean that the extremely competent disciplinarian would not make a good participant in an interdisciplinary effort, but rather that if he is not also extremely adventurous and extremely interested in the project, the rewards which accrue simply due to one's disciplinary competence are likely to pull one away from the interdisciplinary effort. Likewise, the person of extremely broad interests, but lesser disciplinary talent may feel the project is going well, but in fact it never gets beyond the superficial. And the adventurous spirit is needed for learning, where necessary, parts of new disciplines.

Another set of psychological issues involve the simple dynamics of working in a group. It has been remarked over and over by members of Sloan subgroups that they seem to spend almost all semester simply learning what each other is like, everyone getting their biases and interests on the table, and only after this is done do they feel they could really get to work. Whether or not they really could get to work is not at issue here. What is important is that such a "shakedown" of attitudes and modes of behavior is almost always necessary with new groups before they can get to a more substantive level of functioning.

The Institutional Setting. This third category involves the institutional setting for the interdisciplinary work. Under this head is included first of all administrative support for the project. This involves seed money, released time, encouragement, and so on. Closely related to administrative support is the necessity for peer recognition somewhere. This can come from the original parent guild of the participant, from a larger community which deems the interdisciplinary work important, or from the interdisciplinary group itself. These features are connected with the achievement need mentioned under idea dominance and psychological characteristics.

Thus I would predict generally that the more administrative and social support which can be given to interdisciplinary groups, the more successful they are likely to be. Complicating the situation, however, is the need to recognize the operation of the dynamics of the group. With very strong idea dominance, some of the early settling in may be avoided; but in the main, one will simply have to be realistic about how much can be accomplished in a given time under conditions in which the members of the group are, almost by definition, strange to each other.

Epistemological Considerations

I turn now to the category of epistemological considerations. This general area is involved with the modes of inquiry appropriate both to the parent disciplines of participants and to the interdisciplinary effort. In the first place the participants need to recognize that different disciplines do have different cognitive maps and that these maps may well get in the way of successful interdisciplinary inquiry.[2] By cognitive map here I mean the whole cognitive and perceptual apparatus utilized by any given discipline. This includes, but is not limited to, basic concepts, modes of inquiry, what counts as a problem, observational categories, representation techniques, standards of proof, types of explanation, and general ideals of what constitutes the discipline. Perhaps the most striking of these, and also often the least noted, is the extent to which disciplinary categories of observation are theory and discipline relative. Quite literally, two opposing disciplinarians can look at the same thing and not see the same thing.[3] I hope to illustrate this thesis in a few moments.

The present point, however, is that if disciplines do differ in their cognitive maps, then quite plainly until these maps are shared by the interdisciplinary participants, they will be unable to see the relevance of their colleagues' points of view to the problem at hand. If they do not learn the other disciplinary maps, at least some of the discussion will be necessarily misunderstood for it will be processed in terms of the participant's *own* map which may not be the same as that of the person who offered the comment in the first place. Thus learning at least a part of other disciplinary maps is a necessary condition for turning multidisciplinary work into interdisciplinary work.

It might be objected here that learning another discipline's cognitive map cannot possibly be a logically necessary condition for successful interdisciplinary work, since we can point to numerous cases in which the nature of the problem itself clearly called for the insights afforded by another discipline.[4] Thus at a certain stage in the development of biology, the problems clearly called for the insights of physics. The examples could be multiplied. Of course, I do not deny the existence of such historical examples. What I do wish to dispute, however, is that there really was no learning of the cognitive maps of the other relevant discipline. After all, not all biologists saw the need for physics. Could it be that those who did had already learned the necessary minimum about physics?

Alternatively, I would imagine there are cases where people believed that the insights of another discipline were relevant to their current problems, and yet upon investigation and greater familiarity with the other discipline they found that their early faith was misplaced. History seldom records such failures, but they would seem to indicate that problems "call" for other disciplines only when enough is known of the other disciplines to make the ca ll *appropriate*. In short, my claim that learning (or having learned) at least a part of other disciplinary maps is a necessary condition for interdisciplinary work is a conceptual rather than an historical claim.

I would also hypothesize that a failure to undertake such learning helps explain the relatively naive character of so much interdisciplinary work. Failing to realize the significant differences in cognitive maps and yet faced with the necessity for communicating with each other on *some* level or other, the participants retreat to the level of common sense which *is* shared by all. But ipso facto, such a level cannot make use of the more powerful insights of the disciplines. On the other hand some very successful interdisciplinary work has occurred because the overlap of cognitive maps was large to begin with as, for example, in nuclear engineering or biophysics. The problem is paramount when the maps are far apart as, for example, when the team involves humanists and scientists.

Given this difference of cognitive maps, the question arises of what kind of learning of another's disciplinary map is required for the interdisciplinary team member. Harry Broudy gives us a clue here. He has distinguished four uses of learning—the associative, the replicative, the applicative, and the interpretive.[5] Roughly these uses of learning are as follows. One uses learning associatively when on the occasion of use, the learning provides a context of associations. Aesthetic learning in the appreciation of art often functions associatively. One uses learning replicatively when one replicates the learning on the occasion of use in just the form in which it was learned. Spelling is a prime example of replication. One uses learning applicatively when one *does* something in light of the learning. A great deal of expertise is required here both to know the theory, how to apply it, and when to apply it. Persons exercising their full disciplinary competence probably are using their learning applicatively. Finally, one uses learning interpretively when the situation of use is interpreted with the aid of the learning. It is *seen* in light of the learning.

Broudy also suggests that the interpretive uses of learning or knowledge should be understood primarily in terms of Polanyi's concept of tacit knowing.[6] I cannot even begin to do justice here to Polanyi's rich and fertile discussions of tacit knowing. It will be sufficient for my purposes to note two things. First, I take my development in the remainder of this paper to be in the spirit of Broudy's interpretive use of learning and Polanyi's notion of tacit knowing.

Second, I shall make direct use of one central feature of tacit knowing: the contrast between tacit and focal knowing as that is exemplified by the Gestaltist's figure-ground relationship. Polanyi's claim is roughly that the figure in perception is known focally while the ground is known tacitly. Furthermore, as one shifts to perceiving the ground focally, the former figure recedes into the ground and becomes tacit. It is clear that tacit knowing would prove to be a valuable addition to Broudy's theory of interpretive uses of knowledge. For if the interpretation is tacit it would explain both the importance of the interpretive use as well as the difficulty of justifying that use in an age in which everything seems to have to be made focal in behaviorist terms in order to be recognized as important.

Tacit knowledge used interpretively can also be seen as extremely suggestive for my problem of how much and what kind of the others' disciplines must be learned for successful interdisciplinary work. One needs to learn enough so that this knowledge can be used to interpret the problem in the other disciplinary categories. Interpretive knowledge is almost surely used tacitly by the disciplinarian and this explains why it is so easy to overlook its importance in interdisciplinary work. Further, one often retreats to a common sense which is tacitly used by all when the going gets rough. My claim is that one *can* and probably must make this interpretive knowledge focal so that all can learn it well enough to enable it to function tacitly from then on in the operation of the group.

The minimal constituents of the amount of learning needed of the others' disciplines seem to be the following: First one must learn the observational categories of the other discipline and, second, one must learn the meanings of the key terms in the other discipline. Note that this would seem to allow one to interpret the problem in the others' terms but stops short of the full-fledged knowledge of theory, modes of inquiry, and ideals of the discipline, which the disciplinarian himself would possess. It would allow one, however, to understand the import of certain claims or recommendations made from the disciplinary point of view. Such knowledge by the participants in an interdisciplinary group is certainly not sufficient for success, but as I have argued, it is necessary and, clearly, has been largely overlooked in the past.

Let me try now to illustrate what I mean by observational categories and meanings of key concepts. Consider the following so-called "ambiguous figures."[7]

Do you see the martini in the first figure? Now, how about the torso of the girl wearing a bikini. Do you see the duck-rabbit in the second figure? Now consider the third figure of the young-old woman. This one is hard for many. The old woman is looking down and to the left. The young woman is looking away from the viewer and to the left. The old woman's mouth is the choker around the young woman's neck. Notice how, as Polanyi claims, what is focal for one interpretation becomes tacit for another. Note too how the cognitive concept seems to give meaning to the lines or parts of the drawings rather than the other way around. Imagine what it would be like to be a member of an interdisciplinary group discussing a problem in which the young-old woman, or something analogous, played a part. What would happen if your discipline allowed you to see the young woman, while another's discipline interpreted it as an old woman and you didn't realize the difference? Would you be tempted to retreat to your own narrow discipline and categorize those other folks as just silly? My suggestion here is quite simple. It often happens that when different disciplines look at the same thing (the same lines on the paper) they *observe* different things. Thus, it is necessary for people engaged in interdisciplinary work to understand each others' observational categories.

The second example concerns different meanings of key concepts and comes from a discussion section of a course I teach. I was sitting in on the section as an observer and the teaching assistant was trying to explain the difference between facts and values. He gave as an example, "Blacks score ten to fifteen points below whites on standard I.Q. tests," and asked whether this was a statement of fact or a statement of value. A classmember responded that it was a statement of value. This was *not* the correct answer. As discussion proceeded, it became clear that a very understandable difference of meaning was being attached to the concepts "fact" and "value" by the student and by the T.A.

By "fact" the T.A. meant any statement which *purported* to describe what is the case, whether we know if it is true or not. Thus controversial claims and even false claims were all facts to him at least as opposed to values which purport to say what *ought* to be the case. For the student, fact was limited to true, noncontroversial facts and all else was value. Again if different disciplines have different meanings for the same terms and this is not taken into account, one can predict almost certain failure for interdisciplinary projects.

But now if the interpretive use of tacit knowledge is what is required in the interdisciplinary situation, almost by definition it will be a difficult task to determine when the appropriate knowledge of observational categories and theoretical meanings will have been attained—at least short of full disciplinary training. This problem is particularly vexing when one considers just how systematically ambiguous varying interpretations of the world might be among several disciplines. Think of the young-old woman again. Two different disciplinarians might talk about "the woman" which both of them see for a long time without realizing they were talking about different things. For a long time some very intelligent people thought, and perhaps some still do think, that former President Nixon was really talking about a humanitarian response to Hunt's plight rather than hush money on that infamous March 21 tape.

The solution to this problem of how to tell when someone has learned a set of observational categories and theoretical meanings is in principle deceptively simple: introduce what would be a disturbance into the situation being observed and see if the other person counteracts the disturbance.[8] If the disturbance is counteracted, the appropriate categories and meanings probably have been learned. What does this mean? Consider again the young-old woman. If one is attempting to determine whether someone has learned to see the old woman, one might suggest that despite her age, she certainly has a lovely nose. If one can actually see the old woman, that should, for most, constitute a disturbance which would be resisted by some disclaimer as, "You call *that* nose lovely? You're out of your mind." In the case of the teaching assistant and the student who disagree on the meaning of "fact," the assistant can introduce examples of true facts, false facts, and controversial facts to see what sort of resistance the student puts forth. If all of these count as facts while a paradigmatic value statement is not, and vice versa, then the student probably understands the fact-value distinction.

A real life example occurred once in one of our general sessions during the Sloan project. Professor Nicholas Britsky was speaking to us on how the artist views the world and was showing us a series of slides of his own and others' work. Recall that we were a thoroughly interdisciplinary group with scientists, engineers, social scientists, and humanists. Professor Britsky came to a slide of one of his own abstract works. He was asked whether a certain predominant color area on the canvas could have been anywhere else, and his response was negative. Some in the audience agreed. To move that area would have constituted a disturbance from the perspective of the observational categories of those who understood and appreciated the art work. Others could not see the difference that would have been made. They had not yet assimilated the appropriate observational categories. The principle of introducing a disturbance to test for the presence of categorical and meaning knowledge is thus clear even if the application is often extremely difficult.

I have now identified the minimal cognitive level necessary for successful interdisciplinary work—namely, coming to use the observational categories and meanings of the other disciplines interpretively. I have also indicated, in principle, a test for when this use of knowledge has been attained. In conclusion, I want to sketch briefly the key pedagogical tool which I think needs to be employed to bring people to this minimal level of understanding of another's discipline. The tool I have in mind is metaphor—where "metaphor" is conceived of broadly as encompassing visual metaphors and even theories—models as they are often called in the sciences.[9]

Notice that the interdisciplinary situation is, by hypothesis, one which seems peculiarly apt for the kind of language which has surrounded metaphor.[10] The participants are familiar with one set of observational categories and meanings, their own, and they want to gain an insight into another system of observational categories and meanings. Metaphors traditionally have enabled us to gain an insight into a new area by juxtaposing language and concepts familiar in one area with a new area. One begins to see the similarities and differences between the literal uses of the metaphor and the new area to which we have been invited to apply the "lens" or "cognitive maps" supplied by the metaphor.

The notion of correcting disturbances enters again into the actual pedagogical use of metaphor. The students in the group begin by utilizing the inferences, concepts, and observational categories surrounding the literal use of the metaphorical term in the new to-be-learned area. Of course, certain adjustments are made due to the dissimilarities already perceived by the student between old and new areas of discourse. However, since the learning is being conducted in the presence of an already competent disciplinarian, the student who makes a wrong move with the metaphor creates a disturbance for the disciplinarian teacher. The disciplinarian's reaction shows the student that the move under discussion is part of the difference between the literal use of the metaphor and the new use. Gradually both come to react to disturbances in the same way, as already described.

I cannot begin to give many varied illustrations of pedagogically useful metaphors, primarily because it follows from my discussion that only competent disciplinarians can locate their own best metaphors. However, I shall try to give at least two. My own presentation here has used the ambiguous figures as visual metaphors for the important notion of theory-dependent observational categories. I have found by experience that this metaphor is usually extremely good pedagogically.

A second example I still remember from high school geometry. A very dear, old-fashioned teacher used it to explain the concepts of point as location, line as distance, and rectangle as plane surface. She held up a pencil and said, "Imagine this pencil sharpened as sharp as possible—and then sharpened much sharper than that. That's a point." Then she took this "point" in her fingers and drew it apart, saying, "Now, if I take the point and draw it apart like this, that's a line." Then he pulled the line down in front of her saying, "And if I pull this line down like so, that's a plane." For me that metaphor worked beautifully, and I think most disciplinarians would be able to come up with appropriate pedagogical metaphors for their own fields.

An important pedagogical point here is that through use and assimilation, metaphors die and take on simply an alternative technical meaning. When disciplinarians fail to realize that terms which they use in a technical sense—as dead metaphors—may be taken as quite live metaphors by their students, communication problems are almost certain to result. Thus the conscious and imaginative use of appropriate metaphorical devices seems to be required to bring the members of an interdisciplinary group to the requisite minimal level of understanding of each other's discipline. Once more we return to one of Harry Broudy's long-standing interests—the importance of humanistic education in general and, to the extent that metaphor is central to aesthetic education, to aesthetic education in particular. Although in this case, I'm not quite sure that Professor Broudy will approve of *that* much stretching of aesthetic education.

Summarizing, I have argued that for truly interdisciplinary as opposed to multidisciplinary efforts, the factors of idea dominance, psychological characteristics of the participants, and the institutional setting are all extremely important. With respect to epistemological considerations, I have urged that some mixes of disciplines require as a necessary condition for success that the participants must learn the observational categories and meanings of key terms of each other's discipline. This knowledge is then tacitly used in an interpretive way on the problems facing the group. One can tell when this minimal learning has been achieved by noting when disturbances are corrected. Finally, I have suggested that a conscious attention to a very broad notion of metaphor is the key of bridging the gap between the differing categories and concepts of the different disciplines. Only when you see what I see does interdisciplinary work have a chance.

Notes

1. See, for example, Harry S. Broudy, *The Real World of the Public Schools* (New York: Harcourt, Brace, Jovanovich, 1972), Ch. 7, and Harry S. Broudy, "On Knowing With," *Proceedings of the Philosophy of Education Society* (Edwardsville, Ill.: Studies in Philosophy and Education, Southern Illinois University, 1970), pp. 89–103.
2. Thomas Kuhn's work is probably the best known current position on the differences in cognition among different disciplines. See Thomas Kuhn, *The Structure of Scientific Revolutions*, 2nd ed. (Chicago: University of Chicago, 1970).
3. There is a large literature on the theory-dependence of observation. A classical source is N. R. Hanson, *Patterns of Discovery* (Cambridge: Cambridge University Press, 1958). A view which accepts much of the theory-dependency thesis yet objects to some of the more radical interpretations of it can be found in Israel Scheffler, *Science and Subjectivity* (New York: Bobbs-Merrill, 1967). For some of the pedagogical implications of this view, one might consult Hugh G. Petrie, "The Believing in Seeing," in *Theories for Teaching*, ed. by Lindley J. Stiles (New York: Dodd-Mead, 1974).
4. This problem was suggested to me by Dudley Shapere.
5. See Harry S. Broudy, B. O. Smith, and J. R. Burnett, *Democracy and Excellence in American Secondary Education* (Chicago: Rand McNally, 1964).
6. See Broudy, "On Knowing With," *Philosophy of Education Society*; Michael Polanyi, *Personal Knowledge* (Chicago: University of Chicago, 1958); and "The Logic of Tacit Inference," *Philosophy*, Vol. 40 (1966): 369–86, will get one started on Polanyi's views of tacit knowledge.
7. The martini-bikini was drawn for this paper. The duck-rabbit and the young-old woman were taken from N. R. Hanson, *Perception and Discovery*, ed. Willard E. Humphreys (San Francisco: Freeman, Cooper and Co., 1969), p. 90.
8. This notion of a disturbance and counteracting a disturbance which I am here using in what is hoped to be a nontechnical way receives a most illuminating and far-reaching technical treatment in William T. Powers, *Behavior: The Control of Perception* (Chicago: Aldine, 1973). In ten years this book will have generated a revolution in philosophy and psychology.
9. See my paper, "Metaphorical Models of Mastery: Or How to Learn to Do the Problems at the End of the Chapter in the Physics Text," presented to the Philosophy of Science Association meeting, Notre Dame, November, 1974, for a detailed analysis of the role of metaphor in pedagogical situations logically equivalent to the one obtaining for interdisciplinary work. This paper is scheduled for publication in *PSA 74: Boston Studies in the Philosophy of Science*, Vol. 32, 1975. See also Andrew Ortony, "Why Metaphors Are Neces-

sary and Not Just Nice," *Educational Theory*, Vol. 25, No. 1 (Winter 1975): 45–53; and Felicity Haynes, "Metaphor as Interactive," *Educational Theory*, Vol. 25, No. 3 (Summer 1975), 272–277.

10. The account of metaphor upon which I am relying is a fairly standard one as found, for example, in Max Black, *Models and Metaphors* (Ithaca, N.Y.: Cornell University, 1962).

Reading 10 Discussion Questions

1. What are the reasons, according to Harry Broudy, for the importance and necessity of interdisciplinary work?

2. List two reasons why interdisciplinary projects sometimes do not work.

3. What is the distinction between multidisciplinary and interdisciplinary work according to Petrie?

4. From your understanding of Reading 10:

   A) Provide at least one example of interdisciplinary work not discussed in the reading and explain why it is interdisciplinary.

   B) Provide at least one example of multidisciplinary work not discussed in the reading and explain why it is multidisciplinary.

5. Who is responsible for integration in multidisciplinary work?

6. What is meant by epistemology?

7. What are some non-epistemological considerations for doing interdisciplinary work?

8. List at least four psychological characteristics of those who are open to doing interdisciplinary work.

9. What is a cognitive map? List eight elements of a cognitive map.

10. What are the four ways in which we learn?

11. What is meant by tacit learning?

12. According to Petrie, what is tacit in interdisciplinary work?

13. According to Petrie, what are some of the minimum constituents of doing interdisciplinary work?

14. Provide three examples of how different disciplines observe differently that are not discussed in the reading.

Why Do Interdisciplinary Projects Fail?

In "Do You See What I See? The Epistemology of Interdisciplinary Inquiry," Petrie claims that one of the reasons why interdisciplinary projects fail is that they tend not to get off the ground. According to Petrie (1976), "the level of scholarship seldom exceeds that of a glorified bull session" (p. 30). Petrie does not inquire further why that may be the case. Bradbeer (1999) sees the "symptoms of problems in achieving interdisciplinarity in student learning" in three ways:

- Problems in working across disciplines: In particular these are the difficulties that students experience as they move from one discipline to another. These are, in effect, problems in working at the multidisciplinary level.

- Problems of working in different disciplines: The problems here are often those of failing to understand what different disciplines have to offer. These may be regarded as lying somewhere between multidisciplinarity and interdisciplinarity.

- Problems in synthesizing . . . : The ability to synthesize in this way must be regarded as one of the key characteristics of interdisciplinarity. (p. 382)

What exactly is to be synthesized? Bradbeer (1999) wrote "disciplines," which, as Newell has observed, is not adequately precise: It is the ability to synthesize *disciplinary insights* by first evaluating their underlying assumptions that is a key characteristic of interdisciplinary study (W. H. Newell, personal communication, July 30, 2004 personal communication). By now you should be realizing that precision in language is very important for doing interdisciplinary studies if not for all academic work.

Bradbeer (1999) views these three problems as existing "simultaneously at several different levels," the products of the following:

- Differences in disciplinary epistemologies;
- Differences in disciplinary discourses;
- Differences in disciplinary traditions of teaching and learning;
- Differences in students' preferred learning approaches and styles. (p. 382)

According to Bradbeer (1999), the problem of what Petrie calls "a glorified bull session" is the result of clashes between disciplinary "cultures." (p. 382). In other words, different disciplines use different languages, see the world differently, learn differently, think differently, and approach problems differently. There can be little wonder then why interdisciplinary projects do not progress sometimes. How can they progress if team members cannot communicate with one another, let alone understand each other?

Necessary Conditions for Interdisciplinarity

Petrie (1976) cites education scholar Harry Broudy in his assertion that "a complex technological society requires interdisciplinary solutions for its problems" (p. 30). Nevertheless, Petrie (1976) insists that certain conditions must be met for interdisciplinary projects to succeed. He then considers these conditions under the following four categories: non-epistemological considerations, psychological characteristics of participants, institutional setting, and epistemological considerations.

NON-EPISTEMOLOGICAL CONSIDERATION #1: IDEA DOMINANCE

What Petrie means by non-epistemological factors are those not strictly concerned with theories of knowledge. The primary non-epistemological consideration necessary for success in interdisciplinary endeavors, in Petrie's view, is idea dominance. Petrie (1976) defines idea dominance as the following:

> *a clear and recognizable idea which can serve as a central focus for the work. It can be embodied in a single individual who leads the project through force of personality or importance of the perceived mission. The dominant idea may be imposed by some external necessity clearly perceived by all participants. Finally it may be an idea embodied in a new and powerful theoretical concept or model—a concept which does not find a natural home in an established discipline. (p. 32)*

Idea dominance is truly an important factor or reason why some individuals become interdisciplinarians. As we have already seen in the case of Murray (1986), individuals who focus on certain issues, problems, or questions that cannot be easily answered by one discipline are well suited to becoming interdisciplinarians. The author of this textbook became an interdisciplinarian as the result of idea dominance. I became interested in answering the following question: what is the body going to look like in the future? When I started to do my research in 1994, cosmetic surgery had not yet enjoyed the popularity it does currently in the mass media. Indeed, it is now difficult to imagine that in the mid-1990s actual cosmetic surgery, or any other surgery for that matter, was rarely shown on television.

My research question was the result of "confrontations" or encounters with two women who have had cosmetic surgeries publicly for very different reasons. The first encounter was with the French multimedia artist Orlan, who had nine cosmetic surgeries framed as performance art between 1990 and 1993 in a conceptual art project entitled, *The Reincarnation of Saint Orlan*. Orlan used the biotechnology of cosmetic surgery to remake herself—but according to the ideals from the history of Western art. In so doing she has performed a critique of conventional standards of beauty as her appearance resembles more *Star Trek* than *Extreme Makeover*. (For more information about Orlan, including images, see <http://www.orlan.net>. The website is mostly in French but students can navigate around the site to see images from Orlan's surgical performances.)

The second encounter was with Cindy Jackson, "the woman who would be Barbie." Jackson has had multiple cosmetic surgeries and other procedures in an attempt to obtain conventional ideal beauty. Jackson's story is no longer that unusual, as many have followed her footsteps. Indeed, it has become increasingly more common for undergraduate college students to have not one but multiple cosmetic surgeries and other cosmetic procedures during college. The future of the body has arrived, and it looks a lot like Cindy Jackson. (For more information about Cindy Jackson, see <http://www.cindyjackson.com>)

This rather brief personal example of idea dominance is meant to provoke your thinking: what do you think about? What questions do you want answered? Richard W. Jackson's (2004) intellectual autobiography, "The Celtic Question" (see Reading 5) is an excellent example of how one student's "idea dominance" led to his quest for an interdisciplinary education.

NON-EPISTEMOLOGICAL CONSIDERATION #2: THE NEED FOR ACHIEVEMENT

Petrie (1976) includes the need for achievement as a non-epistemological factor even though he admits it is also a psychological achievement. In this context, the need for achievement is linked to idea dominance—an idea cannot remain dominant if it is not succeeding. Reputations will be damaged (of the person with the idea dominance), interest in the project will wane, and doubt will rise as to the feasibility of any project that seems to be going nowhere. Ultimately, as Petrie (1976) points out, "a powerful new theoretical idea will ultimately be shelved if it fails to achieve results" (p. 32).

OTHER CONSIDERATIONS

Petrie (1976) mentions institutional setting as one of the primary factors for success in interdisciplinary endeavors. While adequate administrative support for interdisciplinary studies degree programs is critical for success, institutional setting tends to be more of a concern for faculty than students since faculty need adequate support from their institutions to teach well.

Petrie (1976) furthermore asserts that "peer recognition" is also a necessity. Clearly peer recognition is important for interdisciplinary studies students: Who wants to major in a degree that no one recognizes? Something similar can be said for interdisciplinary studies faculty. Without adequate administrative support and peer recognition it will be very difficult to sustain a need or drive for achievement.

Another important factor for success in interdisciplinary endeavors is psychological in nature. Petrie lists the psychological characteristics of interdisciplinarians, all of which have been discussed in Chapter Four. We will turn next to the central concerns of this chapter: the nature of disciplines and guidelines for doing research on them.

EPISTEMOLOGICAL CONSIDERATIONS: COGNITIVE MAPS OF DISCIPLINES

Petrie's fourth category for interdisciplinary inquiry is extremely helpful for learning more about the nature of disciplines. Petrie is interested in those epistemological structures that make disciplinary knowledge possible. For Petrie, that epistemological structure comes in the form of a cognitive map. According to Petrie (1976), a cognitive map is "the whole cognitive and perceptual apparatus utilized by any given discipline" (p. 35). What does that mean in plain English? Perhaps a more basic understanding of a cognitive map of a discipline is its elements or components.

According to Petrie (1976), while every discipline has its own individual cognitive map, every discipline has the following elements:

- basic concepts
- modes of inquiry
- what counts as a problem
- observational categories

representational techniques
- standards of proof
- types of explanation
- general ideas of what constitutes the discipline (p. 35)

To these elements we can also add the following:

- assumptions and worldviews
- leading theories
- leading thinkers
- leading practitioners
- seminal texts/books
- leading academic journals
- official academic/professional associations

In the next section each of these elements will be discussed in more detail.

Elements of Any Given Discipline

BASIC CONCEPTS

Why is something so "basic" so difficult to understand? A concept is more than an idea or a notion of something. It is, according to Lawson (2004), a "mental construction" or "invention." In other words, we invent concepts—they do not exist in nature by themselves (p. 50). A good example that Lawson deploys to explain the concept of concepts is oxygen. Oxygen is invisible; we cannot see it, smell it, or touch it. Nevertheless, without it, we cannot breathe nor can fire burn. The efforts of scientists such as the Englishman Joseph Priestly and the Frenchman Antoine Lavoisier during the 1700s led to the discovery of the concept of oxygen as each scientist was trying to understand why fire burns.

Concepts are sometimes described as the "building blocks" to theories. Every discipline has basic building blocks or concepts that it builds upon as knowledge is advanced in the given discipline. For example, in biology, which is the study of life, a central concept may be cell, since it is among the most fundamental units of life. While there are single cell organisms, and there are parts of cells, cells are the basic unit to understanding life. In molecular or cellular biology, which has emerged from a sub-discipline in biology to a discipline in its own right, the basic concept is the gene. Often the basic concepts of a discipline correspond to the basic objects of inquiry or those objects that make the basic objects of inquiry possible. For example, if economies are the primary objects of study in economics, some basic concepts would include markets, trade, supply and demand.

What are some basic concepts in the disciplines you are investigating? If you are unable to identify the basic concepts of the disciplines you are studying, you will not be able to understand the discipline. Not only are the concepts the building blocks for theories, they also provide the basic vocabulary for the discipline. Can you imagine doing accounting without an understanding of the concepts of debit and credit? It would be difficult to understand economics without a strong grasp of both supply and demand.

Supply and demand are very basic concepts of economics. While it is important to know what are the basic concepts of a discipline and to study them thoroughly, you should also strive to go beyond the obvious in familiarizing yourself with disciplinary concepts. The more disciplinary concepts you can recognize and understand, the more knowledgeable you will be and the easier it will be for you to understand what experts in the field are saying and writing.

LEADING THEORIES

What is a theory? Klein notes (2001) that "the modern English word *theory* derives from the Latin *theoria*, which in turn, derived from the Greek *theorein*. Its root meaning is looking at or viewing, contemplating or speculating. In general use, a theory connotes a scheme or system of ideas and statements, with associated rules or principles" (p. 44). Theories, according to Lawson (2004), tend to consist of "a group of related concepts that derives meaning from one another and from analogies" (p. 51). Theories explain something, a general or universal phenomenon, usually by identifying relationships among concepts. As political theorist and former president of the American Political Science Association Kenneth N. Waltz (qtd. in Kreisler 2003) puts it:

> *What a theory does is present a mental picture of a part of the world, and in that picture are identified the major causal factors at work. The theory specifies the relations among those, and the necessary relations as they're necessary within the terms of their theory, among those major causal forces, which we often now refer to as variables (adopting a scientific terminology that's not always useful). That's a simple way of putting it. . . . Theory is a simple instrument in which you hope to be able to understand and explain the real world, The emphasis is on explanation, not prediction. Prediction is nice. If you can predict, fine. But the key requirement: if a theory is not able to explain what's going on, then it's not a theory, or it's a worthless theory. It's not a theory at all. (pp. 2–3)*

Examples of leading theories of human development would include Erik Erickson's psychosocial theory and Jean Piaget's cognitive theory.

It is important to be able to make the distinction between a theory and a hypothesis. Often what is considered a theory in everyday language is really an untested hypothesis. A hypothesis is a tentative explanation for a puzzling, particular or unique phenomenon (Lawson 2004, p. 10). For example, there are several leading hypotheses that attempt to explain who killed the late President John F. Kennedy, including the official "single bullet" hypothesis (often referred to as "theory"), which contends that Lee Harvey Oswald acted alone, and the less credible "second gunman" hypothesis that asserts there was a second gunman involved.

MODES OF INQUIRY (OR RESEARCH METHODS)

What research methods are used to carry out research? Does the discipline use qualitative, quantitative, or textual research methods? Does it utilize qualitative and quantitative methods like communication and other social science disciplines? When does it use qualitative and when does it use quantitative methods? If it uses interviews, are those interviews qualitative, quantitative, or both? These are questions you need to be able to answer before you can truly understand how researchers in the discipline conduct research.

WHAT COUNTS AS A PROBLEM?

What counts as a problem in communication, e.g., sexual harassment, may or may not be a problem in geography. Problems can overlap and co-exist, such as in the case of sexual harassment, since it is a problem in management and law as well as in communication.

OBSERVATIONAL CATEGORIES

How is a problem viewed? According to Petrie (1976), "when different disciplines look at the same thing (the same lines on the paper) they *observe* different things" (p. 38). For example, in viewing a photographic portrait, a psychologist may observe the portrait's body language as that of a well-adjusted person, while a sociologist may view the person's tattered clothing as someone who is struggling financially.

REPRESENTATIONAL TECHNIQUES

Any given problem may be represented in multiple ways. Each discipline will tend to have a certain way or ways to representing a problem. For any given problem in a specific discipline, students need to ask the following question: how is the problem represented? Is it represented as an equation? Is it presented as a case study? Is it presented visually in a painting or video? Or is it described in a narrative that is either written or performed? The more you analyze how problems are represented, the more you will understand the nature of the discipline.

TYPES OF EXPLANATION

There are different ways to explain solutions to problems just as there are different ways to represent the problems themselves. It is also important for students to understand how the practitioners of a given discipline explain things. Is the explanation of a problem represented as a proof (to the equation)? Is it presented visually? Is it described in words or in a story?

STANDARDS OF PROOF

Standards of proof are essential to any discipline. Think about the Internet. There are thousands if not millions of web pages and blogs. Anyone can write anything and publish their opinion, which may or may not be sufficiently based on reality. Tabloid magazines often publish rumors as fact. Disciplinary knowledge advances knowledge overall. The results of experiments, for example, need to be reproduced by other scientists before they can be accepted as true. When scholars submit their articles for publication in a peer-reviewed (also called "refereed") academic journal, the article is reviewed by at least three reviewers (or referees). The article is sent to the reviewers without the author's name; their comments and decisions regarding publication are sent to the author anonymously as well. This process is called a blind review, which produces the most objective evaluations possible.

In addition, there are minimum qualifications to be considered an expert in a discipline, or for that matter, to teach in that discipline. In most cases, the minimum qualification to hold a teaching position in a university is a Ph.D. or another terminal degree (such as a M.F.A. for the fine arts). College instructors and professors have on average at least five more years of education than their students, and typically many more.

GENERAL IDEALS OF WHAT CONSTITUTES THE DISCIPLINE

Many disciplines have a code of ethics. All disciplines have mission statements or a statement of purpose. These documents state what are the purpose, ideals and objectives of the discipline. In so doing they can reveal the implicit if not explicit values of a discipline. Determining a discipline's values is "important to interdisciplinarians trying to evaluate the appropriateness of the discipline's perspective in the context of the specific interdisciplinary issue or problem" (W. H. Newell, personal communication, July 30, 2004). For example, the implicit values of social workers may or may not be in conflict with those who study or practice real estate. While social workers may value a low-income housing project in a major city where poor children and their parents are living, real estate developers would prefer to tear down the project and build expensive condominiums for the wealthy. The social workers value helping the disadvantaged, while the real estate developers in this particular instance are not concerned about their welfare at all; they are more concerned about making profits and building new housing on prime real estate.

ASSUMPTIONS AND WORLD VIEWS

Every discipline inculcates its own assumptions and world views. For example, sociology has very different beliefs and views about poverty than economics. Sociology tends to see poverty the result of societal factors, while economics will see poverty as the result of market factors or even as the result of individual irresponsibility or mismanagement.

DISCIPLINARY PERSPECTIVE

As already discussed in Chapter Six, each discipline sees the world differently. Each discipline will thus approach a given problem or issue differently. It is up to the student to understand how each discipline approaches problems.

SEMINAL TEXT/BOOKS

In any disciplines there will be certain books or other texts (e.g. articles, films, reports) that most of the practitioners have read. These texts usually provide a foundational framework for the discipline, or setting out major concepts, theories, or both.

MAJOR THINKERS

Major thinkers are often those individuals who have written seminal texts in a discipline but not always. In one way or another, their ideas have contributed greatly to the discipline.

MAJOR PRACTITIONERS

Certain practitioners are more known for excelling in a given discipline than contributing intellectually. For example, a major business practitioner would be Bill Gates. While Gates has written books, he is more known for his lucrative business practices than his intellectual ideas.

OFFICIAL PROFESSIONAL/ACADEMIC ASSOCIATIONS AND LEADING ACADEMIC JOURNALS

Every discipline (and often sub-discipline) has its own corresponding professional organization to which its practitioners in the discipline belong. For example, your literature professor very likely belongs to the Modern Language Association (MLA) and attends its annual conference. Your literature professor would also receive the official refereed journal of the MLA, *Publications of the Modern Language Association of America* (*PMLA*). The official organization for interdisciplinary studies is the Association for Integrative Studies (AIS). AIS sponsors an annual conference as well as publishes the quarterly *Newsletter of the Association for Integrative Studies* and the annual official, refereed journal, *Issues in Integrative Studies* (*IIS*).

Table 7-1 15 Elements of a Discipline
(What Every Student Should Know about Each Discipline)

Basic concepts
Modes of inquiry (or research methods)
What counts as a problem
Observational categories
Representational techniques
Types of explanation
Standards of proof
General ideals of what constitutes the discipline
Assumptions and worldviews
Disciplinary perspective
Seminal texts/books
Major thinkers
Major practitioners
Professional academic associations
Leading academic journals

Reading 11

In the next reading Dirk Olin gives an account of the development of a new interdisciplinary area or sub-discipline of finance (which in itself can be viewed as a sub-discipline of economics), behavioral finance, which draws from psychology and economics.

READING

PROSPECT THEORY

by

Dirk Olin

From the infamous Dutch tulip hysteria of the 17th century to the Great Depression to the dot-com crash, wild bouts of speculation have occasionally inflated big fat financial bubbles that soaked investors when they burst. Daniel Kahneman, a professor at Princeton who was the first psychologist to win the Nobel in economics (which he was awarded last year for studies he conducted with Amos Tversky), has attributed market manias partly to investors' "illusion of control." Kahneman recently explained the basic weirdness of the dot-com bomb to *The Financial Times:* "A high percentage of investors knew it was a bubble and still invested because they thought they could get out in time." Why did so few heed the alarms? According to Kahneman's "prospect theory," most of us find losses roughly twice as painful as we find gains pleasurable. This radical precept subverts much of "utility theory," the longstanding economic doctrine that says we weigh gain and loss rationally. When combined with the reality that some market winners display the same recklessness as some victorious gamblers—a phenomenon that Richard Thaler, an economist at the University of Chicago, calls "the house-money effect"—the market is often revealed to be downright loony. Indeed, the findings of "behavioral finance" in recent years have increasingly challenged the fundamental rationality assumed by defenders of "efficient markets," those who believe Eugene Fama's famous dictum that prices "fully reflect available information." Fama, another economist from the University of Chicago, is saying that you can't get ahead of the market by building a clever model, because you can't predict the news that will affect prices. (As for the crazy players, Fama has contended that big-time rational arbitrageurs counterbalance them.) So, as stocks have shown some new life this spring, can you put your trust back in the market?

Thumbnail Economics

A fairly straight line of standard economic theory runs from the late 1700's to the 20th century. First came the "invisible hand" that Adam Smith said guided decision-making according to basic market logic. This was refined in the early 19th century by Jeremy Bentham into a philosophy of utilitarianism that assumed, among other things, that consumers knew what was best for themselves. John Maynard Keynes challenged some of that doctrine's underpinnings during the 1930's, when he compared market participants to viewers trying to guess the outcome of a beauty contest. Milton Friedman subsequently helped rescue rationalism during the post-World War II period, arguing that most market participants behave as if they had made rational calculations, even if they were not consciously making those calculations. In 1979, however, Kahneman and Tversky published a paper that included results from subjects who answered two comparative money problems. And their responses appeared to reveal systematic deviations from rationality: In problem No. 1, subjects were given an imaginary $1,000 and asked to choose between (a) a 50 percent chance to gain $1,000 and a 50 percent chance to gain nothing and (b) a sure gain of $500. In problem No. 2, subjects got $2,000 and were asked to chose between (a) a 50 percent chance to lose $1,000 and a 50 percent chance to lose nothing and (b) a sure loss of $500. The results? In the first problem 84 percent chose (b). In the second, 69 percent chose (a). What's odd here is that if the majority opt for the $1,500 of (b) in problem No. 1, the majority therefore ought to take the same $1,500 payout in answer (b) in the second problem. But instead the majority is willing to take the risk to try to "break even" when the problem is framed in terms of losses. Irrationally, people feel differently about losing than they do about gaining, even if either choice produces the same outcome.

Hedging the Theories, or Practical Advice

The Princeton economist Buton Malkiel, whose investing classic, *A Random Walk Down Wall Street,* has just come out in its eighth edition, mostly touts efficient markets. Like Fama, he says he believes that prices tend to go up over time but without any discernible pattern that can be used to predict future movements. Unlike Fama, however, Malkiel concedes that bursts of market irrationality do occur, which is why he calls himself "a random walker with a crutch." "There are lots of good lessons to be taken from behavioral finance," Malkiel says. "But what it doesn't do is provide any kind of clear road map for cool sharp-penciled professionals to beat the market. For example, the existence and extent of bubbles are only discernible in retrospect."

Interestingly, irrational- and rational-market experts provide much the same advice for investors: buy into index funds that are pegged to broad swaths of the market rather than trying to play selected sectors. Then hold. You might expect that advice from the efficiency mavens, but how do the behaviorists—who say you should be able to exploit the crazy market players—square that conservative circle? "While behaviorists think that it is theoretically possible to beat the market," Richard Thaler says, "individual investors do not have the time or training to do that on their own, and finding superior skills among active mutual-fund managers is not easy, either. So a reasonable strategy to adopt is to settle for the average returns and low fees offered by index funds."

An existentialist corollary for your consideration. More than a few philosophers have sermonized that behaving as if an afterlife exists is beneficial to society in the here and now, even if the belief turns out to be unfounded. Now listen to Malkiel: "To the extent that the behaviorists are right, few if any could take those insights and beat the market. In other words, you ought to act as if the markets are efficient."

Of Higher Interest

Fama, E. F. "Market Efficiency, Long-Term Returns and Behavioral Finance," *Journal of Financial Economics,* Vol. 49, pp. 283–306 (1998). For less empirical market studies, on film, see also Oliver Stone's *Wall Street* and John Landis's *Trading Places.*

Kahneman, D., and Tversky, A. "Prospect Theory: An Analysis of Decision Under Risk," *Econometrica,* Vol. 47, pp. 263–292 (1979).

Malkiel, B. G. *A Random Walk Down Wall Street.*

IDENTIFYING ELEMENTS OF A NEW SUB-DISCIPLINE/ EMERGENT DISCIPLINE

Based on Reading 11, you are to determine the cognitive map for behavioral finance. Answer the following questions as thoroughly as you can.

1. What is **the object of study** in behavioral finance? In other words, what is or are its **central question(s)**?

2. What are some **major concepts** of behavioral concepts? For example, market volatility is a major concept of behavioral finance.

    List others here:

3. What are some **major theories** of behavioral finance? For example, Daniel Kahneman's prospect theory explains what causes the phenomenon of "market manias."

    List other behavioral finance or economic theories discussed in the reading here:

4. List at least one **research method** discussed in the article used to study behavioral finance.

5. Who are some of the **major thinkers** of behavioral finance?

6. Who are some of the **major thinkers** of economics?

7. List some of the **seminal texts/books** of behavioral finance:

    List some seminal texts/books in economics:

8. What is a **major assumption/worldview** of behavioral finance?

9. What is a **major assumption/worldview** of economics that is in disagreement with a major collective believe/world view of behavioral finance?

 *Exercise originally developed by Tanya Augsburg. It was modified and enhanced by Kelly Nelson, David Thomas, and Layne Gneiting.*

Worksheet for Researching Disciplines

The following worksheet is in two parts: First you will find the worksheet guidelines that will be helpful to you as you begin to research various disciplines. Following the guidelines is the actual worksheet. Make copies of the worksheet before you start writing in it. Use one worksheet for each investigated discipline. Take the time to find the best possible sources of information. You should choose your sources carefully. Do not rely on either dictionaries or encyclopedias for definitions. Do consult your class notes, textbooks, professors, departmental websites at renowned universities, websites of professional academic associations, and leading academic journals. Do not rely only on Internet sources. Make the time investment to do library research—it will pay off handsomely in dividends as you progress in your education. Be sure to cite correctly, following the citation style your instructor expects you to follow (usually MLA or APA citation style).

In the process of researching and answering each prompt, you will gain a more comprehensive understanding of the discipline. You will have a better understanding of how an expert in the discipline thinks. Ultimately you will have a better understanding of the culture of the discipline. Be sure to vet your findings with the findings of your fellow students and especially with the writings of experts in the discipline you are researching.

GUIDELINES FOR RESEARCHING DISCIPLINES WORKSHEET

Name of Discipline: _____

Discipline Subject Matter:
What is the object(s) of study? What is this discipline about?

Definition of Discipline:
Find an academic definition, by consulting textbooks, academic disciplinary journals, books published by university presses, departmental or professional academic organization web sites. Do not try to define a discipline by looking up the word in the dictionary!

Sub-Fields within a Discipline:
How is this discipline organized or divided? Can this discipline be broken down further into smaller areas (sub-fields)? Carefully describe the purpose or goal of each sub-field. What specific concerns do each sub-field address?

Research Methods:
What methods do researchers use to answer their research questions? You should be able to identify at least one major research method commonly used to do academic research in the discipline. Be specific and use examples that illustrate current research in the discipline.

Key Concepts:
What are some of the key concepts associated with this discipline? You should be able to identify at least three key disciplinary concepts and define them according to how they are defined within the discipline. It is important that you understand how a given discipline defines a specific concept as another discipline may define the concept differently.

Leading Theories:
You should be able to identify and comprehensively describe at least two leading theories associated with the discipline.

Key Books/Seminal Texts:
List three influential, well-known or seminal texts in the field. Be sure to provide a correct, full citation (APA or MLA style) plus a brief description of what each is about and why it is important to the discipline.

Key Thinkers and Practitioners:
List three top thinkers in the discipline. Try to list people who have not authored any of the key books you have listed above. Provide each thinker's name, birth and death year (if deceased), and a brief description of their contribution to the field.

Try to do the same with the top practitioners in the discipline. Do not be alarmed if you have trouble with identifying practitioners. While the practitioners in some discipline will be more commonly known (e.g. business), some more "academic" or scholarly disciplines may rely more on thinking than doing (e.g. physics).

Profesional/Academic Journals:
List at least two titles of academic journals. Note: academic journals are not the same as trade journals. Describe the nature of each publication and its intended audience.

Professional/Academic Associations:
List the names (and web site locations) of several professional academic associations pertaining to the discipline.

WORKSHEET FOR RESEARCHING DISCIPLINES

Name of Discipline: _____

Discipline Subject Matter:

Definition of Discipline Plus Parenthetical Citation(s):

Sub-Fields within a Discipline Plus Parenthetical Citation(s):

Research Methods Plus Parenthetical Citation(s):

Key Concepts Plus Parenthetical Citations:

Key Concept #1 Plus Parenthetical Citation(s):

Key Concept #2 Plus Parenthetical Citation(s):

Key Concept #3 Plus Parenthetical Citation(s):

Leading Theories Plus Parenthetical Citations:

Leading Theory #1 Plus Parenthetical Citation(s):

Leading Theory #2 Plus Parenthetical Citation(s):

Key Books/Seminal Texts:

Key Book/Seminal Text #1:

Why Key Book/Seminal Text #1 Is Important:

Key Book/Seminal Text #2:

Why Key Book/Seminal Text #2 Is Important:

Key Book/Seminal Text #3:

Why Key Book/Seminal Text #3 Is Important:

Key Thinkers and Practitioners:

Key Thinker #1:

Key Thinker #2:

Key Thinker #3:

Key Practitioner #1:

Key Practitioner #2:

Key Practitioner #3:

Professional Academic Journals:

Academic Journal #1:

Academic Journal #2:

Professional Academic Associations:

Professional Academic Association #1:

Professional Academic Association #2:

REFERENCES [APA CITATION STYLE]

OR

WORKS CITED [MLA CITATION STYLE]

Selected Readings

Bradbeer, J. (1999). Barriers to interdisciplinarity: Disciplinary discourses and student learning. *Journal of Geography in Higher Education*, 23 (3), 381–396.

Kegan, R. (1994). *In over our heads: The mental demands of modern life*. Cambridge, MA, and London: Harvard University Press.

Klein, J. T. (2001). Interdisciplinarity and the prospect of complexity: The tests of theory. *Issues in Integrative Studies*, *19*, 43–57.

Kreisler, H. (2003, Feb. 10). Theory and international politics: Conversation with Kenneth N. Waltz, Ford Professor Emeritus of political science, UC Berkeley. Video Transcript [Electronic version]. Institute of International Studies, UC Berkeley. Retrieved July 22, 2004 from <http://globetrotter.berkeley.edu/people3/Waltz/waltz-con0.html>

Lawson, A. (2004). *Biology: An inquiry approach*. Dubuque, IA: Kendall Hunt.

Petrie, H. G. (1976). Do you see what I see? The epistemology of interdisciplinary inquiry. *Journal of Aesthetic Education*, 10, 29–43. [See Reading 10 in this volume.]

PORTFOLIOS FOR INTERDISCIPLINARY STUDIES STUDENTS

Day by day, my future becomes clearer through my portfolio reflections and my collected materials, and with the combination of the skills that I have already and what I have yet to learn, my future seems to be getting brighter.

Paul Rosenberg (2004, p. 202)

Learning Objectives

By reading Chapter Eight of *Becoming Interdisciplinary* you should be able to:

1. Understand what are portfolios.
2. Recognize different kinds of portfolios.
3. Know what is an artifact.
4. Generate your own artifacts.
5. Be familiar with the history of portfolios.
6. Create your own portfolios.

What Are Portfolios?

There are many definitions of portfolios these days. Most are pretty similar, although some are better phrased than others. Kimeldorf (1997) points out that the word derives from Latin: *port* — means to carry and — *folio* means papers. Kimeldorf (1997) defines *portfolio* as "a portable collection of papers and/or artifacts" (p. 12).

While his definition is pretty straightforward it needs some tweaking to take account of the electronic age. Collections of papers no longer have to be physical since they can be virtual and viewed on a computer screen. As Crockett (1998) insightfully points out, any definition of portfolios should place its emphasis on the contents of the portfolio rather than on what or how they are contained (p. 4). So for the purposes of this textbook a working definition of portfolios is the following:

Portfolios are either portable collections or electronic spaces in which you can show specific things, namely artifacts, which communicate both visually and verbally your identity, your interests, your skills, your talents, and your qualifications.

What are artifacts? Artifacts are documented pieces of evidence and samples, usually paper documents, but can be others things too—such as photos or samples of artwork. Artifacts are like pieces of evidence for the "case" you wish to present. The type of case you are making (as well as the type of artifacts you are choosing) depends on the type of portfolio you are putting together. Examples of artifacts will be provided in the next section.

Types of Portfolios Helpful to College Students

There are numerous types of portfolios that students can use during their college career. Sometimes students are asked to use the same portfolio for different functions, which can lead to confusion. Some common types of portfolios are the following:

SELF-DISCOVERY PORTFOLIO

This portfolio allows one to collect and store information regarding personality assessment, value assessment, dreams, and goals. Personal discovery artifacts include mission statements, personality tests such as the Meyers-Briggs, interests indicators such as the Strong Interests Inventory, personal written narratives such as intellectual autobiographies, visual personal narratives such as autobiographical maps, personal strengths and weaknesses inventories, skills lists, lists of goals, dreams, etc.

The Self-Discovery Portfolio answers the question, "Who am I?"

LEARNING OR EDUCATIONAL PORTFOLIO

This portfolio facilitates the collection and storage of artifacts from one's education experience. According to Cole, Ryan, Kirk, & Mathies (2000), educational portfolios should include a clearly defined purpose as well as the following: student-selected artifacts, student reflections on their selected artifacts, artifacts that demonstrate improvement and mastery, and artifacts that demonstrate growth (p. 12). Educational artifacts can include all of the following:

- Sample work from coursework: papers, class projects, tests, presentation materials, etc.
- Syllabi
- Brochures or fliers that describe seminars, special training, and workshops
- Award letters for scholarships
- Recommendation letters
- Reflections on one's education
- Transcripts or list of courses taken with course descriptions
- List of skills and knowledge contents learned in courses
- Evidence of integration skills
- Sample interdisciplinary work from one's education
- Write-ups of extracurricular activities, service learning, internships, co-ops
- Research reports
- Writing Samples
- Evaluations of coursework (graded work) (See ASU Career Services 1998/2002)

If the primary purpose of the learning portfolio is to track a student's progress within a single course, then the portfolio is known as a ***course portfolio***. If the primary purpose of the portfolio is to track a student's progress throughout a particular program, then that learning portfolio is considered a ***program portfolio***. In the case of many interdisciplinary studies programs, a program portfolio is established in the introductory course and then is revisited in the senior seminar. This chapter will be mainly concerned with interdisciplinary studies program portfolios.

The Learning Portfolio says, "Look how far I've come in my (interdisciplinary studies) education. This is what I have learned."

CAREER PLANNING PORTFOLIO

This portfolio can help a student prepare, for and during, one's job search. Information about companies, letters of recommendation, and résumés are among the documents stored in a career portfolio.

The Career Planning Portfolio says, "This is what I am qualified to do and look where I am heading."

SHOWCASE PORTFOLIO (ALSO KNOWN AS PROFESSIONAL PORTFOLIO)

This portfolio is the one that you would take to an interview setting. The showcase portfolio would contain few but highly selective documents that would showcase or best display one's skills and talents. Among the documents to be included would be one's mission statement; one's résumé; samples of excellent coursework; volunteer activity; work experience; lists of skills; lists and descriptions of courses taken. The selection of the most relevant artifacts is crucial for the showcase portfolio. Accordingly, you should revise and/or update your showcase portfolio for each job interview, as its contents should be specific to each position for which you are applying. Your showcase portfolio is more than your own "greatest hits" album; it should contain the "evidence" to make the best possible case for why you are the best candidate for the position(s) you are applying.

The Showcase Portfolio proudly exclaims, "Look how fabulous am I!"

ELECTRONIC PORTFOLIO

This portfolio is an electronic or web-based version of the showcase portfolio. Electronic portfolios can have similar formats as personal web pages that have a home page and additional links to other sections or categories. Electronic portfolios need not be uploaded to the Internet, however. They can be saved on a CD-ROM. Saving your electronic portfolio on disks may be a safer option if you are concerned about identity theft or having your work stolen or plagiarized. If you prefer to have your electronic portfolio online, you may want to consider having your personal documents password protected. Even with password protection you should avoid uploading any document that contains your home address or personal telephone numbers. Most importantly, you must take care not to upload any document that contains your college ID number or your Social Security Number!

You can find out more information about creating your own electronic portfolio at the following websites:

- Albion College digital portfolio site available at:
  <http://www.albion.edu/digitalportfolio>
- GateWay Community College electronic portfolio site available at:
  <http://www.gwc.maricopa.edu/class/e-portfoio/index.html>
- Kalamazoo College portfolio page available at
  <http://www.kzoo.edu/pfolio/index.html
- LaGuardia Community College portfolio site available at
  <http://www.eportfolio.lagcc.cuny.edu>

The Electronic Portfolio boldly announces to the world, "Look how super-fabulous am I!"

Combination or Hybrid Portfolios

There are other types of portfolios that are a combination or a hybrid of the portfolios listed above. For example, the contents of program portfolios usually do not remain constant. What types of artifacts are combined in a hybrid portfolio that a student has at any given moment really depends on where the student is in the program at that particular time. A portfolio created during an introductory course may emphasize personal discovery and/or career exploration while trying to link one's personal interests with one's educational and professional goals. Thus an introductory-level program portfolio may have the following components:

Personal Discovery + Learning + Career Planning Portfolios

By the time students register for what is often the final course of their college years, i.e., their interdisciplinary studies senior seminars, their concerns often shift as students tend to be preoccupied with their lives after graduation. While students may be asked to revisit and to complete the portfolios they initiated in their introductory courses, the contents of their portfolios may change drastically to reflect their growing professional concerns. Thus a learning program portfolio produced for a senior interdisciplinary studies seminar may have the following components:

Learning + Career Planning + Professional Portfolios

In other words, the interest in personal discovery decreases while the interests in career planning and professional showcasing increase. The learning or educational component also increases: by the time they are in their senior seminar courses students would have completed more coursework since completing their introductory course and thus have produced and collected more educational artifacts. By the time they graduate interdisciplinary studies students should have an abundant amount of interdisciplinary artifacts demonstrating interdisciplinary thinking, interdisciplinary skills, interdisciplinary team projects, interdisciplinary research, and other interdisciplinary work.

If students keep all their educational artifacts in their program portfolios, their portfolios can become massive, heavy tomes by the time they reach what is often the final course of their college careers. Their program portfolios may become too unwieldy to bring to class, let alone to a job interview. Thus it is a good idea to create a showcase portfolio that is a summary or condensation of the hybrid portfolio.

Other Kinds of Useful Portfolios

Of course there are many other types of portfolios as well that are extremely helpful for personal use and getting organized. The following list is only suggestive:

- Personal Portfolio
- Wellness Portfolio
- Personal Finances Portfolio
- Business Plans Portfolio
- Stock Research Portfolio
- Hobbies Portfolio
- Recipes Portfolio
- Travel Portfolio
- Volunteer Work Portfolio
- Multiple Intelligence Portfolio

A Short History of Portfolios

Portfolios have been around for a long time. Artists have used them as early as the seventeenth and eighteenth centuries, first to secure commissions and then to get into art academies. As other careers and jobs emerged, other people began to use portfolios, especially those who do freelance work. For example, graphic artists and writers also create and maintain collections of their work in portfolios. Fashion models rely on "books" that showcase their best photographs to secure further work. Anyone wanting to go into advertising needs to have a creative portfolio that contains sample ads and related projects.

By the late 1980s and early 1990s educators borrowed the concept of portfolios for various purposes. Many prospective teachers create portfolios to demonstrate their teaching skills for job searches. Once they begin teaching, many teachers use portfolios as teaching assessment tools. Indeed, there exists a great amount of literature regarding teaching portfolios for teachers at the elementary, secondary and university level. Portfolios have even entered the elementary and secondary classrooms as tools for assessing students' work, so it is not surprising that portfolios would become a tool for college students as well.

What is surprising is that portfolios have not yet become a standard practice among college students, although that is beginning to change. Art and design students have been required to have portfolios to gain admission to art schools for quite some time. The portfolios are also required to help art and design students prepare to become creative professionals as the basis of many creative careers is in freelance work rather than steady jobs. Many writing composition courses now require course portfolios that document the progress of students' writing skills during the course of a semester or two. For the most part, however, college students have been introduced to the idea of portfolios through university career service programs where portfolios have recently been embraced as a vital career planning tool.

Why Do Interdisciplinary Studies Students Need Portfolios?

Clearly one does not have to be a student majoring in interdisciplinary studies or an interdisciplinary program to benefit from being required to create and maintain portfolios throughout their education. Interdisciplinary studies programs that require portfolios for their majors require either program portfolios that tracks students' progress throughout their education, specific course portfolios, or even hybrid interdisciplinary program portfolios that help students integrate the personal, the educational, and the professional.

More and more interdisciplinary studies programs are requiring program portfolios for their majors. In effect, such programs require that their students create, maintain, and revisit a program portfolio as they complete their coursework for their degrees. These portfolios are not only incorporated within the curriculum but are usually an integral component of it. Interdisciplinary studies program portfolios are particularly designed to facilitate students to integrate their personal, educational, and career interests.

Some universities, such as Truman State University in Missouri, require portfolios from all their graduating students. Among the numerous artifacts Truman State requires of its graduates is an interdisciplinarity artifact demonstrating the student's ability to integrate knowledge. More information about Truman State University's Portfolio Project can be found at <http://assessment.truman.edu/components/Portfolio/index.htm>.

Portfolios are also excellent tools for preparing for life after graduation. As Bridges (1994) points out, the concept of a "job" is a relatively recent one that is a direct consequence of industrialization and the rise of the factory. For most of the twentieth century, most employed individuals worked at a single job for their entire careers. Towards the end of the twentieth century, the concept of the job has become increasingly obsolete as most organizations went through major restructuring. At many organizations work no longer is organized around jobs but around work that needs to be done (Bridges 1994).

Currently at the dawn of the twenty-first century people now work as members of project teams that exist only as long as the project. No longer do individuals expect to work for the same organization or, for that matter, to do the same type of work for the duration of their working years. The reality of the twenty-first century workplace is that employees are increasingly becoming "portfolio professionals" who can now expect to change careers an average of seven times. Maintaining a career portfolio helps employees document all their accomplishments in the workplace as well as their transferable skills that are necessary for advancing or changing careers.

Portfolios: A Necessity in the Postmodern World

Portfolios are increasingly becoming a necessity in today's job market. As it is more and more commonplace for people to switch not only jobs but also careers, it is becoming increasingly more crucial to be able to document your skills and accomplishments. In order to be able to claim that you are an interdisciplinarian, you will have to be able to prove it by documenting your ability to integrate, i.e., your integrative skills, which can be demonstrated by your interdisciplinary artifacts. Moreover, it is vital to be able to show how the skills you utilize at one job or career can be transported to another job or career.

In his description of what he terms "the postmodern condition," Lyotard (1983) asserts that we are now living in an age of self-legitimation, which means that there is a decreasing reliance on outside accreditation for professional identities. Think about it: more and more people are outsourcing, becoming consultants, and/or starting their own business. What qualifies them to do so?

In contrast, what makes a doctor a doctor? A lawyer a lawyer? Their degrees and certification allow them to practice their professions. Without a license to practice medicine or law, doctors and lawyers cannot work legally. External accreditation will continue to be a necessity for these professions and many others. A consultant, however, needs no such certification. A consultant will probably have advanced degrees, but the consultant's expertise will be demonstrated from previous work and recommendations—work and recommendations that undoubtedly have been documented in a professional portfolio that is shown to prospective clients.

Putting together your program and showcase portfolios can legitimate you in terms of your unique personal experiences (your biography), your education, your work experiences, and your skills. Your portfolios will demonstrate your experience, your knowledge, your skills, and your accomplishments, which range from completed class projects, evidence of teamwork and other activities, to awards and accolades you have received. Just as you learn in your writing composition and public speaking classes that you must back up any claim you make in your papers and speeches with evidence, so must you back up your claims for any work you wish to do.

Obviously, if you have not placed much effort in your college career you will have a more difficult time putting together a spectacular interdisciplinary studies program portfolio. The old adage that you will reap what you sow certainly applies here. Nevertheless, assembling an interdisciplinary studies program portfolio will still be a worthwhile project even for those students with less than a stellar academic career. The process of making a portfolio and the final result, the portfolio itself, will make abundantly clear what is lacking and where you need to improve. If you do not have many suitable educational artifacts you might want to consider what are your strengths and emphasize those. If you are uncertain about a career choice, analyzing the artifacts you collect for your personal discovery, educational, and career development sections of your program portfolio should identify your strengths and those activities in which you like to engage further.

For most college students, putting together portfolios yields many pleasant surprises, as students are able to identify and demonstrate skills that perhaps they did not even realize that they had. You worked hard for your college degree! Let your portfolios show how much you learned and gained from your education and experiences. Table 8.1 lists the positive outcomes for student portfolios identified by Augsburg and Helms (2000).

Table 8-1 Student Portfolio Outcomes (Augsburg and Helms 2000)

1. Actively engages students in the learning process.
2. Tracks integrative skills.
3. Documents educational experiences and development.
4. Identifies skills and understand their transferability.
5. Makes connections between curricular, co-curricular and work experiences to the world of work.
6. Enhances the academic advising experience for students.
7. Places the responsibility of career development with the student.
8. Identifies and solidifies career goals, choices, and opportunities.
9. Collects and organizes important career and work-related information.
10. Increases self-efficacy by documenting and examining experiences.
11. Can be utilized for making future career transitions.

The Importance of Saving Your Work

When I first started to assign portfolios to students, I was very surprised to learn that many of my students had not saved any work that they had done while in college. It never dawned on them that they should save their work. Some students claimed that the reason they had not saved their work was because no one had told them to do so, let alone explain to them that the papers they wrote in English 101 could be useful to demonstrate how their writing has improved.

Other students told me that the reason why they did not save their schoolwork was limited space. Who wants all that paper lying around? I can understand that way of thinking—to a point. True, many college students move around frequently, so having less stuff to carry around is certainly a plus in their eyes. Portfolios, however, are wonderful organizational and paper management tools. Paper clutter can be alleviated and even avoided altogether with portfolios since paper can be stored neatly in one place.

While I can understand the need to throw paper out, I am unable to understand why students do not save multiple electronic copies of their work. All too often students have only one diskette of all their schoolwork with no backup files. Those students then learn the hard way the consequences when that diskette becomes lost or destroyed by a computer virus: all of their work becomes irretrievably lost.

I would be willing to bet money that if students were told very early in their college careers that they were required to maintain a portfolio to document their education in order to graduate, virtually all college students would have pretty comprehensive educational portfolios by the time they were seniors. The most appropriate time and place to introduce students to educational portfolios are during the freshman orientation week before classes even begin. This way, students are acquainted with the concept of portfolios before beginning their first assignment.

Assembling Your Portfolio

How do you put together a portfolio? First of all, you will need to purchase at least the following materials to create your portfolio:

- A three-ring binder
- Section dividers
- Plastic sheet protectors

What kind of binder you will need depends on what kind of binder you wish to create. Course portfolios are smaller than program portfolios, so usually 1" or 2" binders will be adequate. Program portfolios need to be bigger—3" or 5". Binders shouldn't have flimsy covers. Binders that have a plastic sleeve on the front cover allow greater individualization in appearance. You can slip a piece of paper or a photograph inside the sleeve in order to give your portfolio an individualized decorative cover. Even if you would rather your cover be plain you should at the very least have your name stated on the cover. In contrast, showcase portfolios should be 1" or 2" and be made out of leather or similar looking material for a more professional look.

Since your portfolios will be constantly in flux as you will continually update them, you will need to protect your artifacts by putting each piece of paper in a sheet protector. This way when pages are turned by your readers they are less likely to be ripped. You will then not have to hole punch your artifacts, so they will be less likely to rip and fall out.

THE APPEARANCE OF YOUR PORTFOLIO COUNTS!

The appearances of your portfolios are crucial for the impression you wish to make. Your portfolios will be a reflection of you and your values. How do you value yourself? How do you value your education? Surely you value yourself and your education—you would not be investing so much time, money, and effort if you did not. It makes perfect sense then that your portfolios should reflect your investment (and protect it as well). Your portfolios will also be a visual representation of yourself. Like it or not, you will be evaluated on if not judged by the quality of both the contents and appearance of your portfolio. You really have no other option but to create an exceptional looking portfolio that reflects your individuality and your efforts.

There is no single template for how your portfolios should look, which is why it can be an extremely effective tool for self-marketing. While showcase portfolios should look as professional as possible, they nevertheless should reflect your individuality and creativity. Program portfolios have more leeway for self-expression. While many students prefer a professional look to represent their education, others may prefer a more "scrapbook" feel. Some students use various crafts such as stamps and glitter to create unique covers. Often students put photographs of themselves on the cover, which is terrific. Nevertheless, be certain that the photograph gracing your portfolio cover is appropriate. You will want to present yourself professionally, so avoid goofy, funny, embarrassing, or sexy photographs of yourself. Of course you want to look attractive, but your portfolios are not intended for dating purposes. Unless you plan to become a swimsuit model there is no reason why you should have a cover photograph of yourself in a bathing suit or wearing otherwise revealing attire.

SELECTING ARTIFACTS FOR YOUR PORTFOLIO

You have to decide what goes into your portfolios, particularly your showcase portfolio. What best illustrates your capabilities and potential? What best demonstrates what you have learned and how? That first paper you wrote in college may be worth including if its purpose is to demonstrate pre-growth or how much you have improved. For each artifact you should ask yourself the following questions:

- Why do I wish to include this particular artifact?
- What does it demonstrate and how?

For some artifacts you will have to include both a title and a description of that artifact's significance so that the reader can understand readily its significance (Kimeldorf 1994). Such explanation can be done on a separate page or by attaching a caption to the artifact.

IDENTIFYING SPECIFIC SKILLS AND KNOWLEDGE

As you select your artifacts you will be reflecting on your education and what you have learned. You should also try to identify exactly what you have learned in each of your courses. You have learned some specific knowledge and some specific skills in every class you have taken. Even if you hated a class and can swear you have learned nothing, in actuality you have learned some things. For starters, you probably learned the skill of overcoming adversity. If your professor was problematic you may have learned how to deal with difficult people. Finally, if you hated the course's subject matter or found it boring you have learned some valuable lessons about yourself. You should ask yourself why you disliked the course material. Very likely all of these lessons have influenced your subsequent educational decisions, whether it was to not take any more classes in that discipline or even to changing your major. On a more positive note, what did you learn in your favorite classes? If you enjoyed learning in your favorite classes, was it because you believed that the lessons learned were extremely valuable? What were those valuable lessons? Your favorite classes probably influenced your subsequent educational decisions as well.

Being able to identify and articulate the specific knowledge contents and skills you have is a very important skill that requires some practice. All too often students tend to underestimate rather than overestimate the skills they have acquired, whether those skills were obtained in one's education, work experiences, volunteer experiences, extracurricular experiences, or life experiences. Students underestimate their skills in part because they have yet to identify adequately their own skills. Have you ever made a list of all your skills? You might want to try making lists of skills that you have developed from various activities. For example, students are always amazed to learn how many skills they learn from their freshman writing composition class or from waiting tables. What kind of portfolios artifacts would demonstrate those skills? For example, what kinds of artifacts would document a volunteer activity? What kinds of artifacts would demonstrate teamwork?

Developed by Chris Helms

Identify those skills by making the following two lists of the specific skills and knowledge you have learned in your freshman writing composition class.

Skills Learned in ENG 101   **Knowledge Learned in ENG 101**

Developed by Chris Helms

Identify by making a list of possible portfolio artifacts that demonstrate the skills and knowledge you obtained in your freshman writing composition class that you listed in Exercise 8-1.

ENG 101 Portfolio Artifacts

Organization Strategies

How should you organize your portfolio? You will probably spend a lot of time trying to answer this question. For example, should you organize your portfolio according to chronology or to skills you have been obtaining? Should you include a personal section, an education section, and a career section? Where should you place your awards and achievements? It would make sense to create a separate "Awards and Achievements" section. Your instructor may provide you with specific organizational guidelines. While there are numerous ways you can organize your portfolio, you should probably avoid paginating your portfolio unless your instructor tells you to do so as the page numbers and sequence will very likely change. The following checklists should help you decide what to include in the following three types of portfolios: course portfolio, program portfolio, and the showcase portfolio.

INTRODUCTORY COURSE PROGRAM PORTFOLIO CHECKLIST

Front Matter:
- Title Page
- Table of Contents
- Mission Statement

Interdisciplinary Studies Program/Intro Course Artifacts:
- Your Interdisciplinary Studies Program Information (home page/program description and/or requirements + course info)
- Definition of Interdisciplinarity (Either the textbook's or the one you developed in Chapter Two)
- Metaphor for Interdisciplinarity and Explanation
- Intellectual Autobiography/Personal Narrative (and/or Autobiographical Map)
- Disciplinary Research
- Example of Integrative Process (Integrative Process Worksheet from Chapter Six)

Personal Discovery Artifacts:
- Strong Interests Inventory Test + One-Page Reflection
- Myers/Briggs + One-Page Reflection
- Your Five Top Values + Values Reflection
- Your Top 5 Skills + Skills Reflection/Indication of Where You Obtained Them
- Your Personal Strengths/Weakness Inventory List
- List of Goals

Educational Artifacts:
- Lists of Skills and Knowledge Contents Learned From Coursework
- Educational Reflections
- Investigating Academic Professional Literature
- Discussion/Analysis of an Interdisciplinary Project
- Analysis of an Interdisciplinary Concept(s)
- Interdisciplinary Thinking Educational Artifact

Career Research/Professional Artifacts:
- Résumé
- Career or Business Research
- Informational Interview

General Education Portfolio Artifacts:
- Writing Samples (with favorable evaluations if possible)
- Academic accomplishments within Areas of Emphasis
- Letters of Recommendation
- Academic Transcript
- Awards or certificate of Merit or accomplishment
- Samples of Artwork/Design/Project
- Write-up/Evidence of Volunteer Activity and/or Internships
- Other

APPEARANCE:

Materials:
- Attractive, Appropriate Three-Ring Binder
- Plastic Sheets/Page Covers
- Dividers

_____ Excellent _____ Very Good _____ Fair _____ Needs Improvement _____ No Effort Made

Neatness (no visible price stickers, no blank plastic sheets etc):

_____ Excellent _____ Very Good _____ Fair _____ Needs Improvement _____ No Effort Made

Organization (portfolio is clearly divided into reasonable categories):

_____ Excellent _____ Very Good _____ Fair _____ Needs Improvement _____ No Effort Made

Creativity:

_____ Excellent _____ Very Good _____ Fair _____ Needs Improvement _____ No Effort Made

Overall Effort:

_____ Excellent _____ Very Good _____ Fair _____ Needs Improvement _____ No Effort Made

SENIOR SEMINAR PORTFOLIO/PROGRAM PORTFOLIO CHECKLIST

CONTENTS CHECKLIST:

Front Matter:
- Title Page
- Table of Contents
- Mission Statement

Interdisciplinary Studies Program/Course Artifacts:
- Definition of Interdisciplinarity
- Interdisciplinary Metaphor
- Copy of Interdisciplinary Studies Program Home Page with Program Description and/or Requirements
- Autobiography/Personal Narrative (and/or Autobiographical Map)
- Samples of Interdisciplinary Work
- Sample Syllabi
- Sample Assignments
- Reflections of Courses/What I Have Learned

Personal Discovery Artifacts:
- Strength/Weakness Personal Inventory
- Skills and Knowledge Learned/Developed from Courses
- Skills and Knowledge Developed from Life/Job/Internship Experiences
- Indication of where and how you learned each skill

Career/Professional Artifacts:
- Career/Professional Artifacts:
- Résumé
- List of Professional Goals
- Evidence of Internship Activity
- Evidence of Work Experience
- Work Performance Evaluations

General Portfolio Artifacts:
- Writing Sample (with favorable evaluations if possible)
- Academic accomplishments
- Letters of Recommendation
- Academic Transcript
- Awards or certificate of Merit or accomplishment
- Samples of Artwork/Design/Project
- Write-up/Evidence of Volunteer Activity
- Other

APPEARANCE:

Materials:
- Attractive, Appropriate Three-Ring Binder
- Plastic Sheets/Page Covers
- Dividers

_____ Excellent _____ Very Good _____ Fair _____ Needs Improvement _____ No Effort Made

Neatness:
_____ Excellent _____ Very Good _____ Fair _____ Needs Improvement _____ No Effort Made

Organization:
_____ Excellent _____ Very Good _____ Fair _____ Needs Improvement _____ No Effort Made

Creativity:
_____ Excellent _____ Very Good _____ Fair _____ Needs Improvement _____ No Effort Made

Overall Effort:
_____ Excellent _____ Very Good _____ Fair _____ Needs Improvement _____ No Effort Made

SHOWCASE PORTFOLIO CHECKLIST

Front Matter:
- Title Page
- Table of Contents
- Mission Statement
- Résumé
- Autobiography/Personal Statement
- List of Courses (If Applicable)

Interdisciplinary Studies Program Section:
- Copy of Program Home Page Plus Program Description/Requirements
- Sample Interdisciplinary Work from Introductory Course
- Sample of Interdisciplinary Coursework
- Sample Interdisciplinary Work from Senior Seminar Course
- Reflection: What I Have Learned in My Interdisciplinary Education
- Reflection on My Integrative Skills

Skills:
- Strength/Weakness Personal Inventory
- Skills Learned/Developed from Courses in Emphasis Areas
- Skills Developed from Life/Job/Internship Experiences
- Indication of where and how you learned each skill
- Sample of Integration Skills

Other:
- Writing Samples from Other Coursework (with favorable evaluations if possible)
- Academic accomplishments within Areas of Emphasis
- Letters of Recommendation
- Academic Transcript
- Awards or Certificate of Merit or accomplishment
- Samples of Artwork/Design/Project
- Write-up/Evidence of Volunteer Activity
- Samples from Work Experience
- Other

APPEARANCE:

Materials:
- Professional Quality/Attractive, Appropriate (Leather) Binder
- Plastic Sheets/Page Covers/Dividers

_____ Excellent _____ Very Good _____ Fair _____ Needs Improvement _____ No Effort Made

Neatness:

_____ Excellent _____ Very Good _____ Fair _____ Needs Improvement _____ No Effort Made

Design:

Typography:	treatment of font size and style support your design
Balance of design:	too much white space, not enough white space, centered, graphic/picture placement
Consistency of design:	reader is able to easily access your work, consistent page layout
Conciseness:	no extra artifacts that don't support your message

_____ Excellent _____ Very Good _____ Fair _____ Needs Improvement _____ No Effort Made

Creativity:

_____ Excellent _____ Very Good _____ Fair _____ Needs Improvement _____ No Effort Made

Overall Effort:

_____ Excellent _____ Very Good _____ Fair _____ Needs Improvement _____ No Effort Made

CHECKLIST FOR SHOWCASE PORTFOLIO (QUESTIONS TO ASK YOURSELF)

1. Does your showcase portfolio clearly answer the question, "How do I want prospective employers to think of me and my work?"

    YES!   Yes   Average   no   NO!

2. **Selection:** Do the artifacts in your showcase portfolio represent your qualifications for the position?

    YES!   Yes   Average   no   NO!

3. **Interdisciplinarity/Synthesis/Integration:** Did you represent your education as interdisciplinary adequately? Did you include evidence of interdisciplinary work? Did you indicate that you have done interdisciplinary work/research/projects?

    YES!   Yes   Average   no   NO!

4. **Language Mechanics:** Is your portfolio free of spelling, punctuation, and grammatical errors?

    YES!   Yes   Average   no   NO!

5. **Organization:** Is your showcase portfolio appropriately organized?

    YES!   Yes   Average   no   NO!

Presenting Your Portfolio to Others: Practice Makes Perfect

Once you assemble your program portfolio, you will have an easier time putting together your showcase portfolio. By reviewing all your artifacts you will be in a better position to select what should go into your showcase portfolio. Once you have a showcase portfolio, however, you need to practice presenting it to others. One way to do so is to simulate an interview situation. What kind of interview depends on your goals: if you plan to go to graduate school after graduation, you should prepare for an admissions committee interview. If you plan to enter the workforce, you should prepare for a job interview. If you plan to continue working at the same organization after you graduate, you may want to practice for a meeting during which you will ask for a promotion or a raise. You should practice answering the following questions:

- Can you tell me about yourself?
- What is an interdisciplinary studies degree?
- Why did you major in interdisciplinary studies?
- Can you explain your degree program?
- What did you study/integrate while you were in college?
- What kind of skills did you learn during college?
- What is your biggest strength? Your biggest weakness?
- Why do you want this position? Or, why do you want to go to graduate school?

Some instructors will assign a portfolio presentation along with a portfolio assignment. Some instructors will request that you present your portfolio to them privately in their office, where they will simulate an interview situation by playing the role of the interviewer. Other instructors will ask students to present their presentations in class, which can be a bit nerve wracking for students who feel uncomfortable about public speaking. You can alleviate any nervousness about public speaking by making your presentation seem more like an actual interview. One way to simulate an interview situation is to ask a fellow student or the instructor to play the role of the interviewer. The advantage of doing a portfolio presentation in front of your peers is the potential for constructive feedback from them.

Students watching the other presentations can take written notes on little slips of paper with each presenter's name on them. After each presentation the student audience members can use the slips of paper to indicate whether or not they would "hire" the presenter. The comments can be written anonymously and then given to the instructor after all the presentations are over. The instructor can also create folders for each student, so that students can drop off their notes for each presenter in the appropriate folder. Once the distribution of notes is completed presenters can pick up their folders and can read the anonymous feedback (Augsburg 2003).

Even if you are not assigned a portfolio presentation for class, it is a good idea to practice on your own, enlisting friends or family members for help. If no one can help you, you can always practice in front of the mirror or in front of your pet dog or cat. Before you can practice your presentation you need to know exactly who your interviewer is supposed to be. If you know exactly what type organization you wish to work for after graduation you should at the very least do some Internet research so you can familiarize yourself with the particular industry. Better yet, try to find out which organizations interest you, and learn all you can about them. If you are planning to go to graduate school, you should research what specific graduate programs and schools. In other words, you need to prepare as much as possible for the presentation of your showcase portfolio.

You should practice your presentation while using your showcase portfolio as a visual aid. If your showcase portfolio is electronic, practice accessing your electronic portfolio and navigating your way to your documents. If at all possible try to organize your showcase portfolio in the order of the points you will be making during your presentation. You will be investing a lot of time putting together your program and showcase portfolios. Take the time to make them work for you!

Selected Readings

Arizona Board of Regents for Arizona State University and Its Department/Office of Career Services. (1998/2002). Portfolio development: What to include in your portfolio [Form 274]. Tempe, Arizona: Arizona State University.

Augsburg, T. (2003). Becoming interdisciplinary: The student portfolio in the Bachelor of Interdisciplinary Studies program at Arizona State University. *Issues in Integrative Studies*, 21, 98–125.

Augsburg, T. & Helms, C. (2000). *Student Portfolios Collaboration with Academic Units = Successful Career Planning*. Paper presented at the annual meeting of Rocky Mountain Association of Colleges and Employers (RMACE), Scottsdale, AZ.

Bridges, W. (1994, Sept. 19). The end of the job. *Fortune Magazine*, 62–74.

Cole, D. J., Ryan, C. W., Kick, F. & Mathies, Bonnie K. (2000). *Portfolios across the curriculum and beyond* (2nd ed.). Thousand Oaks, CA: Corwin Press.

Crockett, T. (1998). *The portfolio journey: A creative guide to keeping student-managed portfolios in the classroom*. Englewood, CO: Teacher Ideas Press.

Kimeldorf, M. (1994). *Creating portfolios for success in school, work and life*. Minneapolis, MN: Free Spirit Publishing.

Kimeldorf, M. (1997). *Portfolio power: The new way to showcase all of your job skills and experiences*. Princeton, N.J.: Person's.

Lyotard, J.-F. (1993). *The postmodern condition: A report on knowledge*. Trans. G. Bennington & B. Massumi. Foreword by F. Jameson. Minneapolis: University of Minnesota Press.

Rosenberg, P. (2004). What a long, strange trip. In J. Zubizareta (Ed.), *The learning portfolio: Reflective practices in student, faculty, and institutional learning* (pp. 76–82). Bolton, MA: Anker Publishing.

Zubizareta, J. (Ed.). (2004). *The learning portfolio: Reflective practices in student, faculty, and institutional learning* (pp. 76–82). Bolton, MA: Anker Publishing.

PART THREE

SUPPLEMENTARY READINGS

CLUSTER ONE

ON METHODS OF INTEGRATION: TRANSFER SKILLS

Reading 12

You have been briefly introduced to numerous methods of doing interdisciplinary throughout this textbook, including the following:

1. Metaphor or analogical thinking
2. Newell's 1983 model of the integrative process
3. Disciplinary Research
4. Longitudinal method (tracking your progress as an interdisciplinarian over time with your program portfolio)

Two methods, translation and borrowing, were mentioned in passing in Chapter One and deserve further discussion. A good source on borrowing is Chapter Five in Klein (1990). Future editions of this textbook will address translation and borrowing in more depth. Reading 12, "Teaching for Transfer," by D.N. Perkins and Gavriel Salomon, considers transfer as a general learning method. The method of transfer is related to borrowing in the sense that it is taking something, whether it is knowledge or a skill, from one discipline or knowledge domain and applied in another. Transfer is also related to translation when transferring or borrowing concepts from one discipline or another since a concept in one discipline can be defined or deployed differently in another similar to what happens to a word when it is translated from one language to another.

While Perkins and Salomon wrote for an audience of educators, their ideas about transfer are especially pertinent for interdisciplinary studies majors. Transfer as a method has two special applications: (1) in contemporary art and (2) in the invention and innovation of new ideas or products. In a nutshell, transfer is a technique of innovation. When the artist Orlan framed cosmetic surgery as performance art for her conceptual art project, *The Reincarnation of Saint Orlan*, she was transferring the skills and conventions of surgical performance into the arena of contemporary art. Artist Eduardo Kac collaborated with biologists in order to transfer technological skills and knowledge for the creation of transgenetic mice, fish, plants, and bacteria for his highly conceptual transgenetic art project, *The Eighth Day* (2001). Orlan and Kac's work are only two of many examples from contemporary art.

There are also too many examples from the business world to cite here, but one dramatic example is worth mentioning: the inventor of Velcro®, George de Mestral, after much trial and error, was able to transfer the same hook-like fastening quality that he observed in burrs sticking to his clothes and his dog's fur while walking in the woods to synthetic material. The reading mentions several examples of knowledge and skills transfer. You should start thinking about the types of knowledge and skills transfer you have done throughout your education, as well as brainstorm about possible innovative transfers you can do in the future.

READING

TEACHING FOR TRANSFER

by

D.N. Perkins and Gavriel Salomon

Students often fail to apply knowledge and skills learned in one context to other situations. With well-designed instruction, we can increase the likelihood that they will.

Facing a move across town and concerned with economy, you rent a small truck to transport your worldly possessions. You have never driven a truck before and wonder whether you can manage it. However, when you pick the truck up from the rental agency, you find yourself pleased and surprised. Driving the truck is an experience unfamiliar, yet familiar. You guide the vehicle through the city traffic with caution, yet growing confidence, only hoping that you will not have to parallel park it.

This everyday episode is a story of transfer—something learned in one context has helped in another. The following line of poetry from Shakespeare also shows transfer: "Summer's lease hath all too short a date." Regretting the decline of summer in his Sonnet 18, Shakespeare compares it to, of all things, a lease. The world of landlords and lawyers falls into startling juxtaposition with the world of dazzling days, cumulus clouds, and warm breezes.

Your experience with the truck and Shakespeare's metaphor differ in many ways. From driving a car to driving a truck is a short step, while from leases to summer seems a long step. One might speak roughly of "near transfer" versus "far transfer." In the first case, you carry a physical skill over to another context, whereas, in the second, Shakespeare carries knowledge associated with leases over to another context. One might speak of transfer of skill versus transfer of knowledge, and, although here we will focus on those two, other sorts of things might be transferred as well; for instance, attitudes or cognitive styles. Finally, the first case is everyday, the second a high achievement of a literary genius. Nonetheless, despite these many contrasts, both episodes illustrate the phenomenon of transfer. In both, knowledge or skill associated with one context reaches out to enhance another. (It is also possible to speak of negative transfer, where knowledge or skill from one context interferes in another.)

Transfer goes beyond ordinary learning in that the skill or knowledge in question has to travel to a new context—from cars to trucks, from lawyers to summer, or across other gaps that might in principle block it. To be sure, that definition makes for a fuzzy border between transfer and ordinary learning. For example, if car-to-truck is a gap, so in some sense is automatic transmission to standard transmission, or Ford automatic to Chrysler automatic. But the last two and especially the last do not seem intuitively to be different enough to pose a significant gap. In practice, we have a rough sense of what gaps might be significant and, although that sense may not always be accurate, nothing in this article will depend upon drawing a perfectly sharp line between transfer and ordinary learning.

If transfer figures in activities as diverse as moving across town and writing sonnets, it is easy to believe that transfer has at least a potential role in virtually all walks of life. But transfer does not take care of itself, and conventional schooling pays little heed to the problem. With proper attention, we can do much more to teach for transfer than we are now doing.

Why Is Transfer Important to Education?

Any survey of what education hopes to achieve discloses that transfer is integral to our expectations and aspirations for education. First of all, the transfer of basic skills is a routine target of schooling. For example, students learn to read *Dick and Jane* or *A Tale of Two Cities* not just for the sake of reading other texts but in preparation for a much wider range of reading—newspapers, job applications, income tax forms, political platforms, assembly instructions, wills, contracts, and so on. Students learn mathematical skills not just for the sake of figuring Sammy's age when it is two-thirds of Jane's, but for smart shopping in the supermarket, wise investment in the stock market, understanding of statistical trends, and so on.

Another expectation of education concerns the transfer of knowledge. The "data base" students acquire in school ought to inform their thinking in other school subjects and in life outside of school. For example, European and American history should help students to think about current political events—the traditions that shape them, the economic and political factors that influence them, the reasons why one votes or acts in certain ways in the political arena. Literary studies should help students to think about fundamental problems of life—the cycle of birth and death, the struggle for dominance, the quest for love, and how one's own life incarnates those eternal dramas. Science instruction should help students to understand the world around them—the branch waving in the wind as an oscillator, a city as an artificial ecology, the threat and promise of nuclear power or genetic engineering.

Finally, transfer plays a key role in an aspiration of education that lately has attained great prominence: the teaching of thinking skills. As with basic skills and knowledge, here again the aim is not just to build students' performance on a narrow range of school tasks. One hopes that students will become better creative and critical thinkers in the many contexts that invite a thoughtful approach-making important life decisions, casting votes, interacting with others equitably, engaging in productive pursuits such as essay writing, painting, and so on.

Why Is Transfer Worrisome in Education?

The implicit assumption in educational practice has been that transfer takes care of itself. To be lighthearted about a heavy problem, one might call this the "Bo Peep" theory of transfer: "Let them alone and they'll come home, wagging

---

Must We Choose Between Cultural Literacy and Critical Thinking?

From certain quarters today comes a wave of pessimism about the prospects of transfer and the potentials of teaching for general cognitive skills. One recent and popular spokesperson for a negative position is E. D. Hirsch, Jr. (1987), who offers in his *Cultural Literacy* an eloquent plea for turning away from general skills and equipping youngsters with the varied basic knowledge that makes one culturally literate.

Such a response is quite understandable in the face of the naive approach to problems of learning and transfer typically found in schools. Often, educators have expected broad global nonspecific transfer from highly specialized activities such as the study of Latin or computer programming, as though these activities exercised up some generic mental muscle. Often, educators have not focused on exactly *what* about such activities might transfer nor made efforts to decontextualize the transferable aspects and bridge them to other contexts. Often, educators have sought to impart lengthy lists of "microskills" for reading or other performances, an approach that seems doomed to sink in the quicksand of its own complexity.

On the other hand, Hirsch and others who would turn their backs on general skills overmake their case. Hirsch, for example, adopts a strong local knowledge position, asserting that the prospects for transfer are meager. However, we argue for the considerable potentials of transfer if attention is paid to fostering it. Throughout *Cultural Literacy*, Hirsch periodically snipes at the teaching of critical thinking, intimating that attention to such general skills pays no dividend. But we emphasize that some aspects of critical thinking plainly call for attention—thinking on the other side of the case, for example.

Ironically, in framing his argument, Hirsch commits one of those lapses of critical thinking he sees no need for schools to address: he creates a false dichotomy, treating as contraries factors that are compatible and indeed complementary. This is one of the most common slips of critical thinking, one that well-designed education could help us all to become more mindful of. Specifically, although basic knowledge of our culture has a commonly neglected importance, as Hirsch argues, this does not imply that critical thinking and other kinds of general knowledge and skill are unimportant. Plainly, more than one thing can be important at the same time. Of course, an articulate monolithic view such as his makes better press. It may even work to correct the opposite excess better than would a balanced appraisal. But it rarely captures the real complexity of human skill and knowledge.

—*D.N. Perkins and Gavriel Salomon*

their tails behind them." If students acquire information about the Revolutionary War and the Westward emigration, if they learn some problem-solving skills in math and some critical thinking skills in social studies, all this will more or less automatically spill over to the many other contexts in and out of school where it might apply, we hope.

Unfortunately, considerable research and everyday experience testify that the Bo Peep theory is inordinately optimistic. While the basic skills of reading, writing, and arithmetic typically show transfer (for reasons to be discussed later), other sorts of knowledge and skill very often do not.

For example, a great deal of the knowledge students acquire is "inert" or "passive." The knowledge shows up when students respond to direct probes, such as multiple choice or fill-in-the-blank quizzes. However, students do not transfer the knowledge to problem-solving contexts where they have to think about new situations. For example, Bransford and his colleagues have demonstrated that both everyday knowledge and knowledge acquired in typical school study formats tend to be inert (Bransford et al. 1986, Perfetto et al. 1983). Studies of programming instruction have shown that a considerable portion of beginning students' knowledge of commands in a programming language is inert even in the context of active programming, where there is hardly any gap to transfer across (Perkins and Martin 1986, Perkins et al. 1986). Studies of medical education argue that much of the technical knowledge student physicians acquire from texts and lectures is inert—not retrieved or applied in the diagnostic contexts for which it is intended (Barrows and Tamblyn 1980).

It has often been suggested that literacy is one of the most powerful carriers of cognitive abilities. Olson (1976), for example, has argued that written language permits patterns of thinking much more complex than can be managed within the limited capacity of human short-term memory. Moreover, written texts, in their presentational and argument structures, illustrate patterns of thinking useful for handling complex tasks. Literacy, therefore, ought to bring with it a variety of expanded cognitive abilities. To put the matter in terms of transfer, literacy should yield cognitive gains on a number of fronts, not just the skills of reading and writing per se.

The difficulty with testing this hypothesis is that people usually learn to write in schools, at the same time that they learn numerous other skills that could affect their cognitive abilities. This dilemma was resolved when Scribner and Cole (1981) undertook a detailed study of the Vai, an African tribe that had developed a written language which many members of the tribe learned and used, but that maintains no tradition of formal schooling. Remarkably, the investigators' studies disclosed hardly any impact of Vai literacy on the cognitive performance of Vai who had mastered the written language. The hypothesized transfer did not appear.

Another source of discouraging evidence about transfer comes from contemporary studies of the impact of computer programming instruction on cognitive skills. Many psychologists and educators have emphasized that the richness and rigor of computer programming may enhance students' cognitive skills generally (e.g., Feurzeig et al. 1981, Linn 1985, Papert 1980). The learning of programming demands *systematicity* breaking problems into parts, diagnosing the causes of difficulties, and so on. Thinking of this sort appears applicable to nearly any domain. Moreover, as Papert (1980) has urged, programming languages afford the opportunity to learn about the nature of procedures, and procedures in turn provide a way of thinking about how the mind works. While all this may be true, the track record of efforts to enhance cognitive skills via programming is discouraging. Most findings have been negative (see reviews in Clements 1985b, Dalbey and Linn 1985, Salomon and Perkins 1987).

Another well-investigated aspect of learning has been the effort to teach somewhat retarded individuals the basic cognitive skills of memory. Learning some basic strategies of memory familiar to any normal individual can substantially improve the performance of retarded learners. However, in most cases, the learners do not carry over the strategies to new contexts. Instead, it is as though the memory strategies are "contextually welded" to the circumstances of their acquisition (Belmont et al. 1982).

With this array of findings contrary to the Bo Peep theory, it is natural to ask why transfer should prove so hard to achieve. Several explanations are possible. Perhaps the skill or knowledge in question is not well learned in the first place. Perhaps the skill or knowledge in itself *is* adequately assimilated but *when* to use it is not treated at all in the instruction. Perhaps the hoped-for transfer involves genuine creative discovery—as in the case of Shakespeare's metaphor—that we simply cannot expect to occur routinely.

While all these explanations have a commonsense character, one other contributed by contemporary cognitive psychology is more surprising: there may not be as much to transfer as we think. The skills students acquire in learning to read and write, the knowledge they accumulate in studying the American Revolution, and the problem-solving abilities they develop in math and physics may be much more specific to those contexts than one would imagine. Skill and knowledge are perhaps more specialized than they look. This is sometimes called the problem of "local knowledge"; that is, knowledge (including skill) tends to be local rather than general and crosscutting in character.

The classic example of this problem of local knowledge is chess expertise, which has been extensively researched. Chess is an interesting case in point because it appears to be a game of pure logic. There is no concealed information, as in card games: all the information is available to both players. It seems that each player need only reason logically and make the best possible move within his or her mental capacity.

However, in contrast with this picture of chess as a general logical pursuit, investigations have disclosed that chess expertise depends to a startling degree on experience specifically with the game. Chess masters have accumulated an enormous repertoire of "schemata"—patterns of a few chess pieces with significance for play (de Groot 1965, Chase and Simon 1973). One pattern may indicate a certain threat, another a certain opportunity, another an avenue of escape. Skilled play depends largely on the size of one's repertoire. A chess player may be no more adept at other intellectual pursuits, such as solving mysteries or proving mathematical theorems, than any layperson.

Findings of this sort are not limited to chess. They have emerged in virtually every performance area carefully studied with the question in mind, including problem solving in math (Schoenfeld and Herrmann 1982), physics (Chi et al. 1981, Larkin 1983, Larkin et at. 1980), and computer programming (Soloway and Ehrlich 1984), for example.

In summary, diverse empirical research on transfer has shown that transfer often does not occur. When transfer fails, many things might have gone wrong. The most discouraging explanation is that knowledge and skill may be too "local" to allow for many of the expectations and aspirations that educators have held.

When Does Transfer Happen?

The prospects of teaching for transfer might be easier to estimate with the help of some model that could explain the mechanisms of transfer and the conditions under which transfer could be expected. Salomon and Perkins (1984) have offered such an account, the "low road/high road" model of transfer. The model has been used to examine the role of transfer in the teaching of thinking (Perkins and Salomon 1987), to forecast the impact of new technologies on cognition (Perkins 1985), and to review the findings on transfer of cognitive skills from programming instruction (Salomon and Perkins 1987).

AL the heart of the model lies the distinction between two very different mechanisms of transfer—low road transfer and high road transfer. The way learning to drive a car prepares one for driving a truck illustrates low road transfer. One develops well-practiced habits of car driving over a considerable period. Then one enters a new context, truck driving, with many obvious similarities to the old one. The new context almost automatically activates the patterns of behavior that suit the old one: the steering wheel begs one to steer it, the windshield invites one to look through it, and so on. Fortunately, the old behaviors fit the new context well enough so that they function quite adequately.

To generalize, low road transfer reflects the automatic triggering of well-practiced routines in circumstances where there is considerable perceptual similarity to the original learning context. Opening a chemistry book for the first time triggers reading habits acquired elsewhere, trying out a new video game activates reflexes honed on another one, or interpreting a bar graph in economics automatically musters bar graph interpretation skills acquired in math. This low road transfer trades on the extensive overlap *at the level of the superficial stimulus* among many situations where we might apply a skill or piece of knowledge.

High road transfer has a very different character. By definition, high road transfer depends on deliberate mindful abstraction of skill or knowledge from one context for application in another. Although we know nothing directly of Shakespeare's mental processes, it seems likely that Shakespeare arrived at his remarkable "Summer's lease hath all too short a date" not by tripping over it, but by deliberate authorial effort, reaching mentally for some kind of abstract metaphorical match with the decline of summer. After all, in contrast with the resemblance between car and truck cabs, no superficial perceptual similarity exists between summers end and leases to provoke a reflexive connection.

Whatever the case with Shakespeare, more everyday examples of high road transfer are in order. It is useful to distinguish between at least two types of high road transfer—forward reaching and backward reaching. In forward-reaching high road transfer, one learns something and abstracts it in preparation for applications elsewhere. For instance, an enthusiastic economics major learning calculus might reflect on how calculus could apply to economic contexts, speculate on possible uses, and perhaps try out some, even though the calculus class does not address economics at all and the economics classes the student is taking do not use advanced math. A chess player might contemplate basic principles of chess strategy, such as control of the center, and reflectively ask what such principles might mean in other contexts—what would control of the center signify in a business, political, or military context?

In backward-reaching high road transfer, one finds oneself in a problem situation, abstracts key characteristics from the situation, and reaches backward into one's experience for matches. The same examples applied in reverse can illustrate this pattern. A different economics major, facing a particular problem, might define its general demands, search her repertoire, and discover that calculus can help. A young politician, developing strategies for the coming campaign, might reflect on the situation and make fertile analogies with prior chess experience: capture the center of public opinion and you've captured the election.

As these examples show, whether forward-reaching or backward-reaching, high road transfer always involves reflective thought in abstracting from one context and seeking connections with others. This contrasts with the reflexive automatic character of low road transfer. Accordingly, high road transfer is not as dependent on superficial stimulus similarities, since through reflective abstraction a person can often "see through" superficial differences to deeper analogies.

The low road/high road view of transfer helps in understanding when it is reasonable or not to expect transfer because it clarifies the conditions under which different sorts of transfer occur. To be sure, *sometimes* transfer happens quite automatically in accordance with the Bo Peep theory; but that is by the low road, with the requirements of well-practiced skills or knowledge and superficial perceptual similarity to activate the skills or knowledge. Moreover, the transfer is likely to be "near" transfer, since the contexts have that surface perceptual similarity. High road transfer can bridge between contexts remote from one another, but it requires the effort of deliberate abstraction and connection-making and the ingenuity to make the abstractions and discover the connections.

Can Failures of Transfer Be Explained?

We reviewed a number of worrisome failures of transfer earlier. It is by no means the case, though, that conventional education affords no transfer at all. As mentioned earlier, most students learn to read more or less adequately and do bring those reading skills to bear when introduced to new areas. They do apply their arithmetic skills to income tax forms and other out-of-school tasks. Can the low road/high road model help us to understand why education sometimes succeeds but all too often fails in achieving transfer?

Broadly speaking, the successes fit the description of low road transfer. For example, students fairly readily carry over their basic reading skills to many new contexts. But the surface characteristics of those new contexts strongly stimulate reading skills—text appears in front of one's eyes, so what else would one do but read it? Arithmetic skills also transfer readily to such contexts as filling out income tax forms or checking bills in restaurants and stores. But again, the stimulus demand is direct and explicit: the tax forms provide places for sums, differences, and products; the bill displays an addition.

Consider now one of the failures: the problem of inert knowledge. For instance, when students fail to interpret current events in light of their historical knowledge, what can be said about the problems of transfer? First, there is an issue of initial learning: the skill students have learned through their study of history is not the skill they need when they consider today's newspapers. We want them to make thoughtful interpretations of current events, but they have learned to remember and retrieve knowledge on cue. We can hardly expect transfer of a performance that has not been learned in the first place!

However, that aside, what about the conditions for low and high road transfer? As to the low road, there is little surface resemblance between the learned knowledge and the new contexts of application. Why should the current strife between Iraq and Iran automatically remind a student of certain of the causes of the Civil War, when the surface features are so different? As to the high road, this would require explicit mindful abstraction of historical patterns and applications in other settings, to break those patterns free of their accidental associations in the Civil War or other settings. Conventional history instruction does little to decontextualize such patterns, instead highlighting the particular story of particular historical episodes.

Consider another failure: the impact of programming instruction on general cognitive skills. As to low road transfer, in most of the studies seeking transfer from computer programming, the students have not learned the programming skills themselves very well, failing to meet the condition of practice to near automaticity. Moreover, there is a problem with the surface appearance condition for low road transfer. In the context of programming, one might learn good problem-solving practices such as defining the problem clearly before one begins. However, the formal context of programming does not look or feel very much like the tense context of a labor dispute or the excited context of hunting for a new stereo system. Accordingly, other contexts where it is important to take time in defining the problem are not so likely to reawaken in students' minds their programming experiences.

As to high road transfer from programming, this would demand emphasis on abstracting from the programming context general principles of, for instance, problem solving and transporting those principles to applications outside of programming. However, most efforts to teach programming include virtually no attention to building such bridges between domains, but rather focus entirely on building programming skills. So the conditions for high road transfer are not met either.

Similar accounts can be given of the other cases of failure of transfer discussed earlier. In summary, conventional schooling lives up to its earlier characterization as following the Bo Peep theory of transfer—doing nothing special about it but expecting it to happen. When the conditions for low road transfer are met by chance, as in many applications of reading, writing, and arithmetic, transfer occurs—the sheep come home by themselves. Otherwise, the sheep get lost.

To be sure, meeting the low road and high road conditions for transfer is not the whole story. There remains the deeper problem of "local knowledge." The most artful instructional design will not provoke transfer if the knowledge and skills in question are fundamentally local in character, not really transferable to other contexts in the first place. This problem will be revisited shortly.

Can We Teach for Transfer?

Besides accounting for failure of transfer, the foregoing explanations hold forth hope of doing better: by designing instruction to meet the conditions needed to foster transfer, perhaps we can achieve it. In broad terms, one might speak of two techniques for promoting transfer—"hugging" and "bridging."

"Hugging" means teaching so as to better meet the resemblance conditions for low road transfer. Teachers who would like students to use their knowledge of biology in thinking about current ecological problems might introduce that knowledge in the first place in the context of such problems. Teachers who want students to relate literature to everyday life might emphasize literature where the connection is particularly plain for many students—*Catcher in the Rye* or the adolescent pining of Romeo, for example.

"Bridging" means teaching so as to meet better the conditions for high road transfer. Rather than expecting students to achieve transfer spontaneously, one "mediates" the needed processes of abstraction and connection making (Delclos et al. 1985, Feuerstein 1980). For example, teachers can point out explicitly the more general principles behind particular skills or knowledge or, better, provoke students to attempt such generalizations themselves: what general factors provoked the American Revolution, and where are they operating in the world today? Teachers can ask students to make analogies that reach outside the immediate context: how was treatment of blacks in the U.S. South before the Civil War like or unlike the treatment of blacks in South Africa today? Teachers can directly teach problem-solving and other strategies and provoke broad-spectrum practice reaching beyond their own subject matters: you learned this problem-defining strategy in math, but how might you apply it to planning an essay in English?

Such tactics of hugging and bridging will sound familiar. Teachers already pose questions and organize activities of these sorts from time to time. However, rarely is this done persistently and systematically enough to saturate the context of education with attention to transfer. On the contrary, the occasional bridging question or reading carefully chosen to "hug" a transfer target gets lost amid the overwhelming emphasis on subject matter-specific, topic-specific, fact-based questions and activities.

There is ample reason to believe that bridging and hugging together could do much to foster transfer in instructional settings. Consider, once again, the impact of programming on cognitive skills. As emphasized earlier, findings in general have been negative. However, in a few cases, positive results have appeared (Carver and Klahr 1987; Clements 1985a, b; Clements and Gullo 1984; Clements and Merriman in press; Littlefield et al. in press). These cases all involved strong bridging activities in the instruction.

The same story can be told of efforts to teach retarded persons elementary memory skills. As noted earlier, transfer was lacking in most such experiments—but not in all. In a few experiments, the investigators taught learners not only the memory strategies themselves but habits of self-monitoring, by which the learners examined their own behavior and thought about how to approach a task. This abstract focus on task demands—in effect a form of bridging—led to positive transfer results in these studies (Belmont et at. 1982).

Even without explicit bridging, hugging can have a substantial impact on transfer. For example, inert knowledge has been a serious problem in medical education, where traditionally students memorize multitudinous details of anatomy and physiology outside the context of real diagnostic application. In an approach called "problem-based learning," medical students acquire their technical knowledge of the human body in the context of working through case studies demanding diagnosis (Barrows and Tamblyn 1980). Experiments in science education conducted by John Bransford and his colleagues tell a similar story: when science facts and concepts were presented to students in the context of a story where they figured in resolving a problem or illuminating a question, the students proved much more able to transfer these facts and concepts to new problem-solving contexts (Bransford et al. 1986, Sherwood et al. 1987). In both the medical context and the science work, the instruction hugged much closer to the transfer performance than would instruction that simply and straightforwardly presented information.

Taken together, the notions of bridging and hugging write a relatively simple recipe for teaching for transfer. First, imagine the transfer you want, let us say, interpretation of contemporary and past conduct of societies and nations, or, let us say, problem solving where care is taken to define the problem before seeking solutions. Next, shape instruction to hug closer to the transfer desired. Teach history not just for memorizing its story but for interpretation of events through general principles. Teach programming or mathematical problem solving with emphasis on problem defining. Also, shape instruction to bridge to the transfer desired. Deliberately provoke students to think about how they approach tasks in and outside of history, programming, or math. Steal a little time from the source subject matter to confront students with analogous problems outside its boundary. Such teamwork between bridging and hugging practically guarantees making the most of whatever potential transfer a subject matter affords.

Moreover, there is an opportunity to go even further: aside from how one teaches, one can help students develop skills of *learning for transfer*. Students can become acquainted with the problem of transfer in itself and the tactics of bridging and hugging. Students can develop habits of doing considerable bridging and hugging for themselves, beyond what the instruction itself directly provides. Accordingly, a major goal of teaching for transfer becomes not just teaching particular knowledge and skills for transfer but teaching students in general how to *learn for transfer*.

Is Knowledge Too Local for Transfer?

Encouraging as all this is, it nonetheless leaves untreated the nagging problem of "local knowledge." If by and large the knowledge (including skills) that empowers a person in a particular activity is highly local to that activity, there are few prospects for useful transfer to other activities. What, then, can be said about this contemporary trend in theorizing about expertise and its implications for the potentials of teaching for transfer?

The suggestion is that, while the findings supporting a "local knowledge" view of expertise are entirely sound, the implications drawn from those findings contra the prospects of transfer are too hasty. Despite the local knowledge results, there are numerous opportunities for transfer. At least three arguments support this viewpoint: (1) disciplinary boundaries are very fuzzy, not representing distinct breaks in the kinds of knowledge or skill that are useful; (2) while much knowledge is local, there are at least a few quite general and important thinking strategies; (3) there are numerous elements of knowledge and skill of intermediate generality that afford some transfer across a limited range of disciplines.

The fuzziness of disciplinary boundaries. Even if knowledge and skill are local, are their boundaries of usefulness the same as the boundaries we use to organize disciplines and subject matters? For a case in point, history and current events might be treated in schools as different subjects; and, because they are partitioned off from each other, one might find scant transfer between them without special attention. Yet it seems plain that the kinds of causal reasoning and types of causes relevant to explaining historical happenings apply just as well to contemporary happenings. For another case in point, literature is a subject to study, life a "subject" to live. Yet plainly most literature treats fundamental themes of concern in life—love, birth, death, acquisition and defense of property, and so on. The relationships between literature and life offer an arena for reflection upon both and for transport of ideas from one to the other and back again.

To generalize, a close look at conventional disciplinary boundaries discloses not a well-defined geography with borders naturally marked by rivers and mountain ranges but, instead, enormous overlap and interrelation. If knowledge and skill are local, the boundaries surely are not the cleavages of the conventional curriculum. Yet because those cleavages are there as part of the organization of schooling, tactics of bridging and hugging are needed to take the numerous opportunities for fertile transfer across the conventional subject matters.

The existence of important crosscutting thinking strategies. There are certainly some strategic patterns of thinking that are important, neglected, and cross-disciplinary in character (see, e.g., Baron 1985a,b; Baron and Sternberg 1986; Chipman et al. 1985; Nickerson et al. 1985; Perkins 1986a,b,c). For example, in virtually all contexts people tend not to give full attention to the other side of the case—the side opposite their own—in reasoning about a claim. For another example, people tend to be "solution minded," orienting too quickly to a problem and beginning to develop candidate solutions at once, when often it would be more effective to stand back from the problem, explore its nature, define exactly what the problem is, seek alternative ways to represent it, and so on. For a third, people tend not to monitor their own mental processes very much, when doing so would garner the perspective and leverage of greater metacognitive awareness.

To be sure, exactly how to consider the other side of the case, explore a problem, or self-monitor is somewhat a matter of local knowledge that will differ significantly from context to context. However, the strategy of allocating attention and effort to considering the other side of the case, exploring a problem, or self-monitoring is fully general. Accordingly, developing such strategies in any domain, one can then hope to transfer them to others.

Patterns of thinking of intermediate generality. Finally, if we do not demand universal generality, there are numerous kinds of knowledge and skill of intermediate generality that cut across certain domains and provide natural prospects for transfer. For example, many considerations of measurement, methodology, and the role of evidence apply fairly uniformly across the hard sciences. Any art yields interesting results when examined through the categories of style and form, although to be sure the particular styles and forms of importance will vary from art to art. Psychological concepts such as motive, intention, inner conflict, the unconscious, and so on have an obvious role to play in interpreting literature, history, current events, and everyday life, and indeed perhaps some role to play in examining scientific discovery.

Of course, conventional subject matter boundaries usually inhibit the emergence of these patterns of thinking of intermediate generality because the style of instruction is so very local that it does not decontextualize the patterns. Bridging and hugging are needed to develop out of the details of the subject matters the overarching principles.

Members of the Same Team

Instead of worrying about which is more important—local knowledge or the more general transferable aspects of knowledge—we should recognize the synergy of local and more general knowledge. To be sure, students who do not know much about history are unlikely to enrich their thinking about the causes of the American Revolution by the general strategy of trying to reflect on both sides of the case, American and British. But students who do not have the habit of reflecting on both sides of a case will not get much depth of understanding out of the history they do know. Similarly, students who lack an understanding of key mathematical concepts will not gain much from the general strategy of trying to define and represent a problem well before they start. But students who lack the habit of trying to define and represent a problem well will often misuse the mathematical concepts they know when the problem is not routine.

So general and local knowledge are not rivals. Rather, they are members of the same team that play different positions. Proper attention to transfer will make the best of both for the sake of deeper and broader knowledge, skill, and understanding.

References

Baron, J. B., and R. S. Sternberg, eds. *Teaching Thinking Skills: Theory and Practice.* New York: W. H. Freeman, 1986.

Baron, J. *Rationality and Intelligence.* New York: Cambridge University Press, 1985a.

Baron, J. "What Kinds of Intelligence Components Are Fundamental? In *Thinking and Learning Skills. Volume 2: Current Research and Open Questions,* edited by S. S. Chipman, J. W. Segal, and R. Glaser, pp. 365–390. Hillsdale, N.J.: Lawrence Erlbaum Associates, 1985b.

Barrows, H. S., and R. M. Tamblyn. *Problem-Based Learning: An Approach to Medical Education.* New York: Springer, 1980.

Belmont, J. M., E. C. Butterfield, and R.P. Ferretti. "To Secure Transfer of Training Instruct Self-Management Skills." In *How and How Much Can Intelligence Be Increased?,* edited by D. K. Detterman and R. J. Sternberg, pp. 147–154. Norwood, N.J.: Ablex, 1982.

Bransford, J. D., J. J. Franks, N. J. Vye, and R. D. Sherwood. "New Approaches to Instruction: Because Wisdom Can't Be Told." Paper presented at the Conference on Similarity and Analogy, University of Illinois, June 1986.

Carver, S. M., and D. Klahr. "Analysis. Instruction, and Transfer of the Components of Debugging Skill." Paper presented at the biennial meeting of the Society for Research in Child Development, Baltimore, Md., April 1987.

Chase, W. C., and II. A. Simon. "Perception in Chess." *Cognitive Psychology* 4 (1973): 55–81.

Chi, M., P. Feltovich, and R. Glaser. "Categorization and Representation of Physics Problems by Experts and Novices." *Cognitive Science* 5 (1981): 121–152.

Chipman, S. F., J. G. Segal, and R. Glaser, eds. *Thinking and Learning Skills. Volume 2: Current Research and Open Questions.* Hillsdale, N.J.: Lawrence Erlbaum Associates, 1985.

Clements, D. H. "Effects of Logo Programming on Cognition, Metacognitive Skills, and Achievement." Presentation at the American Educational Research Association conference, Chicago, April 1985a.

Clements, D. H. "Research on Logo in Education: Is the Turtle Slow But Steady, or Not Even in the Race?" *Computers in the Schools* 2, 2/3 (1985b): 55–71.

Clements, D. H. and D. F. Gullo. "Effects of Computer Programming on Young Children's Cognition." *Journal of Educational Psychology* 76, 6 (1984): 1051–1058.

Clements, D. H., and S. Merriman. "Componential Developments in Logo Programming Environments." In *Teaching and Learning Computer Programming: Multiple Research Perspectives*. Hillsdale, N.J.: Lawrence Erlbaum Associates, in press.

Dalbey, J., and M. C. Linn. "The Demands and Requirements of Computer Programming: A Literature Review." *Journal of Educational Computing Research* 1 (1985): 253–274.

De Groot, A. D. *Thought and Choice in Chess.* The Hague: Mouton, 1965.

Delclos, V. R., J. Littlefield, and J. D. Bransford. "Teaching Thinking Through Logo: The Importance of Method." *Roeper Review* 7, 3 (1985): 153–156.

Feuerstein, R. *Instrumental Enrichment: An Intervention Program for Cognitive Modifiability.* Baltimore: University Park Press, 1980.

Feurzeig, W., P. Horwitz, and R. Nickerson. *Microcomputers in Education* (Report No. 4798). Cambridge, Mass.: Bolt, Beranek, and Newman, 1981.

Hirsch, E. D., Jr. *Cultural Lieracy: What Every American Needs to Know.* Boston: Houghton Mifflin. 1987.

Larkin, J. H. "The Role of Problem Representation in Physics. In *Mental Models*, edited by D. Gentner and A. L. Stevens. Hillsdale, N.J.: Lawrence Erlbaum Associates, 1983.

Larkin, J. H., J. McDermott, D. P. Simon, and H. A. Simon. "Modes of Competence in Solving Physics Problems." *Cognitive Science* 4 (1980): 317–345.

Linn, M. C. "The Cognitive Consequences of Programming Instruction in Classrooms." *Educational Researcher* 14 (1985): 14–29.

Littlefield, J., V. Delclos, S. Lever, and J. Bransford. "Learning Logo: Method of Teaching, Transfer of General Skills, Attitudes Toward Computers." In *Teaching and Learning Computer Programming: Multiple Research Perspectives*. Hillsdale, N.J.: Lawrence Erlbaum Associates, in press.

Nickerson, R., D. N. Perkins, and E. Smith. *The Teaching of Thinking.* Hillsdale, N.J.: Lawrence Erlbaum Associates, 1985.

Olson, D. R. "Culture, Technology, and Intellect." In *The Nature of Intelligence*, edited by L. B. Resnick. Hillsdale, N.J.: Lawrence Erlbaum Associates, 1976.

Papert, S. *Mindstorms: Children, Computers, and Powerful Ideas.* New York: Basic Books, 1980.

Perfetto, G. A., J. D. Bransford, and J. J. Franks. "Constraints on Access in a Problem Solving Context." *Memory & Cognition* 11, 1 (1983): 24–31.

Perkins, D. N. "The Fingertip Effect: How Information-Processing Technology Changes Thinking." *Educational Researcher* 14, 7 (1985): 11–17.

Perkins, D. N. *Knowledge as Design.* Hillsdale, N.J.: Lawrence Erlbaum Associates, 1986a.

Perkins, D. N. "Thinking Frames." *Educational Leadership* 43, 8 (1986b): 4–10.

Perkins, D. N. "Thinking Frames: An Integrative Perspective on Teaching Cognitive Skills." In *Teaching Thinking Skills: Theory and Practice*, edited by J. B. Baron and R. S. Sternberg, pp. 41–61. New York: W. H. Freeman, 1986c.

Perkins, D. N., and F. Martin. "Fragile Knowledge and Neglected Strategies in Novice Programmers." In *Empirical Studies of Programmers*, edited by E. Soloway and S. Iyengar, pp. 213–229. Norwood, N.J.: Ablex, 1986.

Perkins, D. N., F. Martin, and M. Farady. *Loci of Difficulty in Learning to Program* (Educational Technology Center technical report). Cambridge, Mass.: Educational Technology Center, Harvard Graduate School of Education, 1986.

Perkins, D., and G. Salomon. "Transfer and Teaching Thinking." In *Thinking: The Second International Conference*, edited by D. N. Perkins, J. Lochhead, and J. Bishop, pp. 285–303. Hillsdale, N.J.: Lawrence Erlbaum Associates, 1987.

Salomon, G., and D. N. Perkins. "Rocky Roads to Transfer: Rethinking Mechanisms of a Neglected Phenomenon." Paper presented at the Conference on Thinking, Harvard Graduate School of Education, Cambridge, Mass., August 1984.

Salomon, G., and D. N. Perkins. "Transfer of Cognitive Skills from Programming: When and How?" *Journal of Educational Computing Research* 3 (1987): 149–169.

Schoenfeld, A. H., and D. J. Herrmann. "Problem Perception and Knowledge Structure in Expert and Novice Mathematical Problem Solvers." *Journal of Experimental Psychology: Learning, Memory, and Cognition* 8 (1982): 484–494.

Scribner, S., and M. Cole. *The Psychology of Literacy.* Cambridge, Mass.: Harvard University Press, 1981.

Sherwood, R. D., C. K. Kinzer, J. D. Bransford, and J. J. Franks. "Some Benefits of Creating Macro-Contexts for Science Instruction: Initial Findings." *Journal of Research in Science Teaching* 24 (1987): 417–435.

Soloway, E., and K. Ehrlich. "Empirical Studies of Programming Knowledge." *IEEE Transactions on Software Engineering* SE-10, 5 (1984): 595–609.

Author's Note: Some of the ideas discussed here were developed at the Educational Technology Center of the Harvard Graduate School of Education, operating with support from the Office of Educational Research and Improvement (contract #OERI 400-83-0041). Opinions expressed herein are not necessarily shared by OERI and do not represent Office policy.

CLUSTER TWO

TRENDS IN THE 21ST CENTURY INTERDISCIPLINARY WORKPLACE

Reading 13

Author Andrew Kimbrell provides some definitions for some commonly used terms for work in "Breaking the Job Lock." Kimbrell addresses what he calls is a "disturbing picture" about the current workplace and offers some suggestions about how we can all create meaningful work for ourselves.

READING

BREAKING THE JOB LOCK

by

Andrew Kimbrell

Imagine a world where pursuing our passions pays the bills

The alarm clock explodes with a high-pitched screech. It's 6:30 a.m.—another dreaded Monday. Kids need to be dressed, fed, rushed off to school. Then there's 40 minutes of fighting traffic and the sprint from the parking lot to your workstation. You arrive, breathless, just in the nick of time. Now is the moment to confront the week ahead. As usual, you're in overload mode. You seem to be working faster and faster but falling farther behind. What's worse, your unforgiving bosses think everything gets accomplished by magic. But you don't dare do or say anything that might jeopardize your job. (It hurts just to think of those swelling credit card balances.) At the end of the day, when you are drained and dragged out, it's time to endure the long drive home, get dinner ready, and maybe steal a few hours in front of the TV. Then to sleep, and it starts all over again.

Sound familiar? Despite utopian visions earlier in this century of technology freeing us all from the toil of work, we are now working harder than ever—with little relief in sight. In a recent poll, 88 percent of workers said their jobs require them to work longer (up from 70 percent 20 years ago), and 68 percent complained of having to work at greater speeds (up from 50 percent in 1977). And as if all this were not grim enough, the most discouraging aspect of our jobs is that they seem to accomplish little of lasting value. Studies consistently show that as many as 80 percent of workers in our society feel their jobs, however fast and furious, are "meaningless." It is a disturbing picture. The "land of opportunity" is fast becoming a nation of stressed-out wage slaves. Yet no one in the American political arena, on the left or on the right, seems to notice what our jobs are doing to us. Everyone from the president on down declares that creating more new jobs is our most important goal. Left unspoken are the physical and mental suffering, the powerlessness and meaninglessness, that will be endemic to so many of these "new," often low-paying jobs.

Certainly, a low unemployment rate is not a bad thing, especially for the poor and poorly skilled among us. But more jobs isn't a panacea for our problems. We must pay more attention to the kind and quality of work at which we spend our days, our weeks, our lives. It's not just about jobs, or even well-paying jobs. It's about *meaningful work*. Economists, politicians, union leaders, employers, activists, the media--everyone needs to help create a new vision of how we earn our livelihoods. We need work that is good for body, mind, and spirit; work that sustains family and community; work that connects us with and helps us protect the natural world.

Re-envisioning Work

An important starting point for any effort to re-envision work is to remember that there is nothing natural or pre-ordained about our modern system of jobs. For most of human history, people worked far differently than we do, usually right at home in the midst of family, community, and nature. Work wasn't separated from the rest of their lives; it wasn't an uninterrupted eight-hour stretch of duty. Many traditional cultures don't even have a word for work, much less wage-based jobs. Indeed, the word *job* in English originally meant a criminal or demeaning action. (We retain this meaning when we call a bank robbery a "bank job.") After the industrial revolution took hold in 18th-century England, the first generations of factory workers felt that wage work was humiliating and undignified. Angry about being driven from their traditional work on the land or in crafts, they applied the word *job* to factory labor as a way of expressing their disgust.

Even today many of us avoid the word *job*, preferring more upscale terms like *occupation* or *career* to describe what we do for 40-plus hours each week. Yet the older meaning of these words also reveals something about the nature of work. *Occupation* originally meant to seize or capture. (It is still used in this sense when, for instance, we speak of the German occupation of France during World War II.) What an apt description of how jobs take over our lives, subjecting us to the demands of outside rulers. The original meaning of *career* fits well with the role we play in the speeded-up global economic rat race. In the 19th century, *career* meant "racing course" or "rapid and unrestrained" activity.

In searching for ways to put meaning back into our work, we might want to revive the term *vocation* (from the Latin for "voice" or "calling"). Today, "having avocation" or "answering a calling" usually means embarking upon a religious life—an unfortunate narrowing of the concept. We all deserve to be involved in work to which we have been called by our passions and beliefs. Following a vocation can lead to a *profession*—literally, a "public declaration" of what we believe and who we are. A profession is what our work should be, but so rarely is.

The Cult of Efficiency

Any attempt to transform our work from a mere job into a profession of deeply felt values sets us on an inevitable path of conflict with the values of the industrialized job system. These values—speed, productivity, efficiency—govern the workplace in remarkably similar ways in both capitalist and socialist economies. Even though we are supposed to be living in the postindustrial era—many of our jobs are now dictated by the demands of computers instead of assembly lines—our lives at work are really not much different from those of 19th-century factory workers. We are still seen as replaceable spare parts for the great machines of production. From the checkout person at the grocery store to the highly trained engineer, we are all expected to work faster, waste less time, produce more.

We are not machines, of course, and the drive for ever greater efficiency in the competitive global economy is taking its toll. More than 80 percent of Americans say their lives are more stressful now than they were five years ago; pressures at work are cited as the primary reason. More and more of us need to be medicated just to get through the workday. More than 45 million American adults are taking prescription psychotropic medications. The largest increase is not in the use of the much publicized antidepressant Prozac, but rather in a variety of drugs used to treat anxiety and stress disorders.

As a society we continue to honor the virtues of caring and empathy in our personal lives, and these must become the cornerstones of a new kind of work ethic. Empathy for the physical and mental needs of workers must replace efficiency as the paramount value of the workplace. After all, no one in their right mind evaluates the importance of their family, friends, or even pets on a strict efficiency basis.

The Dictatorship of the Workplace

Good work involves not only the character and values of work, but also the power relationships in the workplace. Economists and politicians never mention it, but under the job system, virtually every workplace is a dictatorship. Let's face it: Most of us spend the majority of our adult lives as passive subjects in managerial tyrannies. Workers—whatever the color of their collars—have little say in forming workplace policies or conditions.

Even many of the advances for workers, hard-won through decades of labor-movement struggles, have been rolled back in recent years. While this is largely the result of corporate pressure, unions bear some responsibility for their own decline by choosing to focus almost exclusively on wage issues; they seldom explore other ways to improve workers' lives. Pay is important to anyone with a job, but a sense of purpose and accomplishment, an outlet for creativity, an opportunity for flexibility, and co-worker relationships matter, too. As the American labor movement pushes to revitalize itself by reaching out to women, youth, minorities, and the public at large, there's hope that helping workers achieve other elements of good work will find a more prominent place on union agendas.

Over the past 20 years, a variety of employee ownership strategies and more ambitious efforts toward workplace democracy have brought greater equity to many thousands of workers. A new generation of socially responsible businesses have broadened employees' role in decision making—a trend that is now spreading to some mainstream firms. Many people have found that leaving the dictatorship of the workplace and pursuing partnership or self-employment options, while fraught with risks, can be a way to more fulfilling work and lives. For some it simply means repackaging current job skills as a consulting business in order to spend more time with family or favorite pursuits; others, inspired by writers like Wendell Berry and Paul Hawken, have created independent livelihoods that make a contribution to society and the planet. Each of these efforts is a potentially important step in the re-creation of work.

A Nation of Strangers

For years we have heard urgent pleas to "preserve family values" and to "restore a sense of community" in our lives. Yet we rarely hear the advocates of these causes mention that our current job system is one of the chief culprits in destroying traditional bonds of family and community life. For generations workers have been forced to move to wherever jobs could be found, uprooting their spouses and children from family, friends, and community connections. Downsizing, corporate restructuring, shifting production to low-wage areas, and other favorite tools of the globalized economy keep almost all of us anxious and scouting for the next job. Always anticipating the next move to Seattle, Sarasota, or Singapore, we invest little energy in maintaining strong bonds to our extended family, our community, or any particular place. We have become, in investigative journalist Vance Packard's memorable phrase, "a nation of strangers." Witness the throngs at airports each Thanksgiving as millions return "home" to find a 48-hour semblance of family and community.

A new vision of good work involves pressuring corporations to make a firm commitment to the places where they do business, and working to end the game of global economic pinball, where jobs are endlessly bumped from location to location. It also requires that we begin to value family concerns, community connections, and ties to the places we live, above the financial gains of job mobility. This is not an easy commitment to make since it may mean missing out on more money or a job advancement. Yet if we continue to prize career success above all other aspects of our lives, we run the risk of becoming little more than global nomads seeking a buyer for our labor and ourselves.

Get Working

For the vast majority of us, even contemplating liberation from our current jobs seems hopelessly utopian. We'd love to tell our boss to "take this job and shove it," but mortgage and rent notices, insurance premiums, and credit card bills remind us every day why we can't. We're victims of a kind of wage blackmail. For many Americans, this situation is compounded by the fact that buying things we don't really need or even particularly want has become a comfort and compensatory compulsion that helps us cope with jobs offering little meaning.

We can no longer let wage blackmail run our lives. We must seek a vocation that truly expresses our values and fits our needs. Thinking about our true calling, perhaps for the first time, may take considerable time and patience. We've worked for so long at jobs we "have" to do that we often haven't considered the work we want and need to do.

Even when the path becomes clear, embarking on your profession may not be easy. You may have to steal hours from jobs that financial need requires you to keep. You may have to slash your monthly budget to have the time you want. You must also be prepared to face criticism as people scold you for abandoning your responsibilities and sacrificing the well-being of others to "do your own thing."

On the political front, we must push for measures that give workers more paid vacation, greater flexibility in choosing part-time work, a higher minimum wage, and paid leave to care for family. National health insurance is an important step that could free the entrepreneurial energies of workers who stay in their jobs just for the medical benefits.

The calling of good work also involves mentoring young people to seek vocations rather than settling for jobs. Raising children, nurturing families, and volunteering in your community are wonderful vocations in their own right, deserving at least as much respect and support as wage employment. We must also urge teachers, counselors, and clergy to redefine work for future generations, and to understand the vital role good work must play in true education, and in spiritual and mental growth. Ultimately, of course, the most important way we can teach the next generation about good work is by example

For many, the necessities of life, and even following a calling, may still mean working in the corporate job system. Good work in these circumstances requires us to do all we can to revive unions as active forces for workplace democracy. Unions, for their part, should become key players in establishing patterns of worker participation and job flexibility. At the same time we need to promote socially responsible business behavior as the standard, rather than the exception.

We must be patient with ourselves and others as we begin the difficult personal and collective search for good work. Yet we must remain firmly dedicated to the principle, expressed well by economist E.F. Schumacher, that our "real task is to adapt the work to the needs of the worker rather than demand that the worker adapt himself to the needs of the work."

Reading 14

Researchers Barker, Gilbreath and Stone demonstrate that business schools need to take a more interdisciplinary approach to business school education. They identify five skills that employers are seeking in new hires: communication skills, team oriented skills, cross-functional/interdisciplinary perspective, change receptivity, and intercultural awareness. What is of particular interest to interdisciplinary studies students is that these five skills are commonly associated with the learning outcomes of interdisciplinary study. This reading is a good supplement to the discussion of characteristics of interdisciplinarians in Chapter Four.

READING

THE INTERDISCIPLINARY NEEDS OF ORGANIZATIONS

Are new employees adequately equipped?

by

Randolph T. Barker, Glenn H. Gilbreath and Warren S. Stone
School of Business, Virginia Commonwealth University, Richmond, Virginia, USA

Introduction

The global economy obviously is market-driven. History is replete with stories of automobile companies that produced cars that lacked styling appeal for the consumer; politicians who misinterpreted the true beliefs of their constituents; and national economies that failed to adapt to market changes.

In order to maintain a competitive edge, businesses and governments seek out the most talented individuals available in the job market. These organizations expect to provide additional training in specialty areas that may be unique to their business (Pfeiffer, 1994). Businesses do not, however, expect to train new employees extensively in areas of general expertise within a major industry. For example, a major accounting firm should not have to supply training or schooling to a newly-hired college graduate before the employee sits for the CPA examination.

These examples seem obvious to the reader, but to some degree, colleges and universities frequently are guilty of these oversights. These institutions often neglect to maintain meaningful contact with employers to assess the performance of its graduates, and stay abreast of current and future needs. In today's fast-paced, global environment, a critical problem can be existing in an advanced, multifaceted state before the organization discovers it. Businesses cannot wait years for a university to develop an interdisciplinary curriculum relevant to the pressures that it faces on a regular basis.

Literature Review

Many studies suggest that interdisciplinary research contributes to innovative data analysis and interpretation. For example, Storey (1985) refers to management control as addressed in management and social sciences. The management sciences, embracing subjects such as accounting, operations research, systems analysis and industrial engineering, are yielding to the ideas of behavioral science and social accounting adding to their viewpoints of formal theory and logic.

Support for more interaction also appears in management, sociology, and psychology. By examining customer service issues in organizational behavior and marketing literature, Bowen (1990) identifies four areas that promote an interdisciplinary perspective: customer-organization exchanges, customer-contact personnel roles, management influences, and climate and cultural mechanisms. Odegaard (1987) suggests that psychology should draw from multiple approaches and disciplines, especially when dealing with "big problems." Gans (1989) notes that sociologists need to draw from other social sciences to learn from and improve future research.

Many of the difficulties in academic thinking stem from overemphasizing specialization and disregarding the interdependence of the various functions that constitute the management process. Success requires the ability to move across what Leavitt (1986) calls the "harsh terrain" that separates these aspects (Bedeian, 1989). Showalter (1992), focusing on research in production/operations management (P/OM) and management information systems (MIS), notes limited interdisciplinary linkages in academia, though strong linkages exist between P/OM and MIS in business. In addition, Fimbel

(1994) discusses the role of effective communication as it relates to building a power base within an organization. She calls attention to political implications from employee communications, suggesting that greater awareness of other mind-sets and interests increases interdisciplinary understanding.

Current Thinking

Business management education, training, and development in the USA are in a state of reappraisal. Although the USA is renowned for its specialized business training, the rising importance of international business and communications that crosses functional lines causes the business community to rethink its needs, and prompts business schools to reconsider the thrust of their educational programs.

A 1987 survey of 150 CEOs of companies listed in *Forbes* and *Fortune* magazines stresses the executives' interest in a college-level international business component. The executives suggest that new MBAs in the USA do not possess all the characteristics required by potential employers who are international in scope. Specifically, MBAs do not receive important knowledge tools, because their business schools lack the following:

(1) a faculty capable of teaching MBAs the current broad range of international issues;
(2) resources to teach MBAs to adapt to diversity in the workplace;
(3) incentives for professors to teach practical application of theory and publish works relevant to the real business environment;
(4) an interdisciplinary approach to teaching that encourages MBAs to work and communicate across functional lines.

Many undergraduate and MBA programs emphasize specialization of fields, because the curricula that instructors teach are highly specialized. Institutions expect professors to restrict themselves to writing articles within their specific area of knowledge and collaborate with those who share the same interests. Unfortunately, professors write for research publications that are largely ignored by business executives (Dulek and Fielden, 1992).

Lorange (1994), Mason (1992) and Porter *et al.* (1991) cite examples of progressive strategies of prominent US business schools that utilize partnerships with corporations to fund programs and regularly communicate with the business community to stay abreast of their needs. Elliott *et al.* (1994), on the other hand, present a model that criticizes the approach of many US business schools and their reluctance to change. They believe that students are not receiving a proper balance of research, application, and interdisciplinary training. Massy (1994) supports this notion by decrying the rigid system within universities that restricts their ability to change. Increasingly, Americans realize that graduates of our educational systems may not possess the skills and knowledge that match the US business needs. To quote *Fortune Magazine* (July 1991), "Business education has become largely irrelevant to business practice . . . MBAs lack creativity, people skills, aptitude for teamwork, and the ability to speak with clarity and conciseness—all hallmarks of a good manager."

Possible Reasons

Why have educational institutions continued to produce products that do not meet society's needs? Barker (1990) suggests possible reasons within higher education stemming from the self-perpetuating separation between disciplines. These possible reasons include:

- higher education practices;
- discipline/specialization emphases;
- reward system policies;
- awareness limitations; and
- apprehension effects.

Higher education practices. Cultural practices in higher education create a lack of interaction among disciplines. School administrations structure departments by disciplines, instruction, and research. This approach creates a preprogrammed manner of viewing specific issues that contributes to the separation of disciplines (Andrews and Gilbreath, 1993; Barker, 1990; Elliott, 1994: Leonard, 1992).

Businesses and researchers cast a hopeful eye across the Atlantic Ocean looking at the educational practices. Many assume that business schools in the UK and Europe are superior to those in the USA in the following ways:

(1)   In contrast with British and European business schools, US business schools' learning programs are not coordinated with the needs of the business community.
(2)   British and European business schools produce graduates who are more prepared to enter the international business world.
(3)   Higher quality students from the USA are drawn to British and European business schools.
(4)   US business schools over-emphasize research and under-emphasize application in their educational programs. In other words, British and European business schools generate more support from the business community, because they are application-oriented and integrated with the business environment.
(5)   The American Academy of Collegiate Schools of Business (AACSB) accrediting process discourages interdisciplinary interaction and restricts business schools from adapting to the needs of the educational market. Meanwhile, European business schools are free from regulating bodies and better able to respond to market needs (Bickerstaffe, 1994; Porter *et al.,* 1991; Scullion, 1992; Tully, 1988).

The strong business ties to universities in the UK and Europe are not, however, entirely positive. This point is highlighted by business cutbacks caused by the recent recession. For example, INSEAD (European Institute of Business Administration) froze professional salaries in 1993, because of declining executive education revenue from private business sources (*The Economist,* June 4, 1994).

AACSB guidelines provide a level of quality and consistency for member organizations that is absent in the UK and Europe. Certainly, the top business schools there provide a high-quality education. The schools positioned in the lower tiers with strong business partnerships, however, are in danger of becoming company training schools (*The Economist,* June 4. 1994). Despite the criticism of US business schools, it is noteworthy that 77,000 out of 102,000 MBAs annually receive degrees from US institutions. On a worldwide basis, the Graduate Management Admission Test average scores for business students places nine out of the top ten positions. Only INSEAD is ranked among the leaders, and 81 percent of its professors received doctorates in the USA (*The Economist,* June 4, 1994).

Discipline/specialization emphases. There are pressures toward more specialization in the educational disciplines. One cost of specialization is a limited focus. Another cost may be the inability of the organization to see the interdisciplinary factors that could promote interdependence among models, structures, processes, theories, and policies developed (Barker, 1990).

Personal perception and absence of common knowledge of other disciplines also limit interaction. Golembiewski (1985) suggests that public sector managers may reject private sector innovations because they accept negative stereotypes that such changes would not work within their organizations. Shalinsky (1989) in his article discussing language and polydisciplinary groups, suggests that different disciplines do not share a common language, models and tools for analysis. Some rely on numbers, others rely on words for communication.

Reward system policies. The faculty reward system is a drawback to conducting interdisciplinary research in educational institutions. Currently, most promotion and tenure systems encourage junior faculty to write for mainstream publications within their own disciplines and discourage them from collaborating with outside and/or competing areas. Promotion and tenure policies generally encourage younger faculty to conform to the expectations of peers and senior faculty, reinforcing a single discipline research focus (Barker, 1990; Elliott *et al.,* 1994).

Apprehension effects. Perhaps fear of the unknown, characterized by lack of understanding of a language, research methodologies, and unfamiliar literature restrict interaction. Individuals working in a specialized area may consider an outsider venturing into their area a threat. Grant funding requirements also may deter a scholar from venturing into a new area by requiring specific discipline prerequisites in order to receive funding (Barker, 1990).

Purpose

The current research was conducted because of the preceding separation issues, and business environment perceptions. The purpose of the study was to provide additional information for developing a new MBA program offering. Questions guiding this research include:

(1) What are the perceptions of business executives regarding the skills of newly hired recent graduates of business schools?

(2) What approaches can be developed to help business educators address these issues in the future, particularly as they relate to developing new MBA programs?

Methods

Input from business executives was obtained from personal interviews from executives from 12 companies located in the US Mid-Atlantic region, each of which are included in the *Fortune 1000* listing. The organizations represent a variety of product and service industries including tobacco, engineering, retail, automobile, manufacturing, banking and medical. Participants for the interviews were chosen based on the following criteria: upper level position within the organization, extensive exposure to college graduate new hires, extensive experience in leading and working with all levels within their organizations, and employed by a company with national/international business interactions.

Data

Data were gathered through face-to-face, in-depth, structured interviews. Each of the current researchers independently developed possible open-ended interview questions based on the preceding literature. A meeting reduced by consensus the number of questions to eight. Open-ended questions to stimulate responses rather than restrict the range of responses were selected. Two executives not included in the sample were selected for pretesting the resulting interview guide. The researchers clarified the wording of the interview guide based on pilot findings. The questions used during in-depth interviews were:

(1) What strengths do you note in recently graduated new hires?
(2) Do you note any deficiencies in their skills or abilities?
(3) What training do you provide for new hires?
(4) What role of importance does a team orientation play in your organization? Do your new hires possess teamwork skills?
(5) Can you think of additional characteristics you would like to see in new hires?
(6) For your industry, what skills will be needed in five years that are not currently present in new hires?
(7) What is your perception of the ability of new-hires in their ability to integrate and interrelate with personnel outside their functional area?
(8) What international/intercultural characteristics are needed in your new hires?

One of the researchers called each subject to discuss the research orientation and to solicit their participation. Only the general subject area was divulged in order for the participants to focus their comments during the actual interview.

Researchers assured the participants of confidentiality both in the initial telephone calls and at the beginning of the interviews and received permission to record the interviews in writing.

Interviews occurred in the participants' offices with the duration ranging from 25 to 120 minutes. The interviewer asked questions and probed for specificity and clarification. The data from each interview were summarized and the responses for each question examined across all interviewees. To identify major themes in the interviewees' responses, content analysis was conducted. Two of the researchers independently analyzed responses to generate content categories. Inter-rater reliability produced an r of 0.82. The following section contains the results of the data analysis of the interviewees' responses.

Results

The results of the interviews combine all industries and gender responses. All interviewees agreed to the interviews. Responses were omitted only in those instances where remarks were of a proprietary nature. A summary of responses is presented below by interview question.

What strengths do you note in recently graduated new hires?
The most common response given referred to the new-hires' strength of specific technical expertise. The expertise ranged across the areas of computer, accounting, sales, production, and engineering. Only one individual indicated that more technical knowledge was needed. Quantitative skills of these new hires was the strongest skill developed during the course of their education as suggested by all but one of the interviewees.

Do you note any deficiencies in their skills or abilities?
Eleven of the interviewees indicated deficiencies in the areas of speaking, writing, and interpersonal communication. Two interviewees noted that when new-hires write or speak, the information presented is not audience centered. Most referred to the fact that these people did not understand the "big picture" or strategic nature of the organization when analyzing problems and then making recommendations to decision makers. One interviewee said that new-hires do not gain the trust of others through their verbal and nonverbal behaviors because they transmit messages showing concern only for their own needs. Another interviewee suggested that new-hires should be more open-minded in dealing with other people, who come from different parts of the company with different perspectives and approaches to dealing with situations. Finally, two interviewees adamantly explained that they needed to remind new-hires that their personal career objectives were tied to improved corporate effectiveness and efficiency. As one interviewee indicated "If these people do a good job the career will take care of itself."

What training do you provide for new-hires?
Each interviewee indicated that the company provides an orientation training session to help the new-hire with their job responsibilities and to aid the organization's socialization process. One executive said that the organization releases the employee immediately if the new-hire does not display desirable traits during orientation. All interviewees noted that new-hires receive communication training in the areas of writing, speaking, and customer relations emphasizing the organization's approach. Seven of the interviewees stressed cross-functional and process-driven communication.

One executive believed that some universities were not providing all the basic discipline education needed. Thus, the company retrained many new-hires in the discipline fundamentals for which they were hired.

What importance does a team orientation play in your organization? Do your new hires possess this characteristic?
Eight of the interviewees indicated that teams were vital to their organization's success.

A majority saw a need for people to work effectively across functional/discipline lines at some time in their career depending on the task and situation at hand. Two respondents noted some need for teams and two currently saw no present need.

A majority of interviewees indicated that new-hires do not possess a team orientation, but that it was desirable. As one person said during a lengthy interview "we don't have this orientation yet, but we will as we continue to downsize (reduce the number of employees) . . . those employees left and new hires must develop this team approach." One interviewee stated that an organization-wide effort was under way to train all employees about team concepts and communications among teams. Another noted that his three-year development program focuses on interdisciplinary teams. This executive indicated that both new-hires and career employees lack team communication skills. Ten of the interviewees suggested their organizations exposed most of their new-hires to team concepts, but they needed more exposure in this area prior to assuming their position.

Can you think of additional characteristics you would like to see in new hires?
All but one interviewee identified a growing need for stronger communication skills in the areas of speaking, writing and interpersonal/intercultural relations. Ten interviewees indicated that an organizational orientation would increase the perception of new-hires regarding the interdependence among organization roles. Four interviewees saw a need for more computer literacy in discipline areas as well as general computer use through word processing and spread-

sheet applications. All interviewees saw a need for greater change receptivity to change, with nine interviewees reiterating the need for a stronger team approach to work as organizations decentralize their structure.

For your industry, what skills will be needed in five years that are not currently present in new hires?
Answers to this question were similar to the answers to the preceding question. Three interviewees said that a person with stronger strategic orientation would be necessary . . . a person who envisions the scope of present and future problems and applies meaningful solutions. Two noted more computer literacy, and two suggested a foreign language would be helpful. Although listed in answers to the previous question, one interviewee strongly identified a need for better interpersonal skills to facilitate the teamwork process.

What is your perception of new hires regarding their ability to integrate and interrelate with personnel outside their functional area?
Without exception, each of the interviewees perceives new hires as lacking the ability to understand other points of view, because they view the world from the perspective of their own functional areas. Two of the interviewees noted that after some training and time, these people improved in looking beyond their own discipline and "territory." One interviewee believed this "tunnel-vision" caused problems for both the new hire and each person he or she might contact in the organization. Communication, and idea generation suffer from this myopic viewpoint. One person noted that new hires seem to think that all they have to do is perform their function and not deal with the rest of the organization. Another person indicated that this functional view hinders interpersonal communication.

What international/intercultural characteristics are needed in your new hires?
Four interviewees indicated that foreign language skill was needed. Eight of the interviewees saw a need for more cultural sensitivity and adaptation to the variation in problem-solving approaches of other cultures. Four interviewees did not see any application to this question, because most of their companies work as decentralized multinationals. The use of host country nationals automatically removes the language barrier in that country's operations.

In analyzing the responses, we searched for major themes in the content of the interviews indicating skills needed by the new hire. Based on the content analysis five themes emerged:

(1) communication skills in speaking, writing, and interpersonal relations;
(2) team oriented skills;
(3) cross-functional/interdisciplinary perspective;
(4) change receptivity; and
(5) inter-cultural awareness.

These five themes are discussed below.

Discussion of Findings

Communication skills in speaking, writing, and interpersonal relations
Communications skills combine to create a desired political image of an employee within an organization. There are limited opportunities for members of organizations to communicate directly. It is, therefore, critical for individuals to cultivate their desired images through these contacts. In addition, the written word often is the only connection a manager has with certain other colleagues and superiors. It is politically important for managers to convey positive personal styles and acumen through their writings (Fimbel, 1994). In addition, there is a positive link between productivity and effective communication within organizations (Clampitt and Downs, 1993).

Team-oriented skills
Businesses accomplish many of their goals through teamwork (Peters, 1992). Recognizing this fact, colleges and universities such as Columbia, University of Michigan, Wharton, Stanford, and many others teach team concepts (Mason, 1992). Muller *et al.* (1991) encourage American schools to pursue a European strategy for developing team skills. Although European institutions are well known for their teamwork teaching concepts, some US business schools are quite progressive in this area. At the University of Michigan, teams of students work on actual business projects in conjunc-

tion with faculty members. Business executives from top US companies contribute time to speak on issues relevant to the projects, much in the European fashion (*Harvard Business Review*, 1992). Similarly, the University of Tennessee offers a three-credit course that focuses on teamwork problem solving using realistic business problems (Mason, 1992).

Cross-functional/interdisciplinary perspective

The need for interdisciplinary perspectives in business and school curricula is well documented. Storey supports the need for interaction of management and social science variables that may provide for a more adequate theory of management control. Graham (1978) suggests that some complaints against the management sciences stem from a lack of behavioral considerations. Bowen (1990) believes those customer-organization exchanges, customer-contact personnel roles, management influences, and climate and cultural mechanisms contribute to interdisciplinary perspectives. Elliott *et al.* (1994) call attention to the fact that US businesses must recruit managers with broad perspectives who can manage across functional lines. Muller *et al.* (1991) point to a new recommendation from Massachusetts Institute of Technology (MIT) that it should stress interdisciplinary methods in its program. Researchers make valuable contributions to fields outside of their specialty by asking questions from a different disciplinary viewpoint. The narrower perspective of "insiders" may prevent them from asking critical questions that could solve a puzzle (Kuiper, 1994).

Isolation of the faculty is a major concern at higher educational institutions (Massy *et al.*, 1994). In these cases, individuals lacked interaction and communication skills. The University of Tennessee teaches students interdisciplinary applications through a year-long case study course that attacks cross-functional problems.

Change receptivity

Massy *et al.* (1994) state that faculty members who narrowly specialize are reluctant to embrace new theories, discounting possible advancements and leading to inflexibility. Where differences are openly discussed, however, tolerance increases (Barker and Barker, 1994). Mason (1992) attributes much of this resistance to change in higher education and corporate America to complacency, resulting from successes in the 1960s and 1970s. Although organizations recognize the need to manage change, a Gallup poll of 400 *Fortune 1000* senior executives revealed that 62 percent of executives surveyed are reluctant to deal with change (Warbler, 1994).

Intercultural awareness

A growing number of multinational companies in the world focus attention on intercultural awareness (Tully, 1988). European businesses and universities are particularly adept in this area. Inter-cultural concerns pervade course work and training programs. Fluency in at least two languages, cross-cultural training, and cultural sensitivity training (Clark and Arbel, 1993) are recommended for those entering the job market.

Conclusion and Approach for Meeting Organizational Interdisciplinary Needs

The findings of this research document a continuing need to improve the skills of business graduates in the areas of communication, teamwork, and leadership through an understanding of cultural differences and global concerns. In order to produce graduates that meet the demands of the workplace, business schools must be prepared to initiate meaningful change that disrupts the status quo. Faculty members have the obligation and the opportunity to provide exemplary leadership by communicating the benefits of change and dispelling the fears surrounding it. The Executive MBA Program at Virginia Commonwealth University (VCU) illustrates how faculty commitment can lead to a marketable degree program that mirrors the interdisciplinary nature of the business world.

In addition to this research, the university conducted extensive research that suggested an alternative approach to its traditional MBA program. Encouragement from business leaders prompted VCU to offer an MBA Program that integrates accounting, finance, marketing, and management, rather than presenting them as separate subjects. Second, in this program, issues such as communication, system thinking, teamwork, quality, leadership, and global perspective are treated as pervasive elements. Third, the structure of the program fosters an interactive, participative environment that teaches students to address business situations with an interdisciplinary, team approach that closely resembles progressive business practice.

The role of communication cannot be overstated as VCU's faculty and administration overcame their natural inclination to maintain status quo in the development and delivery of instructional material. Executive MBA instructors accept team teaching roles that require them to present material when it will most aid the learning process. For example, if a class studies a business situation that calls for involvement of multiple corporate functional departments, instructors from the corresponding disciplines present possible solutions in rapid succession from their perspectives. In a traditional MBA program, however, the problem would be addressed in single class from the perspective of one instructor within the confines of a single discipline. The intensity of the program allows participants to graduate with marketable business skills in just 18 months, without sacrificing the academic integrity of the university. Successful implementation of an MBA program similar to VCU's Executive MBA advances the broad communication skills of the students and hinges on the ability of the instructors to communicate effectively in the development and delivery phases of the program.

In summary, as academicians, practitioners, business and government executives, it is time to remove the harsh terrain that comes between us if we are to meet the demands of the next millennium. Programs that value interdisciplinary diversity can help accomplish the needs of our organizations. Who knows what we might discover as we continue to communicate and evolve resisting the temptation to reward the status quo?

References

Andrews, R.L. and Gilbreath, G.H. (1991), "Strategies for improving the quality of instruction in higher education," *Proceedings, Southeastern Chapter, The Institute of Management Sciences*, pp. 323–5.

Barker, R.T. (1990), "Building that interaction bridge: effective communication strategies for the behavioral and decision sciences," *ORSA/ TIMS Annual Conference Proceedings*, Las Vegas, Nevada, May 5–7.

Barker S.B. and Barker, R.T. (1994), "Managing change in an interdisciplinary inpatient unit: an action research approach," *The Journal of Mental Health Administration*, Vol. 21 No. 1, pp. 80–91.

Bedeian, A.G. (1989), "Totems and taboos: understanding in the management discipline," *The Academy of Management News*, Vol. 19 No. 4, pp. 1–6.

Bickerstaffe, G. (1994), "Lesson of the master's: MBA degrees", *International Management*, April.

Bowen, D.E. (1990), "Interdisciplinary study of services: some progress, some prospects," *Journal of International Business Studies*, Vol. 20 No. 1, pp. 71–9.

Clampitt, P.G. and Downs, C.W. (1993), "Employee perceptions of the relationship between communication and productivity," *The Journal od Business Communication*, Vol. 30 No. 1, pp. 5–28.

Clark, J.J. and Arbel, A. (1993), "Producing global managers: the need for a new academic paradigm," *Cornell Hotel and Restaurant Administration Quarterly*, Vol. 34 No. 4.

Dulek, R.D. and Fielden, J.S. (1992), "Why fight the system? The non-choice facing beleaguered business faculties: business schools," *Business Horizons*, Vol. 35 No. 5, pp. 13–24.

Elliott, C.J., Goodwin, J.S. and Goodwin, J.C. (1994), "MBA programs and business needs: is there a mismatch?," *Business Horizons*, July/August, pp. 55–60.

Fimbel, N. (1994), "Communicating realistically: taking account of politics in internal business communications," *Journal of Business Communication*, Vol. 31 No. 1, pp. 7–26.

Gans, H.J. (1989), "Sociology in America: the discipline and the public," *American Sociological Review*, Vol. 54, pp. 1–16.

Golembiewski, R.T. (1985), *Humanizing Public Organizations*, Lomond, Mt. Airy, MD.

Graham, R.J. (1978), "Management sciences process—EOQ—one more with feeling," *Interfaces*, Vol. 9 No. 1, pp. 40–4.

Harvard Business Review (1992), "MBA: is the traditional model doomed?," November/December, p. 128.

Kuiper, S. (1994), "The challenge of interdisciplinary research," *The Journal of Business Communication*, Vol. 31 No. 2, pp. 137–51.

Leavitt, H.J. (1986), *Corporate Pathfinders: Building Vision and Values into our Organizations*, Dow-Jones-Irwin, Homewood, IL.

Leonard (1992), *Harvard Business Review*, November–December.

Lorange, P. (1994), "Back to school: executive education in the US business schools," *Chief Executive*, March.

Marbler, K. (1994), "Change management: still a scary subject," *CMA Magazine*, February.

Mason, J.C. (1992), ".Business schools: striving to meet customer demand," *Management Review*, Vol. 81 No. 9, pp. 10–17.

Massy, W.F., Wilger, A.K. and Colbeck, C. (1994), "Overcoming 'hollowed' collegiality," *Change*, July/August, pp. 11–20.

Muller, H.J., Porter, J.L., and Rehder, R.R. (1991), "Reinventing the MBA the European way," *Business Horizons*, Vol. 34 No. 3, pp 83–93.

Odegaard, C.E. (1987), "A historical perspective on the dilemmas confronting psychology," *American Psychologist*, Vol. 42, pp. 1048–51.

Peters, T. (1992), *Liberation Management*, Alfred A. Knopf, New York, NY.

Pfeiffer, J. (1994), "Competitive advantage through people," *California Management Review*, Vol. 36 No. 2, pp. 9–28.

Porter, J.L., Muller, H. ., and Rehder, R.R. (1991), "The new wave in management education," *Across the Board*, June.

Scullion, H. (1992), "Attracting management globetrotters: recruiting international managers," *Personnel Management*, January.

Shalinsky, W. (1989), "Polydisciplinary groups in the human services," *Small Group Behavior*, Vol. 20 No. 2, pp. 203–19.

Showalter, M.J. (1992), "Integration of P/OM and MIS research," *Decision Line*, December/January, p. 17.

Storey, J. (1985), "Management control as a bridging concept," *Management Science*, Vol. 3, pp. 269–91.

The Economist (1994), "The flawed education of the European businessman," June 4, pp. 89–91.

Tully, S. (1988), "Europe's best business schools," *Fortune*, May 23.

Readings 15 and 16

Reading 15, "The Creative Class," and Reading 16, "The Machine Shop and the Hair Salon," are chapters from Richard Florida's important 2002 book, **The Rise of the Creative Class**. In this book Florida demonstrates the need for creativity in the workplace.

In Reading 15, "The Creative Class," Florida describes what is the creative class as well as the characteristics of its members.

In Reading 16, "The Machine Shop and the Hair Salon," Florida discusses what motivates the Creative Class.

READING

THE CREATIVE CLASS

by

Richard Florida

The rise of the Creative Economy has had a profound effect on the sorting of people into social groups or classes. Others have speculated over the years on the rise of new classes in the advanced industrial economies. During the 1960s, Peter Drucker and Fritz Machlup described the growing role and importance of the new group of workers they dubbed "knowledge workers."[1] Writing in the 1970s, Daniel Bell pointed to a new, more meritocratic class structure of scientists, engineers, managers and administrators brought on by the shift from a manufacturing to a "postindustrial" economy. The sociologist Erik Olin Wright has written for decades about the rise of what he called a new "professional-managerial" class.[2] Robert Reich more recently advanced the term "symbolic analysts" to describe the members of the workforce who manipulate ideas and symbols.[3] All of these observers caught economic aspects of the emerging class structure that I describe here.

Others have examined emerging social norms and value systems. Paul Fussell presciently captured many that I now attribute to the Creative Class in his theory of the "X Class." Near the end of his 1983 book *Class*—after a witty romp through status markers that delineate, say, the upper middle class from "high proles"—Fussell noted the presence of a growing "X" group that seemed to defy existing categories:

> [Y]ou are not born an X person . . . you earn X-personhood by a strenuous effort of discovery in which curiosity and originality are indispensable. . . . The young flocking to the cities to devote themselves to "art," "writing," "creative work"—anything, virtually, that liberates them from the presence of a boss or superior—are aspirant X people. . . . If, as [C. Wright] Mills has said, the middle-class person is "always somebody's man," the X person is nobody's. . . . X people are independent-minded. . . . They adore the work they do, and they do it until they are finally carried out, "retirement" being a concept meaningful only to hired personnel or wage slaves who despise their work.[4]

Writing in 2000, David Brooks outlined the blending of bohemian and bourgeois values in a new social grouping he dubbed the Bobos. My take on Brooks's synthesis . . . is rather different, stressing the very transcendence of these two categories in a new creative ethos.

The main point I want to make here is that the basis of the Creative Class is economic. I define it as an economic class and argue that its economic function both underpins and informs its members' social, cultural and lifestyle choices. The Creative Class consists of people who add economic value through their creativity. It thus includes a great many knowledge workers, symbolic analysts and professional and technical workers, but emphasizes their true role in the economy. My definition of class emphasizes the way people organize themselves into social groupings and common identities based principally on their economic function. Their social and cultural preferences, consumption and buying habits, and their social identities all flow from this.

I am not talking here about economic class in terms of the ownership of property, capital or the means of production. If we use class in this traditional Marxian sense, we are still talking about a basic structure of capitalists who own and control the means of production, and workers under their employ. But little analytical utility remains in these broad categories of bourgeoisie and proletarian, capitalist and worker. Most members of the Creative Class do not own and control any significant property in the physical sense. Their property—which stems from their creative capacity—is an intangible because it is literally in their heads. And it is increasingly clear from my field research and interviews that while the members of the Creative Class do not yet see themselves as a unique social grouping, they actually share many similar tastes, desires and preferences. This new class may not be as distinct in this regard as the industrial Working Class in its heyday, but it has an emerging coherence.

The New Class Structure

The distinguishing characteristic of the Creative Class is that its members engage in work whose function is to "create meaningful new forms." I define the Creative Class as consisting of two components. The Super-Creative Core of this new class includes scientists and engineers, university professors, poets and novelists, artists, entertainers, actors, designers and architects, as well as the thought leadership of modern society: nonfiction writers, editors, cultural figures, think-tank researchers, analysts and other opinion-makers. Whether they are software programmers or engineers, architects or filmmakers, they fully engage in the creative process. I define the highest order of creative work as producing new forms or designs that are readily transferable and widely useful—such as designing a product that can be widely made, sold and used; coming up with a theorem or strategy that can be applied in many cases; or composing music that can be performed again and again. People at the core of the Creative Class engage in this kind of work regularly; it's what they *are* paid to do. Along with problem solving, their work may entail problem finding: not just building a better mousetrap, but noticing first that a better mousetrap would be a handy thing to have.

Beyond this core group, the Creative Class also includes "creative professionals" who work in a wide range of knowledge-intensive industries such as high-tech sectors, financial services, the legal and health care professions, and business management. These people engage in creative problem solving, drawing on complex bodies of knowledge to solve specific problems. Doing so typically requires a high degree of formal education and thus a high level of human capital. People who do this kind of work may sometimes come up with methods or products that turn out to be widely useful, but it's not part of the basic job description. What they *are* required to do regularly is think on their own. They apply or combine standard approaches in unique ways to fit the situation, exercise a great deal of judgment, perhaps try something radically new from time to time. Creative Class people such as physicians, lawyers and managers do this kind of work in dealing with the many varied cases they encounter. In the course of their work, they may also be involved in testing and refining new techniques, new treatment protocols, or new management methods and even develop such things themselves. As a person continues to do more of this latter work, perhaps through a career shift or promotion, that person moves up to the Super-Creative Core: producing transferable, widely usable new forms is now their primary function.

Much the same is true of the growing number of technicians and others who apply complex bodies of knowledge to working with physical materials. And they are sufficiently engaged in creative problem solving that I have included a large subset of them in the Creative Class. In an insightful 1996 study, Stephen Barley of Stanford University emphasized the growing importance and influence of this group of workers.[5] In fields such as medicine and scientific research, technicians are taking on increased responsibility to interpret their work and make decisions, blurring the old distinction between white-collar work (done by decisionmakers) and blue-collar work (done by those who follow orders). Barley notes that in medicine, for instance, "emergency medical technicians take action on the basis of diagnoses made at the site," while sonographers and radiology technicians draw on "knowledge of biological systems, pharmacology, and disease processes to render diagnostically useful information"—all of which encroaches on turf once reserved for the M.D.

Barley also found that in some areas of biomedical work, like the breeding of monoclonal antibodies, labs have had increasing difficulty duplicating each other's work: They might use the same formulas and well-documented procedures but not get the same results. The reason is that although the lead scientists at the labs might be working from the same theories, the lab technicians are called upon to make myriad interpretations and on-the-spot decisions. And while different technicians might all do these things according to accepted standards, they do them differently. Each is drawing on an arcane knowledge base and exercising his or her own judgment, by individual thought processes so complex and elusive that they could not easily be documented or communicated. Though counterproductive in this case, this individuality happens to be one of the hallmarks of creative work. Lest you think this sort of thing happens only in the rarefied world of the biomedical laboratory, Barley notes a similar phenomenon among technicians who repair and maintain copying machines. They acquire their own arcane bodies of knowledge and develop their own unique ways of doing the job.

As the creative content of other lines of work increases—as the relevant body of knowledge becomes more complex, and people are more valued for their ingenuity in applying it—some now in the Working Class or Service Class may move into the Creative Class and even the Super-Creative Core. Alongside the growth in essentially creative occupations, then, we are also seeing growth in creative content across other occupations. A prime example is the secretary in today's pared-down offices. In many cases this person not only takes on a host of tasks once performed by a large secretarial staff, but becomes a true office manager—channeling flows of information, devising and setting up new systems, often making key decisions on the fly. This person contributes more than "intelligence" or computer skills. She or he adds creative value. Everywhere we look, creativity is increasingly valued. Firms and organizations value it for the results that it can produce and individuals value it as a route to self-expression and job satisfaction. Bottom line: As creativity becomes more valued, the Creative Class grows.

Not all workers are on track to join, however. For instance in many lower-end service jobs we find the trend running the opposite way; the jobs continue to be "de-skilled" or "de-creatified." For a counter worker at a fast-food chain, literally every word and move is dictated by a corporate template: "Welcome to Food Fix, sir, may I take your order? Would you like nachos with that?" This job has been thoroughly taylorized—the worker is given far less latitude for exercising creativity than the waitress at the old, independent neighborhood diner enjoyed. Worse yet, there are many people who do not have jobs, and who are being left behind because they do not have the background and training to be part of this new system.

Growing alongside the Creative Class is another social grouping I call the Service Class—which contains low-end, typically low-wage and low-autonomy occupations in the so-called "service sector" of the economy: food-service workers, janitors and groundskeepers, personal care attendants, secretaries and clerical workers, and security guards and other service occupations. In U.S. Bureau of Labor Statistics projections from the late 1990s and 2000, the fastest-growing job categories included "janitors and cleaners" and "waiters and waitresses" alongside "computer support specialists" and "systems analysts." The growth of this Service Class is in large measure a response to the demands of the Creative Economy. Members of the Creative Class, because they are well compensated and work long and unpredictable hours, require a growing pool of low-end service workers to take care of them and do their chores. This class has thus been created out of economic necessity because of the way the Creative Economy operates. Some people are temporary members of the Service Class, have high upward mobility and will soon move into the Creative Class—college students working nights or summers as food clerks or office cleaners, and highly educated recent immigrants driving cabs in New York City or Washington, D.C. A few, entrepreneurial ones may be successful enough to open their own restaurants, lawn and garden services and the like. But many others have no way out and are stuck for life in menial jobs as food-service help, janitors, nursing home orderlies, security guards and delivery drivers. At its minimum-wage worst, life in the Service Class is a grueling struggle for existence amid the wealth of others. By going "under cover" as a service worker, Barbara Ehrenreich provided a moving chronicle of what life is like for people in these roles in her book *Nickel and Dimed*.[6]

A study of the Austin, Texas, economy sheds light on the growing gaps between the Creative and Service Classes. Austin is a leading center of the Creative Economy and consistently ranks among the top regions on my indicators. A study by Robert Cushing and Musseref Yetim of the University of Texas compared Austin, which in 1999 had a whopping 38 percent of its private-sector workforce in high-tech industries, to other regions in the state. Between 1990 and 1999, average private-sector wages in Austin grew by 65 percent, far and away the most in the state. During that same time, the gap between wages earned by the top fifth and the bottom fifth of the people in Austin grew by 70 percent—also far and away the most in the state. Remove the high-tech sector from the equation and both effects go away. There is a perfectly logical reason for the gap: High-tech specialists were in short supply so their wages were bid up. And in fairness, it should be noted that Austin's bottom fifth of wage earners weren't left out entirely. Their income did go up from 1990 to 1999, and more than for their counterparts in other Texas regions. Apparently Austin had a growing need for their services, too. But these trends do more than illustrate a widening income gap. They point to a real divide in terms of what people do with their lives—with the economic positions and lifestyle choices of some people driving and perpetuating the types of choices available to others.[7]

Counting the Creative Class

It is one thing to provide a compelling description of the changing class composition of society, as writers like Bell, Fussell or Reich have done. But I believe it is also important to calibrate and quantify the magnitude of the change at hand. In 1996, Steven Barley estimated that professional, technical and managerial occupations increased from 10 percent of the workforce in 1900 to 30 percent by 1991, while both blue-collar work and agricultural work fell precipitously.[8] In a 2001 article, the sociologist Steven Brint estimated that the "scientific, professional and knowledge economy" accounted for 36 percent of all U.S. employment in 1996—a human capital-based estimate including industries where at least 5 percent of the workforce has graduate degrees. His definition includes agricultural services, mass media, chemicals, plastics, pharmaceuticals, computers and electric equipment, scientific instruments, banking, accounting, consulting and other business services, health services and hospitals, education, legal services and nearly all religious and governmental organizations.[9]

Working with colleagues and graduate students at Carnegie Mellon, I developed a detailed statistical portrait of the rise of the Creative Class and the changing class structure of the United States over the twentieth century (see Figs. 13.1 and 13.2). I believe this definition is an improvement over previous concepts of knowledge workers and the like. I base it on the "standard occupational classifications" collected by the U.S. Census and available in its historical statistics from 1900 to the present. (The Appendix of my book *The Creative Class,* provides a complete explanation of all data and sources.) Let's take a look at the key trends.

■   The *Creative Class* now includes some 38.3 million Americans, roughly 30 percent of the entire U.S. workforce. It has grown from roughly 3 million workers in 1900, an increase of more than tenfold. At the turn of the twentieth century, the Creative Class made up just 10 percent of the workforce, where it hovered until 1950 when it began a slow rise; it held steady around 20 percent in the 1970s and 1980s. Since that time, this new class has virtually exploded, increasing from less than 20 million to its current total, reaching 25 percent of the working population in 1991 before climbing to 30 percent by 1999.

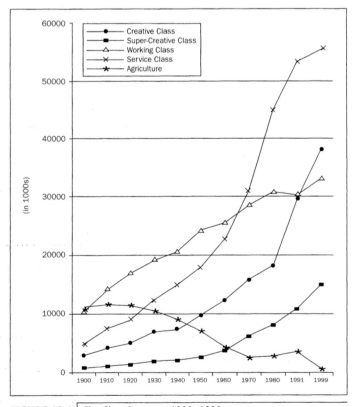

FIGURE 13.1 | The Class Structure, 1900–1999

(SOURCE: See Appendix.)

- At the heart of the Creative Class is the *Super-Creative Core,* comprising 15 million workers, or 12 percent of the workforce. It is made up of people who work in science and engineering, computers and mathematics, education, and the arts, design and entertainment, people who work in directly creative activity, as we have seen. Over the past century, this segment rose from less than 1 million workers in 1900 to 2.5 million in 1950 before crossing 10 million in 1991. In doing so, it increased its share of the workforce from 2.5 percent in 1900 to 5 percent in 1960, 8 percent in 1980 and 9 percent in 1990, before reaching 12 percent by 1999.
- The traditional *Working Class* has today 33 million workers, or a quarter of the U.S. workforce. It consists of people in production operations, transportation and materials moving, and repair and maintenance and construction work. The percentage of the workforce in working-class occupations peaked at 40 percent in 1920, where it hovered until 1950, before slipping to 36 percent in 1970, and then declining sharply over the past two decades.
- The *Service Class* includes 55.2 million workers or 43 percent of the U.S. workforce, making it the largest group of all. It includes workers in lower-wage, lower-autonomy service occupations such as health care, food. preparation, personal care, clerical work and other lower-end office work. Alongside the decline of the Working Class, the past century has seen a tremendous rise in the Service Class, from 5 million workers in 1900 to its current total of more than ten times that amount.

It's also useful to look at the changing composite picture of the U.S. class structure over the twentieth century. In 1900, there were some 10 million people in the Working Class, compared to 2.9 million in the Creative Class and 4.8 million in the Service Class. The Working Class was thus larger than the two other classes combined. Yet the largest class at that time was agricultural workers, who composed nearly 40 percent of the workforce but whose numbers rapidly declined to just a very small percentage today. In 1920, the Working Class accounted for 40 percent of the workforce, compared to slightly more than 12 percent for the Creative Class and 21 percent for the Service Class.

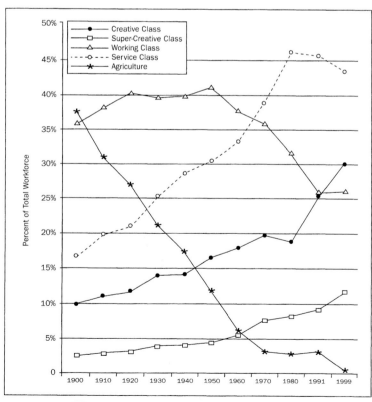

FIGURE 13.2 | The Class Structure, 1900–1999 (Percent of Work Force)

(SOURCE: See Appendix.)

In 1950, the class structure remained remarkably similar. The Working Class was still in the majority, with 25 million workers, some 40 percent of the workforce, compared to 10 million in the Creative Class (16.5 percent) and 18 million in the Service Class (30 percent). In relative terms, the Working Class was as large as it was in 1920 and bigger than it was in 1900. Though the Creative Class had grown slightly in percentage terms, the Service Class had grown considerably, taking up much of the slack coming from the steep decline in agriculture.

The tectonic shift in the U.S. class structure has taken place over the past two decades. In 1970, the Service Class pulled ahead of the Working Class, and by 1980 it was much larger (46 versus 32 percent), marking the first time in the twentieth century that the Working Class was not the dominant class. By 1999, both the Creative Class and the Service Class had pulled ahead of the Working Class. The Service Class, with 55 million workers (43.4 percent), was bigger in relative terms than the Working Class had been at any time in the past century.

These changes in American class structure reflect a deeper, more general process of economic and social change. The decline of the old Working Class is part and parcel of the decline of the industrial economy on which it was based, and of the social and demographic patterns upon which that old society was premised. The Working Class no longer has the hand it once did in setting the tone or establishing the values of American life—for that matter neither does the 1950s managerial class. Why, then, have the social functions of the Working Class not been taken over by the new largest class, the Service Class? As we have seen, the Service Class has little clout and its rise in numbers can be understood only alongside the rise of the Creative Class. The Creative Class—and the modern Creative Economy writ large—depends on this ever-larger Service Class to "outsource" functions that were previously provided within the family. The Service Class exists mainly as a supporting infrastructure for the Creative Class and the Creative Economy. The Creative Class also has considerably more economic power. Members earn substantially more than those in other classes. In 1999, the average salary for a member of the Creative Class was nearly $50,000 ($48,752) compared to roughly $28,000 for a Working Class member and $22,000 for a Service Class worker (see Table 15-1).

I see these trends vividly played out in my own life. I have a nice house with a nice kitchen but it's often mostly a fantasy kitchen—I eat out a lot, with "servants" preparing my food and waiting on me. My house is clean, but I don't clean it, a housekeeper does. I also have a gardener and a pool service; and (when I take a taxi) a chauffeur. I have, in short, just about all the servants of an English lord except that they're not mine full-time and they don't live below stairs; they are part-time and distributed in the local area. Not all of these "servants" are lowly serfs. The person who cuts my hair is a very creative stylist much in demand, and drives a new BMW. The woman who cleans my house is a gem: I trust her not only to clean but to rearrange and suggest ideas for redecorating; she takes on these things in an entrepreneurial manner. Her husband drives a Porsche. To some degree, these members of the Service Class have adopted many of the functions along with the tastes and values of the Creative Class, with which they see themselves sharing much in common. Both my hairdresser and my housekeeper have taken up their lines of work to get away from the regimentation of large organizations; both of them relish creative pursuits. Service Class people such as these are close to the mainstream of the Creative Economy and prime candidates for reclassification.

TABLE 15-1 Wages and Salaries for the Classes

CATEGORY	TOTAL WORKERS	AVERAGE HOURLY WAGE	AVERAGE ANNUAL SALARY
Creative Class	38,278,110	$23.44	$48,752
Super-Creative Core	14,932,420	20.54	42,719
Working Class	33,238,810	13.36	27,799
Service Class	55,293,720	10.61	22,059
Agriculture	463,360	8.65	18,000
Entire US	127,274,000	15.18	31,571

SOURCE: Occupational Employment Statistics (OES) Survey, Bureau of Labor Statistics, Department of Labor, 1999, see Appendix.

Creative Class Values

The rise of the Creative Class is reflected in powerful and significant shifts in values, norms and attitudes. Although these changes are still in process and certainly not fully played out, a number of key trends have been discerned by researchers who study values, and I have seen them displayed in my field research across the United States. Not all of these attitudes break with the past: Some represent a melding of traditional values and newer ones. They are also values that have long been associated with more highly educated and creative people. On the basis of my own interviews and focus groups, along with a close reading of statistical surveys conducted by others, I cluster these values along three basic lines.

Individuality. The members of the Creative Class exhibit a strong preference for individuality and self-statement. They do not want to conform to organizational or institutional directives and resist traditional group-oriented norms. This has always been the case among creative people from "quirky" artists to "eccentric" scientists. But it has now become far more pervasive. In this sense, the increasing nonconformity to organizational norms may represent a new mainstream value. Members of the Creative Class endeavor to create individualistic identities that reflect their creativity. This can entail a mixing of multiple creative identities

Meritocracy. Merit is very strongly valued by the Creative Class, a quality shared with Whyte's class of organization men. The Creative Class favors hard work, challenge and stimulation. Its members have a propensity for goal-setting and achievement. They want to get ahead because they are good at what they do.

Creative Class people no longer define themselves mainly by the amount of money they make or their position in a financially delineated status order. While money may be looked upon as a marker of achievement, it is not the whole story. In interviews and focus groups, I consistently come across people valiantly trying to defy an economic class into which they were born. This is particularly true of the young descendants of the truly wealthy—the capitalist class—who frequently describe themselves as just "ordinary" creative people working on music, film or intellectual endeavors of one sort or another. Having absorbed the Creative Class value of merit, they no longer find true status in their wealth and thus try to downplay it.

There are many reasons for the emphasis on merit. Creative Class people are ambitious and want to move up based on their abilities and effort. Creative people have always been motivated by the respect of their peers. The companies that employ them are often under tremendous competitive pressure and thus cannot afford much dead wood on staff: Everyone has to contribute. The pressure is more intense than ever to hire the best people regardless of race, creed, sexual preference or other factors.

But meritocracy also has its dark side. Qualities that confer merit, such as technical knowledge and mental discipline, are socially acquired and cultivated. Yet those who have these qualities may easily start thinking they were born with them, or acquired them all on their own, or that others just "don't have it." By papering over the causes of cultural and educational advantage, meritocracy may subtly perpetuate the very prejudices it claims to renounce. On the bright side, of course, meritocracy ties into a host of values and beliefs we'd all agree are positive—from faith that virtue will be rewarded, to valuing self-determination and mistrusting rigid caste systems. Researchers have found such values to be on the rise, not only among the Creative Class in the United States, but throughout our society and other societies.

Diversity and Openness. Diversity has become a politically charged buzzword. To some it is an ideal and rallying cry, to others a Trojan-horse concept that has brought us affirmative action and other liberal abominations. The Creative Class people I study use the word a lot, but not to press any political hot buttons. Diversity is simply something they value in all its manifestations. This is spoken of so often, and so matter-of-factly, that I take it to be a fundamental marker of Creative Class values. As my focus groups and interviews reveal, members of this class strongly favor organizations and environments in which they feel that anyone can fit in and can get ahead.

Diversity of peoples is favored first of all out of self-interest. Diversity can be a signal of meritocratic norms at work. Talented people defy classification based on race, ethnicity, gender, sexual preference or appearance. One indicator of this preference for diversity is reflected in the fact that Creative Class people tell me that at job interviews they like to ask if the company offers same-sex partner benefits, even when they are not themselves gay. What they're seeking is an environment open to differences. Many highly creative people, regardless of ethnic background or sexual orientation, grew up feeling like outsiders, different in some way from most of their schoolmates. They may have odd personal habits or extreme styles of dress. Also, Creative Class people are mobile and tend to move around to different parts of the country; they may not be "natives" of the place they live even if they are American-born. When they are sizing up a new company and community, acceptance of diversity and of gays in particular is a sign that reads "non-standard people welcome here." It also registers itself in changed behaviors and organizational policies. For example, in some Creative Class centers like Silicon Valley and Austin, the traditional office Christmas party is giving way to more secular, inclusive celebrations. The big event at many firms is now the Halloween party: Just about anyone can relate to a holiday that involves dressing up in costume.

While the Creative Class favors openness and diversity, to some degree it is a diversity of elites, limited to highly educated, creative people. Even though the rise of the Creative Class has opened up new avenues of advancement for women and members of ethnic minorities, its existence has certainly failed to put an end to long-standing divisions of race and gender. Within high-tech industries in particular these divisions still seem to hold. The world of high-tech creativity doesn't include many African-Americans. Several of my interviewees noted that a typical high-tech company "looks like the United Nations minus the black faces." This is unfortunate but not surprising. For several reasons, U.S. blacks are underrepresented in many professions, and this may be compounded today by the so-called digital divide—black families in the United States tend to be poorer than average, and thus their children are less likely to have access to computers. My own research shows a negative statistical correlation between concentrations of high-tech firms in a region and nonwhites as a percentage of the population, which is particularly disturbing in light of my other findings on the positive relationship between high-tech and other kinds of diversity—from foreign-born people to gays.

There are intriguing challenges to the kind of diversity that the members of the Creative Class are drawn to. Speaking of a small software company that had the usual assortment of Indian, Chinese, Arabic and other employees, an Indian technology professional said: "That's not diversity! They're all software engineers." Yet despite the holes in the picture, distinctive value changes are indeed afoot, as other researchers have clearly found.

The Post-Scarcity Effect

Ronald Inglehart, a political science professor at the University of Michigan, has documented the powerful shift in values and attitudes across the world in more than two decades of careful research. In three periods over the past twenty years, researchers participating in Inglehart's World Values Survey administered detailed questionnaires to random samples of adults in countries around the world.[10] By 1995–1998, the last survey period, the number of nations studied had grown to sixty-five, including about 75 percent of the world's population. Along with specific issues like divorce, abortion and suicide, the survey delved into matters such as deference to authority versus deciding for oneself, openness versus insularity (can strangers be trusted?), and what, ultimately, is important in life. Inglehart and his colleagues have sifted the resulting data to look for internal correlations (which kinds of values tend to go together) and for correlations with economic and social factors such as a nation's level of economic development, form of government and religious heritage. The researchers compared nations to one another, mapping out various similarities and differences—and they also looked for changes over time.

Among other things, Inglehart found a worldwide shift from economic growth issues to lifestyle values, which he sometimes refers to as a shift from "survival" to "self-expression" values. Moreover where lifestyle issues are rising or dominant, as in the United States and most European societies, people tend to be relatively tolerant of other groups and in favor of gender equality. This is very much in line with Creative Class values. In everything from sexual norms and gender roles to environmental values, Inglehart finds a continued movement away from traditional norms to more progressive ones. Furthermore, as economies grow, living standards improve and people grow less attached to large institutions, they become more open and tolerant in their views on personal relationships. Inglehart believes this new value system reflects a "shift in what people want out of life, transforming basic norms governing politics, work, religion, family and sexual behavior."

In their 2000 book *The Cultural Creatives,* sociologist Paul H. Ray and psychologist Ruth Anderson report similar conclusions. They estimate that some 50 million Americans fall into the category of cultural creatives, having neither "traditional" nor conventionally "modern" values. These people tend to be socially active on issues that concern them, pro-environment and in favor of gender equality. Many are spiritually oriented, though rejecting mainstream religious beliefs. Members of this group are more likely than others to be interested in personal development and relationships, have eclectic tastes, enjoy "foreign and exotic" experiences, and identify themselves as being "not financially materialistic." In short, these cultural creatives have values that Inglehart refers to as "postmaterialist."

This shift in values and attitudes, Inglehart argues, is driven by changes in our material conditions. In agricultural societies and even for much of the industrial age, people basically lived under conditions of scarcity. We had to work simply to survive. The rise of an affluent or "post-scarcity" economy means that we no longer have to devote all our energies just to staying alive, but have the wealth, time and ability to enjoy other aspects of life. This in turn affords us choices we did not have before. "Precisely because they attained high levels of economic security," writes Inglehart, "the Western societies that were the first to industrialize have gradually come to emphasize post-materialist values, giving higher priority to the quality of life than to economic growth. In this respect, the rise of post-materialist values reverses the rise of the Protestant ethic."[12] The overriding trend appears to be

> an intergenerational shift from emphasis on economic and physical security toward increasing emphasis on self-expression, subjective well-being, and quality of life. . . . This cultural shift is found throughout advanced industrial societies; it seems to emerge among birth cohorts that have grown up under conditions in which survival is taken for granted.[13]

The Nobel Prize-winning economist Robert Fogel concurs: "Today, people are increasingly concerned with what life is all about. That was not true for the ordinary individual in 1885 when nearly the whole day was devoted to earning the food, clothing, and shelter needed to sustain life."[14] Even though many conservative commentators bemoan these shifts as hedonistic, narcissistic and damaging to society, the Creative Class is anything but radical or nonconformist. On the one hand, its members have taken what looked to be alternative values and made them mainstream. On the other, many of these values—such as the commitment to meritocracy and to hard work—are quite traditional and system-reinforcing. In my interviews, members of the Creative Class resist characterization as alternative or bohemian. These labels suggest being outside or even against the prevailing culture, and they insist they are part of the culture, working and living inside it. In this regard, the Creative Class has made certain symbols of nonconformity acceptable—even conformist. It is in this sense that, they represent not an alternative group but a new and increasingly norm-setting mainstream of society.

Perhaps we are indeed witnessing the rise of what Mokyr calls *homo creativus*. We live differently and pursue new lifestyles because we see ourselves as a new kind of person. We are more tolerant and more liberal both because our material conditions allow it and because the new Creative Age tells us to be so. A new social class, in short, has risen to a position of dominance in the. last two decades, and this shift has fundamentally transformed our economy and society—and continues to do so.

Reading 15 Notes "Creative Class"

1. See Daniel Bell, *The Coming of Post-Industrial Society*. New York: Basic Books, 1973; Peter Drucker, *The Age of Discontinuity*. New York: HarperCollins, 1969; Drucker, *Post-Capitalist Society*. New York: Harper Business, 1995; Fritz Machlup, *The Production and Distribution of Knowledge in the United States*. Princeton: Princeton University Press, 1962.
2. See, for example, Erik Olin Wright, *Classes*. London: Verso, 1990; *Class Counts*. Cambridge, England: Cambridge University Press, 1996; *Class Crisis and the State*. London: Verso, paperback reissue, 1996.
3. Robert Reich, *The Work of Nations*. New York: Alfred A. Knopf, 1991.
4. Paul Fussell, *Class: A Guide Through the American Status System*. New York: Summit, 1983.
5. Steven Barley, *The New World of Work*. London: British North American Committee, 1996.
6. Barbara Ehrenreich, *Nickel and Dimed: On Not Getting By in America*. New York: Henry Holt & Company, 2001.
7. As cited in Bill Bishop, "As City Booms, Poor Get Poorer." *Austin American-Statesman*, January 2, 2000.
8. Barley, *The New World of Work*, p. 7.
9. Steven Brint, "Professionals and the Knowledge Economy: Rethinking the Theory of the Postindustrial Society." *Current Sociology*, 49(1), July 2001, pp. 101–132.
10. See Ronald Inglehart, "Globalization and Postmodern Values." *The Washington Quarterly*, 23(1), Winter 2000, pp. 215–228; *The Silent Revolution: Changing Values and Political Styles in Advanced Industrial Society*. Princeton: Princeton University Press, 1977; *Culture Shift in Advanced Industrial Society*. Princeton: Princeton University Press, 1990; *Modernization and Postmodernization: Cultural, Economic and Political Change in Forty-Three Societies*. Princeton: Princeton University Press, 1997; and "Culture and Democracy," in Lawrence Harrison and Samuel Huntington (eds.), *Culture Matters: How Values Shape Human Progress*. New York: Basic Books, 2000, pp. 80–97.
11. Paul H. Ray and Sherry Ruth Anderson, *The Cultural Creatives: How 50 Million People Are Changing the World*. New York: Harmony Books, 2000. See introductory chapter, pp. 7–42, especially the "Values and Beliefs" charts, pp. 28–29. Inglehart is cited in the Preface, p. xii.
12. Inglehart, "Globalization and Postmodern Values," p. 225.

13. Inglehart, "Culture and Democracy," p. 84.
14. Robert Fogel, *The Fourth Great Awakening and the Future of Egalitarianism*. Chicago: University of Chicago Press, 2000, p. 191.

READING 16

THE MACHINE SHOP AND THE HAIR SALON

by

Richard Florida

DURING THE LATE 1990s I served on the board of Team Pennsylvania, an economic development advisory group convened by then-Governor Tom Ridge. At one of our meetings, the state's Secretary of Labor and Industry, a big burly man, banged his fist on the table in frustration. "Our workforce is out of balance," he steamed. "We're turning out too many hairdressers and cosmetologists, and not enough skilled factory workers" like welders and machine-tool operators to meet the labor market's needs. "What's wrong?" he implored the group.

The problem is not limited to Pennsylvania. There have been acute shortages of skilled factory workers across the United States and many find this perplexing. Machinists, for example, earn good wages and benefits. They do important work. For many years, a machinist's job was considered an elite career for anyone not college-bound. It is the sort of "good job" that politicians and editorial writers fretted that our economy was losing. Yet as older machinists retire, there are not enough young people to fill the positions that exist. Trade schools that teach skills like machining and welding have had to cut back or close their programs for lack of interest. Meanwhile, young men and women flock to beauty academies.

At the Team Pennsylvania meeting, the clear diagnosis was that (a) guidance counselors at high schools have been steering the kids wrong, because (b) our job projections have been off. If we fixed the projections and worked with the high schools—and maybe did some public-image work—surely droves of young people would come back to those good, secure manufacturing jobs.

After the meeting, I laid out the problem to my first-year public policy students at Carnegie Mellon. Then I asked them: If you had just two career choices open to you, where would you work—in a machine shop, with high pay and a job for life, or in a hair salon, with less pay and where you were subject to the whims of the economy? Later I started putting the same question to audiences across the country.

Time and again, most people chose the hair salon, and always for the same reasons. Sure, the pay isn't as good, but the environment is more stimulating. It's more flexible; it's clean; you're scheduled to meet your clients and then left alone with them, instead of grinding away to meet quotas and schedules with bosses looking over your shoulder. You get to work with interesting people and you're always learning new things, the latest styles. You get to add your own touches and make creative decisions, because every customer is a new challenge, and you're the one in charge. When you do good work, you see the results right away: People look good; they're happy. If you are really talented, you can open your own salon. Maybe even become a hairdresser to the rich and famous, like Christophe, who kept Air Force One on the runway while he gave Bill Clinton a hair-cut, and get written up in celebrity magazines. Even when I pressed the issue of pay, most said the pay differential really didn't matter. In almost every case, the content of the job and the nature of the work environment mattered much more than compensation.

I don't think guidance counselors can change this. The people in my straw poll who chose the hair salon saw it as the more creative, exciting and satisfying place to work. It offers intrinsic rewards—rewards inherent in the nature of the job. I suspect that similar motives drive many of the people who choose the hair salon in real life—as well as the growing numbers of young people who are "good with their hands" but choose to wrap their hands around a tattooing needle, DJ turntable or landscaping tools rather than the controls of a turret lathe. Moreover, these values and attitudes have continually turned up in more structured interviews and focus groups I conducted with Creative Class people and others across the United States. The same values also top the list in various statistical surveys of what people desire in their jobs—including two major recent surveys of information-technology workers.

Why are people's desires so different from what the pundits and policymakers say we should want? The reason is basic. These new attitudes reflect both the changing nature of work and the shifting desires of the Creative Class. Conventional wisdom says people work for money; they will go where the financial opportunities are best and the shot at financial security is greatest. In the halcyon days of the New Economy, this was widely assumed to be true even of high-tech creative workers, who were working for the chance to translate their stock options into untold wealth. That assumption was wrong. Writing at the apex of the New Economy, Peter Drucker had this to say:

> Bribing the knowledge workers on whom these industries depend will therefore simply not work. The key knowledge workers in these businesses will surely continue to expect to share financially in the fruits of their labor. But the financial fruits are likely to take much longer to ripen, if they ripen at all. . . . Increasingly, performance in these new knowledge-based industries will come to depend on running the institution so as to attract, hold, and motivate knowledge workers. When this can no longer be done by satisfying knowledge workers' greed, as we are now trying to do, it will have to be done by satisfying their values, and by giving them social recognition and social power. It will have to be done by turning them from subordinates into fellow executives, and from employees, however well paid, into partners.[1]

As this chapter will show, even dramatically changing economic conditions seem to have little effect on what most people, particularly creative people, want out of their work. Motivating creative people has always required more than money. It depends on intrinsic rewards and is tied to the very creative content of their work.

What Money Can't Buy

Of course people work to make money: It's necessary but not sufficient. During the NASDAQ crash, when mass layoffs were rampant at high-tech firms, I received the following e-mail from someone who had survived a round of head-cutting at the high-tech consulting company Sapient Systems: "Many of those I knew [who were laid off] have had little problem getting new jobs," he explained—but "we had a lot of really good people who wanted to work at Sapient because of the culture, and when they were let go it was like losing family." Then he added: "One of the most important things at Sapient is culture and hiring only the best people. Sapient does not pay the best, intentionally, because if you pay top dollar, then you get mercenaries and mercenaries don't help develop culture."[2] This was an astounding statement. Here was an employee writing at the darkest hour, with heads rolling all around him, and he was praising his employer for having the wisdom not to pay too highly. He also hints at another key point. For many people, the big worry during the high-tech downturn was not the loss of stock-option value or job security. It was that they might have to settle for "just a job," and perhaps not enjoy all the intrinsic rewards they'd grown accustomed to.

I am hardly the first observer to notice that money isn't the only thing people want Yet my research has convinced me that many firms, scholars and business pundits still overrate money as a motivating factor, especially in the world of creative work. What I find generally is the following:

- Yes, people want enough money to live in the manner they prefer.
- Even if earning enough to pay the bills, they will be unhappy if they feel they are not being paid what they're worth, as gauged, for instance, by how much work they think they do or by what their colleagues are paid.
- But while the absence of enough money is sufficient, in itself, to make them unhappy with their work, money alone will not make most workers happy, or committed, or motivated.

Creative people require more than *compensation* for their time—a quid pro quo trade of time and effort for cash and other financial considerations. "You cannot motivate the best people with money," says Eric Raymond, author of *The Cathedral and the Bazaar* and a leading authority on open source software. "Money is just a way to keep score.

The best people in any field are motivated by passion."[3] Yes, but passion for what? There is no one-size-fits-all answer. Passion varies because people are different. A number of books and studies on workplace motivation have tried to sort people into various groups on the basis of what they value most, and we'll look at some of these efforts shortly. I would also point out that people are complex. Most of us have mixed motives.

The *Information Week* Surveys

For all the attention given to workplace motivation over the years, surprisingly little hard numerical research or analysis has been done on what motivates today's creative workers.[4] In the summer of 2001, I had a chance to address this issue by analyzing data from what I believe are among the largest and most comprehensive extant surveys on the subject. As a columnist for *Information Week,* a print/on-line magazine covering the information-technology industry, I have access to the publication's research data. Every year *Information Week* conducts a Salary Survey that asks readers detailed questions not only about their pay and benefits, but about their job satisfaction and a host of work-related factors. Some 20,000 information-technology (IT) workers completed the survey in both 2000 and 2001. Of these, approximately 11,000 identified themselves as IT staff and 9,000 as management. The sample is not scientifically random, since people self-select by choosing to respond. But it is extremely large and it reaches far beyond the computer and software industries per se, including IT workers in virtually every sector of the economy.

IT workers provide an interesting vantage point from which to examine these issues. On the one hand, they have been said to be a fairly conventional sector of the Creative Class. They are certainly a good deal more mainstream than artists, musicians or advertising copywriters. On the other, IT workers are said to care a great deal about money. They are a high-paid segment of the workforce to begin with, and during the late 1990s, companies went to great lengths to provide bonuses, stock options, six-figure salaries and other financial incentives to lure them. My colleague Kevin Stolarick and I combed through the raw data from the *Information Week* surveys and repeatedly resifted it to seek a better understanding of what IT workers value.

One key question in the survey asked: "What matters most to you about your job?" It then listed thirty-eight factors from which respondents could check one or more. Just from glancing at the initial results, one bottom line is clear: Money is an important but insufficient motivator (see Fig. 16.1). Base pay ranked fourth as a key factor, selected by 38.5 percent of respondents. Nearly twice as many selected "challenge of job/responsibility," making it the top-ranked factor. Interestingly, the ability to share in the financial upside through stock options did not even make the top twenty: Fewer than 10 percent of all people selected it.

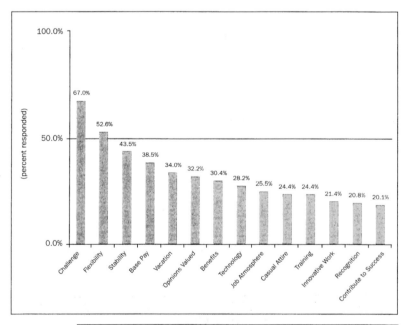

FIGURE 16.1 | What Matters Most to IT Workers (Based on 38 Individual Job Factors) IT workers value challenge, flexibility and stability over pay.

(SOURCE: *Information Week* Salary Survey, 2001, analysis by Richard Florida and Kevin Stolarick.)

When we sorted the thirty-eight individual job factors in the *Information Week* survey into eleven broad clusters, challenge remained by far the top-ranked factor, followed by flexibility and job stability (see Fig. 16.2). Compensation was again fourth, followed by peer respect, technology and location; and further down the list were company orientation, organizational culture, career orientation and benefits.

The things that matter to IT workers tend to stay fairly constant as economic conditions change. To determine this, I compared the *Information Week* surveys for two consecutive years. The surveys are taken early in the year and the one for 2000 was done before the high-tech downturn, when the stock-option dream was supposedly hottest. The 2001 survey came after the NASDAQ crash had supposedly wiped out the dream. The same three general attributes—a challenging job, a flexible workplace and job stability—topped the list in both years. Only a small percentage of people in each survey, the roughly 10 percent cited above, ranked stock options as being very important. Both before and after the crash, pay was generally important, but not nearly so much as intrinsic rewards. What people value and desire in their work is not contingent on the stock market or the rise and fall of the tech sector.

Beyond the Dollar

In the *Information Week* surveys as well as my own field research and statistical studies, certain job factors and workplace attributes keep showing up as highly valued. I digest them to a top-ten list as shown below. The list is not ranked. Suffice it to say that most people value one or more of these factors to varying degrees, with the mix varying from person to person. But note that nine of the ten highly valued job factors are intrinsic.

- *Challenge and responsibility*—being able to contribute and have impact; knowing that one's work makes a difference.
- *Flexibility*—a flexible schedule and a flexible work environment; the ability to shape one's work to some degree.
- *A stable work environment and a relatively secure job*—not lifetime security with mind-numbing sameness, but not a daily diet of chaos and uncertainty either.
- *Compensation*—especially base pay and core benefits: money you can count on.
- *Professional development*—the chance to learn and grow, to expand one's horizon for the future.
- *Peer recognition*—the chance to win the esteem and recognition of others in the know.

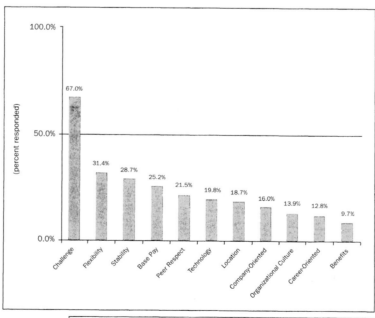

FIGURE 16.2 | What Matters Most to IT Workers (Out of 11 Key Categories)
Challenge far outranks other criteria when individual job factors from the survey are clustered.

(SOURCE: *Information Week* Salary Survey, 2001, analysis by Richard Florida and Kevin Stolarick.)

- *Stimulating colleagues and managers*—creative people like to be around other creative people, and they prefer leaders who neither micromanage nor ignore them.
- *Exciting job content*—the chance to work on projects and technologies that break new ground or pose interesting intellectual problems.
- *Organizational culture*—an elusive term that can include some factors already mentioned, plus more; perhaps best put for now as simply a culture in which the person feels at home, valued and supported.
- *Location and community*—a big factor.

These factors can and frequently do overlap. Any sorting of human motives and values into categories is arbitrary; there are many ways to slice the pie. Keeping that in mind, let's bring the picture to life by looking in more detail at a few of these factors.

Challenge and Responsibility

Participants in my focus groups and interviews like to be on the front lines, doing work that makes a difference. They talk about wanting to work on "exciting projects," "great technology" and "important stuff." And it's very important for them to work on things that will see the light of day. One of the most frustrating events is having a project dropped, pecked to death or strangled in red tape. One person commented, "I would go crazy if I could not contribute. I would die if I had to deal with constant bureaucracy and could not contribute directly."[5] My respondents display a general disdain for the bureaucratic strictures and long career development paths of the past. I believe this was a key factor driving people to small companies during the high-tech boom. In a small firm, everyone counts. One young woman in Des Moines, Iowa, described the mind-numbing boredom of her first job after college. She worked in an insurance company and her entry-level post was essentially that of a better-paid secretary. "They had me Xeroxing paper all day and answering phones," she said. "So I quit, even though the pay was great, I had normal hours, and a secure job." She left for a job in a smaller company, where she could "use my skills, make a contribution, and not be bored silly all day."[6]

The young chief technology officer of a Seattle software startup offered yet another take on the subject. A boyish thirty-something of Asian-American descent, he had earned his Ph.D. in computer science at Carnegie Mellon and taught at Harvard. He then gave up a successful and promising career at the top of academia for the high-risk world of a startup because he wanted to see his ideas have an effect in the real world. "It's not enough to just publish papers and advance theory," he told me. "I did that. For me and for an increasing number of people of my generation, you have to show the impact of your work in the commercial market. You have to show that your technology can make a real difference in the market and in people's lives."[7]

Flexibility

The people in the focus groups and interviews blanched at the very idea of a 9-to-5 schedule or a standard dress code. How you use your time and how you dress and adorn yourself are intensely personal aspects of life. People are no longer so willing to compromise on these matters simply to get a job. Many spoke of wanting to be able to "bring themselves to work"—their real identities and selves—rather than create a separate, instrumental self to function in the workplace. This is nothing new. Creative people from artists to professors and even scientists in corporate R&D labs have always demanded flexibility of this sort.

Flexibility means more than the freedom to show up at the office at 10 A.M. wearing a nose ring. Creative people want the freedom and flexibility to pursue side projects and outside interests—some of which are directly related to their work, others perhaps less so, like being a musician or artist or being involved in community affairs. Regardless of whether they are directly work related, creative people see such activities as an important element by which they cultivate their creativity. In a detailed ethnographic study of high-tech design firms in Chicago, the sociologist Richard Lloyd quoted one person as saying: "The place where I'd want to work would support my creative endeavors and the kinds of creative things that I did on the side, and would recognize the fact that if I was continually building my skills with my own stuff, it would also benefit the company."[8]

Another key aspect of flexibility is having input in designing your workspace--and your role in the organization. Scientists have long controlled their work environments setting up their own labs and designing their own experiments. The people in my focus groups and interviews want the same kinds of freedoms. In her research on high-tech startup firms, Laurie Levesque of Carnegie Mellon found that this process of role-making is highly valued by creative employees and their employers alike. Levesque studied eight firms in depth, interviewing both top executives and employees on their roles in the organization.[9] The most salient attributes, cited as desirable by both executives and workers, were "flexibility," meaning adapting to different responsibilities, and "defining one's own role" in the organization. Many of the employers said a key criterion for hiring an individual was that person's penchant for "wearing many hats." This was important because employers were often too busy to constantly monitor employees. The employees, meanwhile, thrived on "ambiguity" and the ability to "create" their own role in the enterprise, which they defined as being able to take on tasks and, on their own, figure out what they needed to accomplish. As one high-tech worker told Levesque: "My role is unclear, and that's how I like it." Much of this looseness is a function of size. Small emergent companies by their nature have less structure or hierarchy. People can make it up as they go along. But as a company grows, division of labor develops and people get pigeonholed in particular roles: Structure emerges inexorably.

Peer Recognition

As Eric Raymond notes, peer recognition and reputation provide powerful sources of motivation for open source software developers.[10] Most are paid nothing for the time they devote to such work. They post their contributions for free so that their peers will recognize them as competent and successful developers. They have evolved a complex, self-organizing, self-governing system of peer review that works much like that in academic science. The only difference is that open source software is a commercial activity.

Peer recognition has always been a strong motivator for thinkers and scientists. The sociologist Robert Merton long ago pointed to its importance in the work life of scientists, who he said were motivated more by reputation than by money.[11] Building on Merton's idea, the economists Partha Dasgupta and Paul David argue that peer recognition is the primary force in the "new economics of science" because it motivates scientists to be lauded as the first to discover something new.[12] The economist Scott Stern has calculated that academic scientists actually "pay" to engage in science—sacrificing roughly 25 percent of their potential private-sector pay in order to pursue self-defined projects at prestigious universities.[13]

In one sense, these scientists are the polar opposite of the chief technology officer (CTO) at the Seattle software company, who left academia because he wanted his work to have commercial impact. But in another sense, they are the same. Both are choosing jobs that let them do what they want to do. Neither is motivated primarily by money or security, whether in the form of academic tenure or a fat corporate pension plan. The university researchers want to be able to do what interests them intellectually rather than what pays off commercially, whereas the CTO wants to see if he can do something practical, turning his research into a product that people will actually buy and use.

And when you're doing what you really want, for whatever personal reasons, it is the respect of your peers, the excitement and the challenge of the activity that really matter. This is the kind of work that keeps me at my keyboard for hours, hardly noticing that it's long past bedtime, or hardly caring that I've missed the chance to go to a party or have some other kind of "fun." The fun is the work itself—and this, I think, is a key element of the passion that Eric Raymond talks about. Can this passion come dangerously close to workaholism? Of course it can. But for me and many others, it is far better than work that has you counting the minutes until it's time to stop.

Location and Community Involvement

In contrast to the many techno-futurists who say the wired and wireless information age has made location and community irrelevant, the creative workers I talk with say they are vitally important. These people insist they need to live in places that offer stimulating, creative environments. Many will not even consider taking jobs in certain cities or regions—a stark contrast to the organizational age, when people moved to chase jobs and gladly let firms shuttle them from one backwater to another as part of the price of climbing the corporate ladder. I also meet Creative Class people who use location as their primary criterion in a proactive sense: They will pick a place they want to live, then focus their job search there.

Consider that nearly 20 percent of workers in the *Information Week* survey reported that geographic location of their workplace (18.7 percent) and the amount of time they have to commute (18.8 percent) are important factors. Both factors ranked ahead of the potential for promotion, bonus opportunities, financial stability, company prestige, stock options, on-site childcare, telecommuting and the ability to work from home. Other surveys, covering many types of workers, reinforce the importance of location. In a 2001 survey of U.S. workers by the public opinion firm Zogby International, nine out of ten reported quality of life (i.e. in the surrounding community) as being important in their decisions to take their current jobs. In a survey of 960 people looking to switch jobs, reported in the *Wall Street Journal* in July 2001, location ranked second only to salary (chosen by 25 percent versus 32 percent) as the prime motivation for switching.[14]

There are many reasons location is deemed so important, . . . Let me note for now that members of the Creative Class are highly mobile and not bound to any particular place. My focus groups and interviews provided many examples of people who made employment decisions "for the money" and later left for "better locations." And every year I receive calls from former students who want to forego the high-paying consulting jobs they've landed for greater job quality and improved quality of life.

People also want to be involved in their communities. Numerous Creative Class people I have spoken with seek latitude to use work time and resources for community projects. To some degree, this is nothing new. Executives and highly skilled employees have long been enlisted to lead charitable campaigns, or to serve on the boards of nonprofit institutions. But Creative Class people today have new ideas on how to engage in community-building and civic action. They seek direct involvement on their own terms, in part because it is part of their creative identity—a point I will return to later . . . For now the key point is: People use these extracurricular activities as a way of cultivating their interests, values and identities both in the workplace and in society more generally. In my view, they reflect a broader process of self-actualization and an attempt to use work as a platform for pushing forward an overall creative identity.

The Financial Side of Things

Compensation, of course, still matters, and it involves more than base pay. The past decade has seen a rapid run-up in the use of alternative forms such as stock options. and bonuses. Many commentators favor these new forms, saying they align individual and organizational interests and provide more incentive for work effort. Furthermore, it has long been argued that workers trade off financial compensation against job security. Tenured professors, for instance, sacrifice short-term income for the long-term compensation that a secure lifetime position affords. Others trade job security for higher immediate pay and more risk. Either way, one could well say that security or stability is a form of compensation itself. It's the perceived ability to enjoy a fairly long-term income stream; one can project it, calculate it and weigh it against other forms.

So how do workers value these various forms of compensation? The *Information Week* survey data offered a number of insights.

- Job stability was more highly valued than any form of direct compensation. More than 40 percent of workers chose it as a key factor.
- Base pay was slightly less important, with 38.5 percent saying it is a key factor.
- Vacation and time off ranked next highest, chosen by slightly more than a third.
- Benefits (such as medical insurance and pension plans) matter almost as much as vacation time.
- Bonuses are not critical. The American Compensation Association reports that 83 percent of companies offer bonuses to upper management, 80 percent to middle management, and 74 percent to technical staff. Despite their extensive use, bonuses rate just twentieth of thirty-eight factors in the *Information Week* survey, with just 18 percent of workers identifying them as important. They rank lower than location, commute distance, casual attire and job atmosphere
- Stock options are one of the least important factors in job satisfaction. Long offered to top management, they became popular for other employees as well during the New Economy boom because they allegedly enable employees to share in the company growth and thus better align individual and company interests. Compensation experts and financial economists have long predicted that such equity-based compensation will eclipse other forms of pay for top executives, outstanding technologists and other key people. Stock options are frequently said to serve three interrelated functions: to lure top candidates, to provide additional incentives for top people, and as "golden handcuffs" to keep key people on the job until they become vested. Yet despite all the hype, stock options ranked thirtieth in the *Information Week* surveys, with less than 10 percent of workers saying they are important.

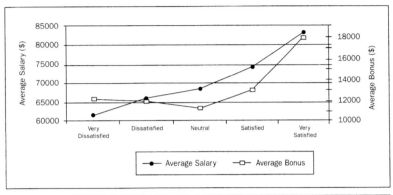

FIGURE 16.3 | Job Satisfaction Rises Alongside Pay

(SOURCE: *Information Week* Salary Survey, 2001.)

The question remains: How does compensation interact with other factors to shape satisfaction? More than half of all IT workers were satisfied with their compensation and nearly two-thirds were satisfied overall. Of those who were satisfied with their compensation, roughly nine in ten were also satisfied with their jobs overall. But the story runs deeper. As Figure 16.3 shows, overall job satisfaction climbs steadily with compensation. The most satisfied workers are also the ones who make the most money. Perhaps they feel they can "afford" to focus on the other intrinsic aspects of their work because they are paid well. Or perhaps these workers have been performing better than their peers for a long time and so have earned raises, management approval and greater control over their jobs.

Whatever the cause, dissatisfied workers rate pay as one of the key elements of their being dissatisfied, as Figure 16.4 shows. Furthermore, people looking for work are also frequently looking for higher pay. More than three-quarters of the IT workers who were looking for work in 2000 and 2001 said "higher compensation" was the main reason, followed by dissatisfaction with management (42.4 percent), "more interesting work" (39.5 percent) and "more responsibility" (31.1 percent). Job stability ranked lower (18.5 percent), and stock options (13.4 percent) and the chance to join a startup company (2.9 percent) were among the lowest-rated answers. So pay is much more relevant to being dissatisfied with your job than to being satisfied.

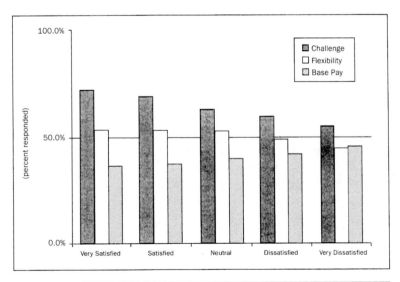

FIGURE 16.4 | Challenge, Flexibility and Pay
Satisfied workers prefer challenge and responsibility; dissatisfied workers want higher pay.

(SOURCE: *Information Week* Salary Survey, 2001.)

Money, therefore, is important, but not the whole story. Creative people want challenging work and the ability to do their jobs flexibly, and as with anyone else, those who receive low pay are more likely to be unhappy. As Eric Raymond said, pay is essentially just a way to keep score. But Peter Drucker said it even better: bribing creative people just won't work.

Herding Squirrels

Unlike the traditional Working Class, Creative Class workers expect to be treated as distinct individuals. Harnessing them to do productive work thus can be very challenging, and there is no shortage of theories on how to wrangle a diverse herd of creative people into doing what the organization wants to have done, . . . Let's close this chapter, meanwhile, with a look at some attempts to simplify the problem by classifying workers into broad attitudinal groups. *The McKinsey Quarterly's* much-cited 1998 War for Talent Study surveyed more than 6,000 executives in seventy-seven large U.S. companies and found that while all survey respondents "care deeply about culture, values and autonomy," they could be divided into four distinct groups.

- "Go with a winner": This group preferred growth and advancement in a highly successful company and were less concerned with mission or location.
- "Big risk, big reward": A second group valued compensation and career advancement over the company's success or its active role in their professional development.
- "Save the world": Members of this group desired an inspiring mission and exciting challenges, caring less about compensation and personal development.
- "Lifestyle": This group valued flexibility, compatibility with their boss, and location over company growth or excitement.[15]

The 2001 *Towers Perrin Talent Report* likewise sampled a large group of professionals in various fields, dividing them by preference as follows:

- The largest group (42 percent) reported "work-life balance" as their priority.
- Twenty-eight percent said their chief desire was to develop their skills and advance in the company or companies they work for.
- Some 12 percent identified themselves as "fast-trackers" seeking quick advancement and high rewards.
- Another 12 percent saw themselves as "experimenters," interested in trying many things over the course of a career.
- Just 6 percent said they are "free agents" who desire to move quickly from job to job in search of greater financial rewards.[16]

Working from the raw data in the *Information Week* Salary Surveys, Kevin Stolarick and I sorted IT workers into six broad preference groups. Our percentages add up to more than a hundred, as many people fell into more than one category, and people in all the groups desired challenge in their work.

- About a third of the IT workforce sample (34.5 percent) value "flexibility" over other factors. Important job factors for them include a flexible work schedule and the ability to work from home when they like.
- Another third (34 percent) are "compensation-driven," favoring base pay, benefits and vacation time.
- About 20 percent are "technologists," motivated principally by the opportunity to work with leading-edge technology and highly talented peers, among other things.
- Roughly 15 percent are "professionals" who desire skill development, effective supervision and recognition for work well done.
- "Company men" (14 percent) tend to align their interests with the overall success of the company.
- "Entrepreneurs" (11 percent) are the smallest group. Among other things, they rate stock options as important, and prefer to work in startup companies.

Employers seeking to align such workers' needs with those of the organization must consider two additional points. The first is that while motivations have undoubtedly always varied, these variations can no longer be ignored as they could be in the past. The nature of the work, and thus of the workers, has changed. Second, employees' preferences are frequently mixed and subject to change over time. Our Seattle software CTO who left the faculty at Harvard apparently had felt, for a long stretch of his life, that academic research suited him. But he began to feel he had been there, done that, and so moved on to fulfill another yearning. Creative workers do not merely move up the scale in Abraham Maslow's classic hierarchy of needs. Most are not very worried about meeting the basic needs of subsistence; they're already on the upper rungs of the ladder, where intrinsic rewards such as esteem and self-actualization are sought. And having reached the high end, they can and do move laterally from seeking one form of esteem or actualization to another.

In *The Fourth Great Awakening,* Robert Fogel notes that in the advanced industrial nations, growing segments of the population work for challenge, enjoyment, to do good, to make a contribution, and to learn.[17] Such motivations, he suggests, will eventually eclipse compensation as the most important motivators for work. In the fast-growing Creative Class, where the job description includes creativity, I would say the surveys show this has already happened. It is even happening in the factory, where the rank and file do not merely follow orders and routines but are asked to take an active part in continuously rethinking and improving their work. If the trend continues, we may even hope to see young people migrating back to the machine shop. But only if the machine shop embraces the new values and structures of the creative age, acting on people's intrinsic motivations and allowing them to nurture and express their creativity— only, that is, if it becomes more like the hair salon.

Reading 16 Notes "The Machine Shop and the Hair Salon"

1. Peter Drucker, "Beyond the Information Revolution?" *The Atlantic Monthly,* 284, October 4, 1999, pp. 47–57, quote from p. 57.
2. This e-mail was forwarded to me by one of my students in spring 2001.
3. William C. Taylor, "Eric Raymond on Work:" *Fast Company,* November 1999, p. 200. Also see Eric Raymond, *The Cathedral and the Bazaar: Musings on Linux and Open Source by an Accidental Revolutionary.* Sebastopol, Calif.: O'Reilly and Associates, Inc., 1999.
4. *Information Week,* Annual Salary Survey, 2000 and 2001.
5. Personal interview by author, summer 2000.
6. Personal interview by author, winter 2000.
7. Personal interview by author, spring 2000.
8. Richard Lloyd, "Digital Bohemia: New Media Enterprises in Chicago's Wicker Park Neighborhood:" Paper presented at the annual conference of the American Sociological Association, August 2001.
9. Laurie Levesque, "A Qualitative Study of Organizational Roles in High Tech Start-up Firms." Paper presented at the Annual Conference of the Academy of Management, Toronto, 2000; *Role Creation Processes in Start-up Firms.* Pittsburgh: Carnegie Mellon University, Graduate School of Industrial Administration, doctoral dissertation, 2001; "Creating New Roles: Understanding Employee Behavior in High Tech Start-ups." Paper presented at the Annual Conference of the Academy of Management, Washington, D.C., 2001.
10. Raymond, *The Cathedral and the Bazaar.*
11. See Robert Merton, "Priorities in Scientific Discovery: A Chapter in the Sociology of Science." *American Sociological Review,* 22(6), 1957, pp. 635–659; and *The Sociology of Science.* Chicago: University of Chicago Press, 1973.
12. See Partha Dasgupta and Paul David, "Information Disclosure and the Economics of Science and Technology" in G. Feiwel (ed.), *Arrow and the Ascent of Modern Economic Theory.* New York: New York University Press, 1987; and "Toward a New Economics of Science." *Research Policy,* 23(3), May 1994, pp. 487–521. Also see Paula Stephan, "The Economics of Science?" *Journal* of *Economic Literature,* 34, 1996, pp. 1199–1235.
13. Scott Stern, "Do Scientists Pay to Be Scientists?" Cambridge, Mass.: National Bureau of Economic Research, Working Paper 7410, October 1999. Also see Michelle Gittleman and Bruce Kogut, "Why Do Firms Do Research (By Their Own Scientists?): Science, Scientists and Innovation Among US Biotechnology Firms?" Paper presented at the Annual Conference of the Academy of Management, Toronto, 2000; and "Does Good Science Lead to Valuable Knowledge: Biotechnology Firms and the Evolutionary Logic of Citation Patterns." Philadelphia: Wharton School, University of Pennsylvania, Jones Center, Working Paper 2001–04, 2001.
14. Though neither are scientific surveys, they do highlight the importance of location. The Zogby survey findings are reported in "U.S. Workers Face Care Dilemma: Love It or Leave It? National Survey Finds," PR Newswire Association Inc., February 12, 2001. The second survey, cited by the *Wall Street Journal,* is based on a sample of 970 job seekers by CareerEngine.com in summer 2001, see Kemba Dunham, "The Jungle: Focus on Pay, Recruitment and Getting Ahead." *Wall Street Journal,* July 3, 2001.
15. Elizabeth Chambers, Mark Foulon, Helen Handfield-Jones, Steven Hanklin and Edward Michaels, "The War for Talent." *The McKinsey Quarterly,* 3, 1998, pp. 44–57.
16. *The Towers Perrin Talent Report: New Realities in Today's Workplace.* New York: Towers Perrin, 2001.
17. Robert Fogel, *The Fourth Great Awakening and the Future of Egalitarianism.* Chicago: University of Chicago Press, 2000.

CLUSTER THREE

TYPES OF INTELLIGENCE
FOR THE INTERDISCIPLINARY WORKPLACE

Reading 17

The readings in Cluster 3 are intended to help you in your self-assessment. While being familiar with the characteristics of interdisciplinarians is important, it is also important to know about a current buzzword in the workplace: EQ. EQ or emotional intelligence is extremely desirable, and Anne Fisher's interview with Daniel Goleman, the author of **Emotional Intelligence** (1995), reveals why EQ is so important in the workplace.

READING

SUCCESS SECRET: A HIGH EMOTIONAL IQ

by

Anne Fisher

Psychologist and bestselling author Daniel Goleman says his research proves that business prizes emotional intelligence over expertise in its managers.

What separates people who do well in life from people who fail or who simply never seem to get very far, despite obvious smarts and skills? In his groundbreaking 1995 bestseller, *Emotional Intelligence* psychologist Daniel Goleman drew on a wealth of new research to argue persuasively that what we usually think of as intelligence—as measured by IQ—is far less important as a predictor of a person's path in life than one's supply of attributes he calls emotional intelligence: self-awareness, impulse control, persistence, confidence and self-motivation, empathy, and social deftness. Now Goleman has written a sequel, *Working With Emotional Intelligence*, that zeroes in on how these qualities, or the lack of them, can make or break your career. Goleman, who is CEO of Emotional Intelligence Services in Sudbury, Mass., recently talked with *FORTUNE*'s Anne Fisher about why emotional intelligence is more essential now than ever—and how to tell whether your emotional intelligence could stand some improvement.

In an era that seems preoccupied with technology and technical skills, why place a premium on "soft" stuff like emotional intelligence? How important is it really?

The data that argue for taking it seriously are based on studies of tens of thousands of working people, in every kind of professional field, and the research distills precisely which qualities mark a star performer. The rules for work are changing, and we're all being judged, whether we know it or not, by a new yardstick—not just how smart we are and what technical skills we have, which employers see as givens, but increasingly by how well we handle ourselves and one another. In times of extremely rapid and unpredictable change, like right now, emotional intelligence more and more comes to determine who gets promoted and who gets passed over—or even who gets laid off and who doesn't.

This is true at every level of the organization. For instance, one study of what corporations seek when they hire MBAs shows that the three most desired capabilities are communication skills, interpersonal skills, and initiative—all elements of emotional intelligence. And the higher you go up the corporate ranks, the more these things matter.

How do you know that?

We've been able to quantify it in a couple of ways. I did one study where I gathered from HR training and development specialists their competence models—which are essentially lists of the most desired traits—for 181 jobs in 121 companies worldwide, with their combined work force numbering in the millions. Once we separated out the purely technical skills from the emotional competencies, and compared their relative importance, we found that two out of three of the abilities considered vital for success were emotional competencies like trustworthiness, adaptability, and a talent for collaboration.

That finding has been supported by other in-depth studies showing that emotional competencies are twice as important to people's success today as raw intelligence or technical know-how. And in any kind of managing or leadership position, emotional intelligence is of paramount importance. Often when you see people get promoted on the basis of technical ability and then fail in that new job, it's because they were promoted for essentially the wrong reason. They lack emotional competencies that are crucial at that higher level. More and more companies are realizing this and altering how they train and promote people accordingly.

Which emotional competency is most important to someone who has, or wants to get, a high-level executive job?

It's hard to single out one trait as most important because different aspects of emotional intelligence come into play depending on the circumstances. But one distinguishing characteristic is, how persuasive are you? Can you get "buy-in" for your ideas from the people around you? The most effective leaders have a very finely honed political awareness and ability. The word "political" is loaded, I know, because it carries negative connotations of empty charm, manipulativeness, or someone who is good at managing up but not down and is really interested only in his or her own gain. But "political" in the sense I mean is a knack for articulating a mission or a goal and knowing how to bring everyone on board to get it accomplished. Can you take the pulse of a group, understand its unspoken currents of thought and concerns, and communicate with people in terms they can understand and embrace? That is great leadership. And it takes huge social intelligence, including a strongly developed sense of empathy.

Beyond taking a quiz like the accompanying one we've devised, how can a person gauge his or her own EQ?

It's very tough to measure our own emotional intelligence, because most of us don't have a very clear sense of how we come across to other people, and that is much of what ultimately matters here. What you really need is to have someone else, or preferably a cross section of people you work with, rate you on the various components, such as trustworthiness, reliability, flexibility, how good you are in a crisis, and how open you are to new ideas and new ways of doing things. This is why 360-degree performance evaluations are so helpful. A 360, in which you are getting honest feedback from people above, below, and beside you, can give you a very clear sense of where you need to improve. The areas to focus on especially are the ones where your boss and your peers see you very differently from how you see yourself.

What about people who work for companies that don't offer 360-degree evaluations?

Clearly it will take a little more work on your part, but you can set up your own. Pick some people whose judgment you respect—including perhaps your immediate boss, a couple of peers who are neither your best buddies nor biased in any other obvious way, and maybe one or two people below you in the organization who have worked closely with you. Ask them to rate you according to the quiz, or use the more detailed list from the book. You may be very surprised by their answers, and by how much the score they give you varies from the score you give yourself. You want to be on the lookout especially for points of agreement, areas where, for instance, your boss and your subordinates all see the same shortcoming in you. Maybe nobody thinks you listen very well, or everybody more or less agrees that you tend to lose your temper pretty easily. Whatever the specific problem, that's where you need to direct your attention.

Let's suppose I give myself a high rating on, for example, being open to new ideas—yet my colleagues see me as rigid and inflexible. How do I go about fixing that?

You can do it. Emotional intelligence is not a fixed quantity, and in varying degrees we're all increasing it as we go through life. To change a particular tendency, what you need at the outset is motivation. You have to want to do it, not just because someone tells you that you should, but because you see the importance of it. Most shortcomings in emotional intelligence are the result of habits of mind that are deeply rooted because they are learned very early in life. For example, a reluctance to consider new ideas may come from some experience in your childhood that taught you that new ideas are too dangerous or risky, that if you go out on a limb you may fall off and get hurt.

There are two basic steps in transforming any mental habit. The first is to notice when you are falling into it. Monitor yourself. The next time someone proposes something new and you catch yourself automatically thinking "No," stop and think. Jot down some notes, if that helps you. Why does this particular idea make you uncomfortable? What's the context of the discussion? What are the emotions that go along with resisting the idea? Do you feel threatened by it in some way? Why? Don't judge yourself or tear yourself down. Just try to analyze your own reaction to the situation.

What's the second step?

Practice a different response. This will feel strange at first, and it is a real effort, because you are dismantling an old habit and building a new one. You might even deliberately set up a situation where a lot of new ideas will be thrown at you—for instance, call a meeting with the express purpose of getting your team to brainstorm about different ways of doing things. Then concentrate on keeping your mind open to what people suggest. It does take time for new mental habits to form. It doesn't happen instantly. But by being aware, you can do a little better each time you try.

It helps to have some support. Many executives hire a coach to help them alter a specific behavior. A more practical approach for most people is to find a role model in your own workplace, a colleague who is especially strong in a trait you'd like to develop, and emulate that person. Watch how he or she handles a given situation and see how closely you can adapt your own style. As you feel you're getting better at the competency you're trying to develop, ask the people around you for feedback. You might even encourage a colleague to give you a signal when he or she sees you slipping back into your old habit.

Should companies be developing formal training programs to help people strengthen emotional competencies?

Lots of them are already doing so, yet it is such a complicated task that right at this moment millions and millions of dollars are being wasted on programs that have no lasting impact, or little effect at all, on building emotional competence. It amounts to a billion-dollar mistake.

Heads of development at plenty of FORTUNE 500 companies know this, but the ones who wanted to have their own programs have been frustrated because they lacked standards and yardsticks for training in "soft" skills. That's why I co-founded the Consortium for Research on Emotional Intelligence in Organizations. It's a coalition of researchers and practitioners from business schools, consulting firms, corporations, and the federal government. We've come up with basic guidelines for the best practices in teaching emotional competencies, and these are described in my book. If it's done right, this kind of training yields remarkable results.

Can you give us an example?

Sure. The Weatherhead School of Management at Case Western Reserve University has developed an innovative course called Managerial Assessment and Development that incorporates most of the consortium guidelines. Since 1990 this course has been offered to several groups of students, mostly men and women in their 20s and 30s pursuing an MBA after several years on the job. Each student starts the course by choosing a specific set of competencies he or she wants to strengthen. Instead of the familiar one-size-fits-all approach to management training, students construct a highly individualized learning plan. The class then meets for three one-hour sessions a week over nine weeks.

To gauge how well it works, Weatherhead has put its students through a set of rigorous assessments, using measures of applied emotional intelligence that the consortium gleaned from corporate employers. When the ratings are compared with the assessment scores the students earn when they start the program, they show an average 86% improvement. And even more significantly, follow-ups three years later have consistently shown these gains holding on the job. So based on results like this, it's clear that, if they're given the right tools, people can master the emotional-intelligence capabilities the working world demands.

Reading 18

In the following excerpt from her 1996 book, **Thinking in the Future Tense**, Jennifer James summarizes Howard Gardner's theory of multiple intelligence. Knowing about multiple intelligence will be helpful to students in their self-assessments. The short quiz at the end of the reading will help you evaluate your own strengths and weaknesses.

READING

MASTERING NEW FORMS OF INTELLIGENCE

by

Jennifer James

THE FUTURE WILL REQUIRE a higher and more socialized process of reasoning and more sophisticated reactions. We once believed that reason and logical analysis could solve all problems. A rational mind was all that we needed. In school, if we were good at narrow problem-solving we did well on IQ tests. High scores on aptitude tests made us believe that storing information—the kind that could be called up on demand—was the best use of the mind.

This old blueprint for intelligence may have served us reasonably well at one time. But not now, and not in the future. Now it limits our thinking. It leaves us aware only of the known, the understood, and the controllable. It suffocates fresh perceptions. It treats new information as just more data to be fed into well-established formulas of thought. Anything that doesn't fit is rejected. We are unaware of the subtle biases in our perception and thought.

We need a new vision of intelligence, one that integrates the right brain of images and creativity with the left brain of words and calculations, in the context of the social environment. You could call it "middle brain" intelligence, somewhere between reason and creative freefall. It is a fluid thought process that leads us to question our usual assumptions, to rein in our judgments, to take a fresh look at our world and what we really know about it. It is the core of a twenty-first-century mind and an essential skill for anyone who aspires to effective leadership.

Our brain has almost infinite capacity, the processing power of a hundred billion personal computers joined together. Yet even with that enormous capacity, too often we feel overloaded and we close down the system rather than learning to use our minds in new ways. Take a close look at a widely used aptitude test, the Scholastic Assessment Test (SAT), and you will get a better sense of how narrowly we define intelligence. The SAT *does* measure literacy, memory, vocabulary, general comprehension, pattern identification, spatial ability, reasoning, and math. But it *does not* measure many of the skills—actually, forms of intelligence . . . It doesn't, for example, measure perceptive ability, verbal communication skills, teamwork or relationship abilities, ingenuity, intuition, creativity, flexibility, mental health, multicultural awareness, varieties of experience, or ethical codes. Nor does it measure what is now being called emotional intelligence. If you come up with a creative answer or work out problems with a team, you flunk the SAT. The test favors homogenous groups with common experiences.

The SAT was developed in 1926, modeled after army tests from World War I, to measure the potential of the college-bound population. The baseline of "potential" in the 1920s was white, male, and agrarian/industrial. The SAT has been modified since then, but because of cost and standardization, no new baseline has been established. If you do well on the SAT, you may have the mind of a 1926 white guy from Massachusetts who would succeed as a World War I army officer. Your thinking and leadership skills are important and relevant, but may not be all that is needed to cope with our vastly different challenges today.

Not long ago, researchers examined the characteristics of students who won educational awards based on their performance on standardized tests such as the SAT. The study, done by an organization called FairTest, concluded that the same type of minds that could be found in college in 1920 are still being favored today.[1] Interestingly, many of these minds are now in the bodies of Asian Americans.

The anachronisms in the way we measure intelligence can also be found in IQ tests, which have not changed in any major way since the 1950s. In fact, they measure a very narrow range of intelligence. You don't have to understand the effect of your behavior on others or the environment. You can be a rabid racist or a psychopath planning your next murder and still get a high score on most IQ tests. You can be "intelligent" and run your corporation in a manner that exploits instead of supports the community. You can be a Mensa member with a very high IQ and not be able to hold a job or relate to anyone.

Understanding Who Is Smart

The debate over intelligence is a debate over higher standards. Over the past forty years, researchers of all kinds have uncovered the weaknesses of our tests and shown new respect for a broader-based definition of intelligence that reflects more than traditional fact retention and computation skills. Educators, in particular, are looking for a battery of tests that is more productive of real-world success. The designers of a school testing program in California, for example, put a premium on the skills required for "reasonably deciding what to think and do."[2] Among other things, students had to be able to determine the relevance of information, distinguish between fact and opinion, identify unstated assumptions, detect bias or propaganda, come up with reasonable alternatives or solutions, and predict possible consequences. Intelligence is the ability to make adaptive responses in new as well as old situations.

At Harvard, philosopher Nelson Goodman wanted to understand why some people were "creative" and others were not. In his work, Goodman expanded the concept of intelligence from "How smart is he or she?" to "*How* is he or she smart?" Motivation and interest in the task at hand—along with traits such as concentration, intention, purpose, drive, and tenacity—emerged as important influences.

Howard Gardner, a psychologist who helped to conduct this research, thought of intelligence as the ability to solve problems or create products. He devised the following list of eight primary forms of intelligence (to which I have added one of my own):[3]

1. Verbal/linguistic intelligence. This form of intelligence is revealed by a sensitivity to the meaning and order of words and the ability to make varied use of the language. Impromptu speaking, storytelling, humor, and joking are natural abilities associated with verbal/linguistic intelligence. So, too, is persuading someone to follow a course of action, or explaining, or teaching. Will Rogers had this form of intelligence. Good journalists also have it.

2. Logical/mathematical intelligence. This form of intelligence is easiest to standardize and measure. We usually refer to it as analytical or scientific thinking, and we see it in scientists, computer programmers, accountants, lawyers, bankers, and, of course, mathematicians, people who are problem solvers and consummate game players. They work with abstract symbols and are able to see connections between pieces of information that others might miss. Einstein is one of the best examples of someone with this form of intelligence.

3. Visual/spatial intelligence. Persons with this form of intelligence are especially deft at conjuring up mental images and creating graphic representations. They are able to think in three-dimensional terms, to re-create the visual world. Picasso, whose paintings challenged our view of reality, was especially gifted at visualizing objects from different perspectives and angles. Besides painters and sculptors, this form of intelligence is found in designers and architects.

4. Body/kinesthetic intelligence. This form of intelligence makes possible the connections between mind and body that are necessary to succeed in activities such as dance, mime, sports, martial arts, and drama. Martha Graham and Michael Jordan delighted audiences with their explosive and sensitive uses of the body. Because they know how we move, inventors with this form of intelligence understand how to turn function into form. They intuitively feel what is possible in labor-saving devices and processes.

5.   Musical/rhythmic intelligence. A person with this form of intelligence hears musical patterns and rhythms naturally and can reproduce them. It is an especially desirable form of intelligence because music has the capacity to alter our consciousness, reduce stress, and enhance brain function. For example, students who had just listened to Mozart scored higher on standard IQ tests than those who had spent the same period of time in meditation or silence. Reseachers believe that the patterns in musical themes somehow prime the same neural network that the brain employs for complex visual-spatial tasks

6.   Interpersonal intelligence. Managers, counselors, therapists, politicians, mediators, and human relations specialists display this form of intelligence. It is a must for workplace tasks such as negotiation and providing feedback or evaluation. Individuals with this form of intelligence have strong intuitive skills. They are especially able to read the moods, temperaments, motivations, and intentions of others. Abraham Lincoln, Mohandas Gandhi, and Martin Luther King, Jr., used interpersonal intelligence to change the world.

7.   Intrapersonal intelligence. Sigmund Freud and Carl Jung demonstrated this form of intelligence, the ability to understand and articulate the inner workings of character and personality. The highest order of thinking and reasoning is present in a person who has intrapersonal intelligence. We often call it wisdom. He or she can see the larger picture and is open to the lure of the future. Within an organization, this ability is invaluable.

8.   Spiritual intelligence. This form of intelligence is tentative; Gardner has yet to decide whether moral or spiritual intelligence qualifies for his list. It can be considered an amalgam of interpersonal and intrapersonal awareness with a "value" component added.

9.   Practical intelligence. Gardner doesn't list this form of intelligence, but I do. It is the skill that enables some people to take a computer or clock apart and put it back together. I also think of practical intelligence as organizational intelligence or common sense, the ability to solve all sorts of daily problems without quite knowing how the solutions were reached. People with common sense may or may not test well, but they have a clear understanding of cause and effect. They use intelligence in combination with that understanding.

Qualities of Mind

Rate yourself on each of these forms of intelligence. What are your strengths and weaknesses? How are they reflected in the kind of work you do and your relationships with others?

	LOW				MODERATE					HIGH
	1	2	3	4	5	6	7	8	9	10
1. Verbal/linguistic										
2. Logical/mathematical										
3. Visual/spatial										
4. Body/kinesthetic										
5. Musical/rhythmic										
6. Interpersonal										
7. Intrapersonal										
8. Spiritual										
9. Practical										

Don't let this list intimidate you. There is increasingly strong evidence that intelligence can be taught, despite ongoing arguments about genetic predetermination. Also, the levels of each of these forms of intelligence can vary from one person to the next. Albert Einstein had a high degree of logical and spatial intelligence, but his lack of personal skills was legendary. He left those details to others.

Reading 18 Notes from "Mastering New Forms of Intelligence"

1.   FairTest, Cambridge, Mass.
2.   "California Learning Assessment System," *New York Times,* May 4, 1994.
3.   Gardner, Howard, *Frames of Mind* (New York: Basic Books, 1985).

References

Arizona State University Career Services. (1998). Portfolio development: What to include in your portfolio [Form 274]. Tempe, Arizona: Arizona State University.

Armstrong F. (1980). Faculty development through interdisciplinarity. *JGE, The Journal of General Education*, 32 (1), 52–63.

Augsburg, T. (2003). Becoming Interdisciplinary: The student portfolio in the Bachelor of Interdisciplinary Studies program at Arizona State University. *Issues in Integrative Studies*, 21, 98–125.

Augsburg, T. & Helms, C. (2000). *Student Portfolios Collaboration with Academic Units = Successful Career Planning.* Paper presented at the annual meeting of Rocky Mountain Association of Colleges and Employers (RMACE), Scottsdale, AZ.

Baldick, C. (1990). The concise Oxford dictionary of literary terms. Oxford and N.Y.: Oxford University Press.

Barker, R. T., Gilbreath, G. H., & Stone, W. S. (1998). The interdisciplinary needs of organizations: Are new employees adequately equipped? *Journal of Management Development*, 17 (3), 219–232. [See Reading 14 in this volume.]

Bateson, M. C. (1994). Constructing continuity. *Peripheral visions: Learning along the way* (pp. 77–94). New York: Harper Collins. [See Reading 3 in this volume.]

Baxter Magolda, M. B. (1999). *Creating contexts for learning and self-authorship: Constructive-developmental pedagogy.* Nashville, TN: Vanderbilt University Press.

Baxter Magolda, M. B. (2001*). Making their own way: Narratives for transforming higher education to promote self-development.* Sterling, VA: Stylus.

Benson, T. C. (1982). Five arguments against interdisciplinary studies. *Issues in Integrative Studies,* 1, 38–48. [See Reading 7 in this volume.]

Berger, M. (1977, Nov. 9). Isaiah Berlin, philosopher and pluralist, is dead at 88. *The New York Times*, p. A1. [See Reading 1 in this volume.]

Bradbeer, J. (1999). Barriers to interdisciplinarity: Disciplinary discourses and student learning. *Journal of Geography in Higher Education,* 23 (3), 381–396.

Bridges, W. (1994, Sept. 19). The end of the job. *Fortune Magazine*, 62–74.

Briggs, A., & Micard, G. (1972). Problems and solutions. In *Interdisciplinarity: Problems of teaching and research in universities* (pp. 85–299). Paris: Center for Educational Research and Innovation.

Calhoun, C. (2001). Foreword. In K. W. Worcester, Social Science Research Council, 1923–1998 (pp. 4–10) [Electronic Version]. New York: Social Science Research Council. Retrieved on July 7, 2005 at <http://www.ssrc.org/inside/about>

Centre for Educational Research and Innovation. (1972). *Interdisciplinarity: Problems of teaching and research in universities.* Paris: OECD Publications.

Cole, D. J., Ryan, C. W., Kick, F. & Mathies, Bonnie K. (2000). *Portfolios across the curriculum and beyond* (2nd ed.). Thousand Oaks, CA: Corwin Press.

Connolly, W. E. (1993). *The terms of political discourse* (3rd ed.). Oxford, UK and Cambridge, M.A.: Blackwell.

Crockett, T. (1998). *The portfolio journey: A creative guide to keeping student-managed portfolios in the classroom.* Englewood, CO: Teacher Ideas Press.

Davidson, D. (1979). What metaphors mean. In S. Sacks (Ed.), *On metaphor.* Chicago and London: University of Chicago Press.

Elkins, J. (2001). *Why art cannot be taught.* Urbana and Chicago: University of Illinois Press.

Fisher, A. (1998, Oct. 26) Success secret: A high emotional EQ. *Fortune*, 293–298. [See Reading 17 in this volume.]

Flexner, S. B. (Ed.). (1987). *The Random House dictionary of the English language* (2nd ed.). Unabridged. New York: Random House.

Florida, R. (2002). *The rise of the creative class.* New York: Basic Books.

Foucault, M. (1979). *Discipline and punish: The birth of a prison.* Trans. Alan Sheridan. New York: Vintage.

Frank, R. (1988)."Interdisciplinary": The first half-century. *Issues in Integrative Studies*, 6, 139–151.

Gaff, J. G., Ratcliff, J. L. & Associates. (1997). *Handbook of the undergraduate curriculum: A comprehensive guide to purposes, structures, practices, and change.* San Francisco: Jossey Bass.

Gallie, W. B. (1962). Essentially contested concepts. In M. Black (Ed.), *The importance of language* (pp. 121–146). Englewood, N.J.: Prentice-Hall.

Gunn, G. (1992). Interdisciplinary studies. In J. Gibaldi (Ed.), *Introduction to scholarship in modern languages and literatures* (pp. 239–261). New York: Modern Language Association.

Haskins, C. H. (1940). *The rise of universities.* New York: Peter Smith.

Hastings, R. (1936). *The universities of Europe in the middle ages.* Vol. 1. London: Oxford University Press.

Hershberg, T. (1981). The new urban history: Toward an interdisciplinary history of the city. In T. Hershberg (Ed.), *Philadelphia: Work, space, family, and group experience in the nineteenth century* (pp. 3–42). New York and Oxford: Oxford University Press.

Hursh, B., Haas, P., & Moore, M. (1983). An interdisciplinary model to implement general education. *Journal of Higher Education,* 54 (1), 42–49.

Ibarra, H. & Lineback, K. (2005). What's your story? *Harvard Business Review,* 83 (1), 64–71.

James, J. (1996). *Thinking in the future tense.* New York: Simon & Schuster.

Kegan, R. (1994). *In over our heads: The mental demands of modern life.* Cambridge, MA, and London: Harvard University Press.

Kimbrell, A. (1999, Jan./Feb.) Breaking the job lock. *Utne Reader,* 47–49. [See Reading 13 in this volume.]

Kimeldorf, M. (1994). *Creating portfolios for success in school, work and life.* Minneapolis, MN: Free Spirit Publishing.

Kimeldorf, M. (1997). *Portfolio power: The new way to showcase all of your job skills and experiences.* Princeton, N.J.: Person's.

Klein, J. T. (1990). *Interdisciplinarity: History, theory and practice.* Detroit: Wayne State University Press.

Klein, J. T. (1993). Blurring, cracking, and crossing: Permeation and the fracturing of discipline. In E. Messer-Davidow, D. R. Shumway, & D. J. Sylvan (Eds.), *Knowledges: Historical and critical studies in disciplinarity* (pp. 185–211). Charlottesville: University of Virginia Press.

Klein, J. T. (1996). *Crossing boundaries: Knowledge, disciplinarities, and interdisciplinarities.* Charlottesville and London: University of Virginia Press.

Klein, J. T. (2001). Interdisciplinarity and the prospect of complexity: The tests of theory. *Issues in Integrative Studies,* 19, 43–57.

Klein, J. T. (2004). Unity of knowledge and transdisciplinarity: Contexts of definition, theory, and the new discourse of problem solving." In G. H. Hadorn (Ed.), *Unity of knowledge* (in *Transdisciplinary research for sustainability*). In *Encylcopedia of life support systems* (EOLSS). Developed under the Auspices of the UNESCO, EOLSS Publishers, Oxford, UK [<http://www.eolss.net>].

Klein, J. T. (2005). *Humanities, culture, and interdisciplinarity.* Albany, NY: State University Press of New York.

Klein, J. T., & Newell, W. T. (1996/1998). Advancing interdisciplinary studies. In W. T. Newell (Ed.), *Interdisciplinarity: Essays from the literature* (pp. 3–22). New York: College Entrance Examination Board. Originally published in J. G. Gaff, J. L. Ratcliff, & Associates (Eds.), *Handbook of the undergraduate curriculum* (pp. 393–415). San Francisco: Jossey-Bass.

Kreisler, H. (2003, Feb. 10). Theory and international politics: Conversation with Kenneth N. Waltz, Ford Professor Emeritus of political science, UC Berkeley. Video Transcript [Electronic version]. Institute of International Studies, UC Berkeley. Retrieved July 22, 2004 from http://globetrotter.berkeley.edu/people3/Waltz/waltz-con0.html

Lakoff, G. & Johnson, M. (1980). *Metaphors we live by.* Chicago: University of Chicago Press.

Lattuca, L. R. (2001). *Creating interdisciplinarity: Interdisciplinary research and teaching among college and university faculty.* Nashville: Vanderbilt University Press.

Lawson, A. (2004). *Biology: An inquiry approach.* Dubuque, IA: Kendall Hunt.

Lejeune, P. (1975). *Le pacte autobiographique.* Paris: Éditions du Seuil.

Lewis, D. (2003, February 28). Fred Rogers, host of *Mister Rogers' Neighborhood,* dies at 74. *The New York Times,* p. A1. [See Reading 2 in this volume.]

Lyotard, J.-F. (1984). *The postmodern condition: A report on knowledge.* Trans. G. Bennington & B. Massumi. Foreword by F. Jameson. Minneapolis: University of Minnesota Press.

McAdams, D. P. (1993). *The stories we live by: Personal myths and the making of the self.* New York and London: The Guilford Press.

Meeth, L. R. (1978). Interdisciplinary studies: A matter of definition. *Change: The Magazine of Higher Learning,* 10 (6), 10.

Menard, L. (2001). Undisciplined. *The Wilson Quarterly,* 25 (4), 51–60.

Mickenberg, D. (2003, Jan. 17). Creating art in the microcosm of Auschwitz. *The Chronicle of Higher Education,* p. B 15.

Moran, J. (2002). *Interdisciplinarity.* New York: Routledge.

Murray, T. H. (1986). Confessions of an unconscious interdisciplinarian. *Issues in Integrative Studies,* 4, 57–69. [See Reading 4 in this volume.]

New College. (n. d.). Ways of knowing. [Electronic version]. University of Alabama. Retrieved July 17, 2005 from <http://www.as.ua.edu/nc/>

Newell, W. H. (1983). The case for interdisciplinary studies: Response to professor Benson's five arguments. *Issues in Integrative Studies* 2, 1–19. [See Reading 8 in this volume.]

Newell, W. H. (1998). Professionalizing interdisciplinarity: Literature review and research agenda. In. W. H. Newell, (Ed.), *Interdisciplinarity: Essays from the literature* (pp. 529–563). New York: College Entrance Examination Board.

Newell, W. H. (2001). A theory of interdisciplinary studies. *Issues In Integrative Studies,* 19, 1–25.

Newell, William H. (in press). Decision-making in interdisciplinary studies. In Göktug Morçöl (Ed.), *Handbook of decision making.* New York: Marcel Dekker.

Newell, W. H., & Green, W. J. (1982). Defining and teaching interdisciplinary studies. *Improving College and University Teaching,* 30 (1), 23–30.

Newell, W. H., Hall, J., Hutkins, S., Larner, D., McGuckin, E., & Oates, K. (2003). Apollo meets Dionysius: Interdisciplinarity in long-standing interdisciplinary programs. *Issues in Integrative Studies,* 21, 9–41.

Nissani, M. (1995). Fruits, salads, and smoothies: A working definition of interdisciplinarity. [Electronic version] *Journal of Educational Thought,* 29, 119–125. Retrieved August 1, 2005 from <http://www.is.wayne.edu/mnissani/PAGEPUB/SMOOTHIE.htm>

O'Mallery, S. (2004). *"Are you there alone?" The unspeakable crime of Andrea Yates.* N.Y.: Simon and Schuster.

Olin, D. (2003, June 8). Prospect theory. *The New York Times*, Section 6, p. 33. [See Reading 11 in this volume.]

Orrill, R. Foreword. In W. H. Newell, (Ed.), *Interdisciplinarity: Essays from the literature* (pp. *xi–xii*). New York: College Entrance Examination Board.

Perkins, D. N. & Salomon, G. (1988). Teaching for transfer. *Educational Leadership, 40* (8), 22–32. [See Reading 12 in this volume.]

Petrie, H. G. (1976). Do you see what I see? The epistemology of interdisciplinary inquiry. *Journal of Aesthetic Education*, 10, 29–43. [See Reading 10 in this volume.]

Petr, J. L. (1983). The case for/against interdisciplinary studies: A comment on the debate. *Issues in Integrative Studies*, 2, 20–24.

Rosenberg, P. (2004). What a long, strange trip. In J. Zubizareta (Ed.), *The learning portfolio: Reflective practices in student, faculty, and institutional learning* (pp. 76–82). Bolton, MA: Anker Publishing.

Sacks, S. (Ed.) (1979). *On metaphor*. Chicago and London: University of Chicago Press.

Sherif, M., and Sherif, C.W. (1969). Interdisciplinary coordination as a validity check: Retrospect and prospects. In M. Sherif and C.W. Sherif (Eds.), *Interdisciplinary relationships in the social sciences* (pp. 3–20). Chicago: Aldine Publishing.

Simpson, J.A. and Weiner, E. S. C. (Eds.). (1989). *Oxford English Dictionary* (2nd ed.). Oxford: Clarendon Press; New York: Oxford University Press.

Swoboda, W. W. (1979) Disciplines and interdisciplinarity: A historical perspective. In Joseph J. Kockelmans (Ed.), *Interdisciplinarity and higher education* (pp. 49–92). University Park: The Pennsylvania State University Press.

Szostak, R. (2002). How to do interdisciplinarity: Integrating the debate. *Issues in Integrative Studies*, 20, 103–122.

Von Oech, R. (1990). *A whack on the side of the head: How you can be more creative* (Rev. ed.). N.Y.: Warner Books, 1990.

Williams, P. & Associates. (2005, Jan. 6). Conviction overturned for mom who drowned 5 kids. [Electronic version]. MSNBC News. Retrieved January 7, 2005 at <http://www.msnbc,.msn.com/id/6794098>

Wilson, E. O. (1998). *Consilience: The unity of knowledge*. N.Y.: Knopf.

Worcester, K. W. (2001). Social Science Research Council, 1923–1998. [Electronic version]. New York: Social Science Research Council. Retrieved July 7, 2005 at <http://www.ssrc.org/inside/about>

Zubizareta, J. (Ed.). (2004). *The learning portfolio: Reflective practices in student, faculty, and institutional learning* (pp. 76–82). Bolton, MA: Anker Publishing.

Credits

Grateful acknowledgment is made to the following writers, agents, and publishers for permission to publish or to reprint previously published material.

Allred, Joseph. "Sample Integrative Process Worksheet." Copyright © 2005 by Joseph Allred. Reprinted with permission. (Student work)

Randolph T. Barker, Glenn H. Gilbreath, and Warren S. Stone."The Interdisciplinary Needs of Organizations: Are New Employees Adequately Equipped?" *Journal of Management Development* 17:3 (1998): 219–232. Reprinted with permission.

Bateson, Mary Catherine. "Constructing Continuity." *Peripheral Visions: Learning Along the Way*. NY: HarperCollins, 1994. 77–94. Copyright © 1994 by Mary Catherine Bateson. Reprinted with permission.

Benson, Thomas C. "Five Arguments Against Interdisciplinary Studies." *Issues in Integrative Studies* 1 (1982): 38–48. Copyright © 1982 by the Association for Integrative Studies. Reprinted with permission.

Berger, Marilyn. "Isaiah Berlin, Philosopher and Pluralist, Is Dead at 88" *The New York Times* (9 Nov. 1997): A1. Copyright © 1997 by The New York Times Company. Reprinted with permission.

Fisher, Anne. "Success Secret: A High Emotional EQ." *Fortune* (Oct. 26, 1998): 293–298. Reprinted with permission.

Florida, Richard. Chapter 4, "The Creative Class," and Chapter 5, "The Machine Shop and the Hair Salon," In *The Rise of the Creative Class*. NY: Basic Books, 2002. 67–82; 85–101. Copyright © 2002 by Richard Florida. Reprinted with permission.

Gneiting, G. Layne. "Autobiographical Map." Copyright © 2005 by G. Layne Gneiting. Reprinted with permission.

Jackson, Richard W. "The Celtic Question." Copyright © 2004 by Richard W. Jackson. Reprinted with permission. (Student work)

James, Jennifer. "Mastering New Forms of Intelligence." *Thinking in the Future Tense*. NY: Touchstone, 1996. 179–185. Copyright ©1996 by Jennifer James, Inc. Reprinted with permission.

Kimbrell, Andrew. "Breaking the Job Lock." *Utne Reader* (Jan/Feb 1999): 47–49. Reprinted with permission.

Lewis, Daniel. "Fred Rogers, Host of 'Mister Rogers' Neighborhood,' Dies at 74," *The New York Times* (28 Feb. 2003): A1. Copyright © 2003 by The New York Times Company. Reprinted with permission.

Murray, Thomas H. "Confessions of an Unconscious Interdisciplinarian." *Issues in Integrative Studies* 4 (1986): 57–69. Copyright © 1986 Association for Integrative Studies. Reprinted with permission.

Newell, William H. "The Case for Interdisciplinary Studies: Response to Professor Benson's Five Arguments" *Issues in Integrative Studies* 2 (1983): 1–19. Copyright ©1983 by the Association for Integrative Studies. Reprinted with permission.

Olin, Dirk. "Prospect Theory." *The New York Times* Section 6 (8 June 2003): 33. Copyright © 2003 by The New York Times Company. Reprinted with permission.

Perkins, D. N. and Gavriel Salomon. "Teaching for Transfer." *Educational Leadership* 40: 8 (September 1988): 22–32. Copyright ©1988 by the Association for Supervision and Curriculum Development. Reprinted with permission.

Petrie, Hugh G. "Do You See What I See? The Epistemology of Interdisciplinary Inquiry," *Educational Researcher* 5:2 (1976): 9–15. Also: *Journal of Aesthetic Education* (Jan. 1976): 29–43. Copyright © 1976 by American Educational Research Association. Reprinted with permission.